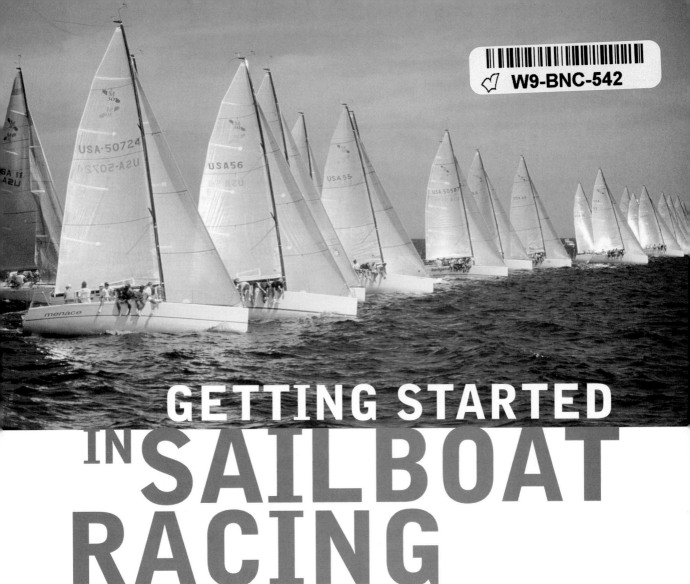

GETTING STARTED
IN SAILBOAT
RACING

International Marine / McGraw-Hill

Camden, Maine • New York • Chicago • San Francisco • Lisbon • London • Madrid •
Mexico City • Milan • New Delhi • San Juan • Seoul • Singapore • Sydney • Toronto

ADAM CORT and RICHARD STEARNS

The **McGraw·Hill** Companies

2 3 4 5 6 7 8 9 10 DOC DOC 0 9 8 7 6

Library of Congress Cataloging-in-Publication Data
Cort, Adam.
  Getting started in sailboat racing / Adam Cort and Rich Stearns.— 1st US ed.
      p.   cm.
  Includes bibliographical references and index.
  ISBN 0-07-142400-8
  1. Sailboat racing. 2. Sailing. I. Stearns, Rich. II. Title.
  GV826.5.C58 2004
  797.124—dc22   2004010952

Questions regarding the content of this book should be addressed to:
International Marine
P.O. Box 220
Camden, ME 04843
www.internationalmarine.com

Questions regarding the ordering of this book should be addressed to:
The McGraw-Hill Companies
Customer Service Department
P.O. Box 547
Blacklick, OH 43004
Retail customers: 1-800-262-4729
Bookstores: 1-800-722-4726

Photographs by Walter Cooper unless noted otherwise.
Illustrations by Joseph Comeau.
Previous page photo by Onne van der Wal/Corbis

Contents

Introduction

There are few things in this world more satisfying than sailboat racing. There's the challenge of handling your boat in close quarters with other boats, the thrill of competition, the visceral beauty of being part of a fleet, the excitement of thundering to windward, neck and neck with another well-found vessel, and the view of the water around you littered with sailboats as far as the eye can see.

Unfortunately, the excitement of the racecourse is something many sailors never experience. Cruisers who wouldn't think twice about crossing hundreds of miles of open water blanch at the idea of racing around the buoys. Daysailors who are perfectly comfortable sailing their sloops through a crowded mooring field think they aren't ready to mix it up with the "big boys." Many are worried about what their fellow sailors might think and about making themselves look foolish. Others worry about safety. It can be scary sailing at high speed in a very small area with dozens of other boats.

Still, for all its "terrors," the racecourse is, in reality, a remarkably safe place, and getting out there is more than worth the risk of losing a little gelcoat or tasting an occasional helping of humble pie. In fact, once you begin racing, you might wonder how anyone can truly appreciate the art of sailing without putting him- or herself to the test in a competitive environment. Uffa Fox, the famed English yachtsman and naval architect, perhaps put it best in his classic work, *According to Uffa*, when he admonished the novice sailor to get out on the racecourse as soon as possible, because, as he wrote, "once you race, every fault is pointed out in the way other boats sail away from you, and when you do anything well this too is revealed as you start sailing away from the rest of the fleet."

The purpose of this book is to explain the fundamentals of racing, so that daysailors and cruisers will feel confident enough not only to crew on a racing boat, but to enter their own boat in a race. It does not cover sailing basics, because it is assumed that the reader is already familiar with his or her boat. Likewise it does not teach the nuances of higher-level strategy or sail tuning, because that will needlessly complicate the basic issues of getting around the buoys.

What this book *will* do is provide the sailor with everything he or she needs to negotiate the racecourse safely and efficiently, and maybe even come in first place from time to time. If you aspire to win an Olympic medal in the 470 class, you will need more than this book (unless you are *very* good). But then again, you will never win that medal if you don't get out on the course in the first place.

Chapter 1 opens with a brief summary of a hypothetical race, and the subsequent chapters break down the racing experience into bite-size pieces. This not only makes the process easier to understand, but reflects the nature of the typical race, since it consists of a number of distinct and very specific parts. There are, of course, the rules (which are not half as complicated as some might think), the start, the windward leg, mark roundings, downwind sailing, the finish, and basic overall strategy. We've also included a chapter on how to get involved; i.e., finding races and figuring out what kind of racing is best for you.

Historically, sailboats have existed not just for pleasure, but to get something done. Even the dowdiest cruiser has at its heart a clipper ship or fishing schooner just begging to be the first one in. Few of us will ever have the chance to round Cape Horn or survive killer storms at sea. But in the spirit of Admiral Horatio Nelson at the Nile, we can beat the pants off that fellow with the gaudy yellow spinnaker! Now let's get out there, put that boat to work, and have some fun!

Chapter 1

WELCOME TO THE RACECOURSE

To those not familiar with the sport, sailboat racing can seem like a study in controlled chaos, with very little in the way of control. One moment you'll see clumps of boats sailing off in opposite directions, spreading themselves so thin it's hard to tell if they are even part of the same group. Next they'll all hoist their spinnakers at the same time and sail along in a neat and tidy line. The start in particular can seem like a kind of waterborne madness. Aboard the committee boat, where the race committee administers the race, horns blare and flags go rushing up and down halyards, while the fleet of competitors circles about in what appears to be impossibly tight quarters, like hyperactive terriers sniffing the wind. A small powerboat with a couple of bright-orange inflatable

The Race Committee

The race committee is an integral part of every sailboat race. It administers the race, sets the start and finish lines, decides on the type of course that will be sailed, and determines the compass headings of the different legs and the times of the starts and finishes. The actual composition of the race committee can vary widely depending on the type of race. Less formal races may have just a couple of people on board the committee boat. More important races will have a full crew of six or more registering the boats as they come out for the race, hoisting flags, blowing horns, shooting off guns, and sometimes hailing the fleet by radio to let it know what's going on. The race committee also decides when the conditions are safe or adequate for racing, and takes note whenever one boat protests another, so that the dispute can be resolved by a separate protest committee on shore.

buoys charges off to windward. Then all of a sudden a flag comes down, there's yet another blast of the horn or maybe even a gun, and some of the boats that had been milling about, apparently aimlessly, begin charging off in the same direction. Amazing! How did they know it was their turn? How do they keep from bumping into each other? And how do they even know where they're going?

Fortunately, as is the case with most racing sports—whether it be a NASCAR oval or a high school track—the courses in sailboat racing are generally very simple, and the rules not much worse. What follows is a brief narrative of a hypothetical sailboat race, along with an explanation of the different kinds of courses used in sailboat racing. The one big difference between sailing and many other racing sports is that there are no lanes or other obvious dividers to keep the boats from crashing into each other. The rules, however, make short work of this problem, with help from the fact that boats can be easily differentiated from one another by the angle of sail. Another difference is that the course for a sailboat race can be tough to spot, since it is delineated by just a handful of buoys, or marks, spread over what can sometimes be miles of open water. To address this problem, the sport has evolved a system of flags, horns, guns, and other signals that clearly communicate where you're supposed to go. It's all very "Age of Nelson stuff," one more reason why sailboat racing is so cool.

A HYPOTHETICAL RACE

Whether it's a national championship regatta with just one type of boat competing or a casual Wednesday night jaunt around the buoys with all different kinds of boats competing in a number of different groups, or classes (also referred to as sections), every sailboat race has a certain kind of energy to it—especially for someone venturing out onto the racecourse for the first time. In fact, the excitement begins as soon as you reach the dock. There's an electricity in the air as dozens of sailors in sunglasses and racing caps hurry back and forth carrying brightly colored sail bags, spinnaker poles, and other pieces of hardware.

Casting off your lines you either motor or sail out to the committee boat, which waits at anchor like some kind of Pied Piper or a shepherd out tending his flock. Then you check in by sailing close alongside and calling out your sail number. The number of boats quickly multiplies, and they all begin sailing back and forth, while the crew on the committee boat gauges the wind direction, decides how to orient the racecourse, and drops an inflatable orange buoy into the water maybe 50 or 100 yards away to create a starting line (this distance can fluctuate dramatically depending on the size of the fleet). Minutes later the aforementioned flags and horns make their appearance. One of the crew aboard your boat notes that the committee is calling for a "windward-leeward" course consisting of four stages, or legs, going directly up- and downwind, and the first section of the fleet goes charging off to windward, hell-bent for leather. After that comes another set of flags and another section takes off. Then it's your turn. Throwing in a few quick tacks and jibes, you bunch up along the line with the other boats in your class, in what you are sure is going to be a terrible pileup. Then, at the sound of a horn, you all charge off to windward in the same direction as the other boats before you, some of which already appear to be little more than dots on the horizon.

Classes and Sections

Although some regional or national championship regattas will have just one type of boat racing, most regattas are comprised of a number of different types of boats sailing in different groups variously referred to as sections or classes. Generally each class will get its own individual starting sequence, although sometimes two or more classes with only a few boats each will start at the same time. A class can be made up of identical boats, as is the case with one-design boats, or similar boats, as is the case with boats that have similar handicap ratings (see chapter 12, Getting Involved, for more about boat classes and handicapping rules). In most regattas, there will be prizes for the winners, and possibly second- and third-place finishers, in each section. The overall winner of a regatta will be the boat that posts the best record in its class.

A fleet of Lightnings drives toward the line in moderate conditions a few seconds before the start. Note the pin-end buoy in the foreground and the committee boat off in the distance.

At this point, things settle down for a bit. The boats in your class slowly separate as they tack back and forth in an effort to sail as quickly as possible to where the first mark, or windward mark, has been dropped in the water a mile or two directly to windward, indicating the turning point at the end of the first leg of the race. On occasion you find yourself either crossing tracks with or sailing parallel to another boat, while at other times it feels like you've got the course to yourself. Eventually, someone sights the mark—still little more than an orange speck on the horizon—and before you know it things are starting to get complicated again as you prepare to hoist the spinnaker for the next leg. Your widely separated competitors begin to converge, many of them lining up close-hauled on starboard tack and quickly advancing toward the buoy. Others angle in on port tack and tack over onto starboard at the last minute. Then it's like the start all over again. What seems like the entire fleet jostles for position, as the different crews hoist their spinnakers as quickly as possible and maneuver their boats as efficiently as they can, both through the crowd and around the buoy.

After that there's another period of relative calm as the fleet makes its way back downwind, once again spreading out as the boats jibe back and forth to make the most of the wind. Then it's time to look out for the leeward mark (the buoy delineating the turning point at the end of the downwind leg), decide on the fastest way to get there, and bunch up again with the rest of the boats for the next mark rounding, an exercise that is further complicated by your having to both take down the spinnaker and hoist the jib as quickly as possible, because the next leg is once again directly to windward. Hopefully by this time the boats in both your class and the entire fleet are spread out enough that it won't be too terribly crowded at the mark, and you can make a nice clean rounding. If not, well, a little chaos at the leeward mark is all part of the fun.

Once you've got the rounding behind you it's time for another long beat, or upwind stretch to the windward mark, followed by another rounding and spinnaker hoist for another trip downwind. This time, however, instead of heading for a single leeward mark, you set a course for the committee boat, which once again has a second buoy in the water—about 30 yards away this time—to designate the finish line. As you draw near you notice that two of your competitors are nearby, and things onboard your own vessel are as tense as ever

Star boats sail to windward during the first leg of a race.

A trio of Lightnings rounds the windward mark. The lead boat is in the process of hoisting its spinnaker as it starts the downwind leg. Note the pair of starboard-tackers approaching the mark off in the distance.

A quartet of One Design 35s enjoys ideal conditions on the downwind leg.

Home at last! A Mumm 30 crosses the finish line.

as the crew tries to eke out every last bit of speed. Then finally, after what seems an eternity, you are sailing past the committee boat, and a member of the race committee calls out your boat's sail number and honks a horn. Congratulations! You've just completed your first sailboat race! Time to relax and have a cold beer. If, like many novice racers, you are a little confused about what exactly you have just done, don't fret. That's what the rest of this chapter is for.

THE COURSE

Today, nearly all inshore sailboat races take place on one of three basic types of courses: the triangle course, the Olympic course, and the simple windward-leeward course. Note that many racecourses will vary slightly from these basic types, depending on the conditions and types of marks that are used. For example, when using an Olympic course, some race committees will have the boats finish on the downwind leg, or run, if the winds are light and the committee doesn't want the race to last too long. On some courses the race can end at a mark in the center of the course. Contrary to its appearance, the windward-leeward course is the most tactically and strategically difficult, because beats and runs offer the best opportunities to pass other boats (and to be passed if you're not careful). In fact, the simple triangle course has been largely relegated to Wednesday night "beer can" races and other casual venues. Still, all three types offer plenty of challenge.

Whatever the course, the starting line will generally be delineated by an orange flag flown aboard the race committee boat, which is anchored at the starboard end of the line, usually with a small buoy placed alongside to keep boats clear. Another buoy—often referred to as the "pin"—determines the other end. In setting the starting line, the race committee will try to make the line as perpendicular to the wind as possible. In reality, however, the line will almost always be cocked a little one way or the other, so that one end is slightly closer to the windward mark than the other, making it the better—or favored—end (for more information about favored end, see chapter 2, Starting). Some race committees will even skew their lines ever so slightly, favoring the pin end, so there won't be too much crowding at the committee boat. The buoys marking the rest of the course can be drop-in inflatable buoys, permanent race buoys, or standard navigational buoys; i.e., bell buoys, cans, nuns, etc. Drop-in buoys, like those referred to at the start of the chapter, are hauled around the course and anchored at the appropriate points by small powerboats called crash boats. Usually just a few minutes before the start, you will see one of these little guys roaring off directly to windward to drop in the first mark before the gun. Sometimes, if there is a dramatic windshift in the middle of the race, they will move the buoys to avoid a situation in which boats are just beam-reaching back

A crash boat heads back to the dock with a buoy in tow after a day of racing.

Types of Racecourses

Nearly all inshore sailboat races take place on one of three basic types of courses. The triangle course begins with a beat to windward, followed by a pair of reaching legs around a turning, or jibe, mark set off to the side. The Olympic course is basically a triangle course followed by a series of three legs directly up- and downwind. The windward-leeward course is simply made up of anywhere from two to five legs going directly up- and downwind.

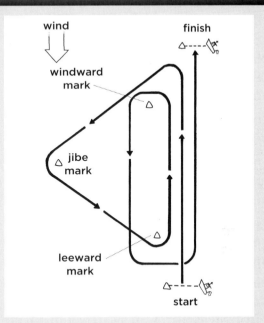

Olympic course

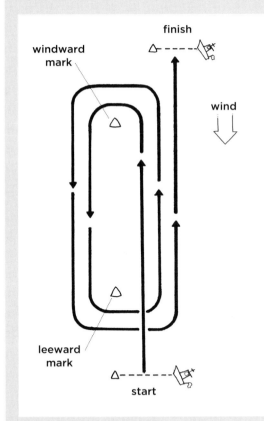

Windward-leeward course

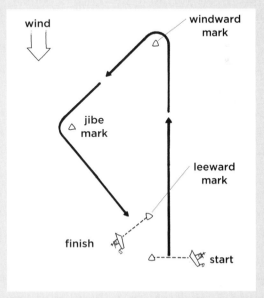

Triangle course

and forth with little possibility for tactical interest or passing. Don't worry. They'll let you know when they move buoys by blowing a horn and waving a letter C signal flag colored with a number of red, white, and blue stripes.

In the case of permanent buoys, the yacht clubs or sailing associations that place them will usually arrange them in a square or star pattern around a central starting buoy. That way, no matter what the wind direction, the race committee will be able to arrange the requisite runs and beats.

Sometimes race committees will create a gate at the leeward mark to accommodate large, crowded fleets. Basically, a gate consists of a pair of leeward marks instead of just one. You can then choose to round whichever one you want, as long as you first pass between the two. This, of course, completely eliminates crowding at the leeward mark . . . uh, well . . . at least in theory. Very few beginners will find themselves facing a situation requiring a gate at the leeward mark (see chapter 6, Leeward Mark Roundings and Finishing, for more information about rounding gates).

FLAGS, GUNS, AND OTHER SIGNALS

The primary flags to be concerned about on the racecourse are those that provide a countdown to the start and those that designate the kind of course the fleet will be sailing. There are a myriad of other flags and sequences of flags, but we will only discuss a few of the more important ones here. Many marine stores carry handy waterproof cheat sheets with all the established signals. Also, the sailing instructions that are provided as a part of every regatta will include a list of the most important signal flags, such as class flags. Class flags may be solid colored standard signal flags or have letters or symbols against a solid background. For those sailors taking part in a season-long series, the yacht club or organizing body will also publish a list of signals and flags—especially if they differ from the norm.

While we are on the subject, the sailing instructions are an important part of sailboat racing, and every crewmember—not just the skipper—should take some time to study them before the beginning of a race. One person—preferably not the skipper—should also be designated as the one in charge of interpreting signals. Again, the instructions will provide a key for determining what flags will be used to designate different courses and divisions. They will also provide the order in which the different classes will start and the time at which each class should, in theory at least, be heading off the line. Don't be one of those crews that finds itself debating whether it finishes on the fourth or fifth leg or whether its section is next in the starting sequence. You've got enough to worry about without being confused over the basic parameters of the game.

As for the starting sequence, which

The *Sailing World*
National Offshore One-Design Regatta
presented by Mount Gay Rum
JUNE 11-13, 2004 CHICAGO YACHT CLUB
Sailing World is the organizing authority of this regatta.

SAILING INSTRUCTIONS

1. RULES
The regatta will be governed by the rules as defined by the Racing Rules of Sailing 2001-2004 (RRS). Classes permitting Category C Advertising (see RRS Appendix 1) are urged to refrain from displaying advertisements for businesses or products competing with those of the primary and support sponsors of the event.

2. ELIGIBILITY
The regatta is open to any boat with a minimum LOA of 24 feet and has sleeping accommodations below decks and is either: a) an active member of a recognized class association for entry in this regatta's One-Design classes, or; b) a boat which meets the criteria established for this regatta by the class coordinator or the Organizing Authority, for entry in a class; and provided that such class is among the first 21 to have eight entries, and further provided that an overall limit of 275 entries is not exceeded. Level classes that combine to meet minimum entry requirements shall be required to accept all entries that have been accepted for those classes. Boats entered in the event that have a valid Area PHRF Rating, and are not entered in a One-Design or Level class, shall be assigned to one of a maximum of four PHRF Handicapped Classes. The composition of PHRF handicapped classes shall be at the discretion of the Organizing Authority, with the assistance of members of the CYC Offshore Racing Committee. Entries with PHRF ratings in excess of 135 shall not be accepted for entry into PHRF rated classes by the Organizing Authority. All decisions made by the Organizing Authority regarding PHRF class assignments and entries shall be final. The Organizing Authority reserves the right to accept entries that do not satisfy these requirements.

3. NOTICE TO COMPETITORS
Notices to competitors will be posted on the official regatta notice board at the Monroe Station of the Chicago Yacht Club.

4. CHANGES IN SAILING INSTRUCTIONS
Any change in the Sailing Instructions will be posted before 0800 hours CDT on the day it will take effect except that any change in the schedule of races will be posted by 2000 hours CDT on the day before it will take effect.

5. SIGNALS MADE ASHORE
Code flag AP Answering Pennant means "The race is postponed. The warning signal will be made not less than 75 minutes after AP is lowered."

6. SCHEDULE OF RACES
Friday, June 11......................1st Warning signal at 1025 hours CDT
Saturday, June 12 ....1st Warning signal at 1025 hours CDT
Sunday, June 13 ....1st Warning signal at 1025 hours CDT

It is the intent of the organizing authority and the Race Committee to run as many races as practical on Friday, June 11 through Sunday, June 13. A maximum of 9 races is scheduled for the series. No warning signal will be made after 1400 hrs on Sunday, June 13. The harbor start is scheduled for 0830 hrs on each day of racing. At the finish of a race, the Race Committee will indicate its intent to conduct a subsequent race with the display of Flag "R."

7. SECTION ASSIGNMENTS AND CLASS FLAGS
Information regarding section assignments, initial starting order, and warning/ class flags will be provided at registration. Competitors are advised that classes may be combined in the starting order yet still be scored separately.

8. RACING AREAS
The diagram contained in the Sailing Instructions provides the approximate starting location for each section.

9. COURSES
9.1 The approximate compass bearing and distance from the starting line to Mark 1 will be displayed from the race committee signal boat for each division.
9.2 The legs of the course to be sailed by the Tartan Ten class and the J105 class shall be the distance posted plus approximately one/half (1/2) mile.
9.3 An "Offset" mark shall be set at approximately 90° to port of mark 1 at a distance of approximately 100 yards. The "Offset" mark will be an inflatable buoy and shall be left to port after rounding mark 1. In the event of a change of course as described in sections 16 and 17, the "Offset" mark may not be in place.

10. MARKS
Marks 1, 2, and G will be orange inflatable marks. New marks, when used in accordance with Instruction 16 "Change of Course After the Start," will be yellow. (Also read Instruction 17.) The starting and finishing marks will also be orange inflatable marks.

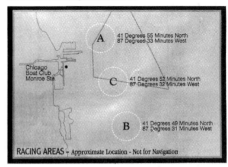

The sailing instructions for a regatta or racing series include information about starting times, the kinds of racecourses you will sail, various signal flags the race committee will use, and more. Everyone on board your boat should be familiar with the sailing instructions, not just the skipper! (COURTESY *SAILING WORLD* MAGAZINE)

consists of a series of flags and horns or gunshots, the committee boat will raise and lower flags in the following order:

Five minutes before the start, or as stated in the sailing instructions: The race committee raises a class, or warning, flag designating which class or section is about to start. At the same time, it fires a gun or sounds a horn to "announce" that the starting sequence has begun.

Four minutes before the start: The race committee sounds another horn and hoists a preparatory flag, usually a blue flag or the P flag (a white flag with a thick blue border). These give the timekeepers on the boats in the starting section the opportunity to make sure they have the right time.

One minute before the start: The race committee lowers the preparatory flag and sounds another horn.

Start: The race committee lowers the class flag and signals the start with a gun or horn.

Note that, in contrast to starting sequences in the past, the start for one class may *not* be the beginning of the next division's sequence. Instead, it may simply serve as a warning for the next division to be on alert. Watch for the class flag. If it goes up at the same moment the division ahead starts, fine. Otherwise, you will have to be patient and keep an eye on the committee boat.

When it is ready, the race committee will start the sequence at the five-minute point by sounding a horn and hoisting the appropriate class flag.

On occasion the race committee will use a flag other than the blue preparatory flag to signal the four- and one-minute points; it will do so to communicate that special penalties are being applied at the start. For example, it might use the I flag (a yellow flag with a black circle in the middle) to signal that any boat crossing the starting line within a minute of the start must sail around either the pin or the committee boat to return to the proper side. It might also use the dreaded black flag to indicate that any boat on the wrong side of the line within a minute of the start is automatically disqualified from the entire race. In many fleets the I flag is assumed. The black flag is usually only employed to control especially large and unruly fleets, say a bunch of J/24 skippers all hungry for a regional championship. The race committee lowers this flag, like the P flag, at one minute to the start; make sure you check the flags early on to avoid any unpleasant surprises after the finish.

Bear in mind that, although many race committees will radio or hail the fleet via megaphone to draw attention to any unusual flags or the fact that a competitor has crossed the starting line early, it is not required to do so. Hailing by the race committee is only a courtesy. Ultimately, it is the responsibility of each individual sailor to watch for any unusual flags that might be flying or changes in the starting sequence.

One time, for example, there were five different classes starting in a National Offshore One-Design (NOOD) regatta off Chicago Harbor. The Tartan Ten fleet, with 48 boats, was starting third in the sequence. In the first four races of the regatta, the class flag went up at the same moment as the start of the class before the Tens. But in the fifth race, the race committee decided not to raise the class flag immediately, because the breeze had picked up and it wanted to give the other sections a bit more of a head start. (The Tartan Ten is especially fast in heavy air.) Unfortunately, because it was windy, there was a lot of noise and confusion; over half the Tartan Ten fleet started five minutes after the previous section's start anyway, only to slow down, peel away, and sail back to the starting area as they realized their mistake. By the time many of these boats got back, there was less than one minute to go to the start and the I flag, which had been raised to keep the unruly fleet in check, had already been taken down. As a result many of them, unaware of the new conditions, just dipped across the line and went charging off toward the windward mark, violating the rules. At the end of the race these boats didn't receive a finish signal, because they hadn't properly started. They had all been over the line early—a hard way to learn a lesson in a major regatta.

Note that, before the actual sequence begins, the race committee will post a set of large numbers designating the compass heading of the first beat (which then determines the position of the entire course; all other marks are relative to the starting line and windward mark) and a letter designating the course type. For example, a race committee might display a letter "W"—to signify a windward-leeward course with four legs—with the number 270 immediately below, indicating that the heading on the first leg is due west. Even if you can't see the mark (which is usually the case unless you are racing dinghies close inshore) you will still know exactly where to go. Because the course is a windward-leeward, the headings on the second and fourth legs are simply the reciprocal of the first and third, i.e., 90 degrees, or due east. If the course includes a triangle, the sailing instructions will designate the angles that must be sailed relative to the windward leg. If you are sailing around a series of fixed marks, all the compass headings will be included in the sailing instructions. Again, it's all fairly straightforward. This is sailing after all, not rocket science.

OTHER FLAGS

Beyond the basic starting sequence, race committees also use flags to communicate other kinds of information, the meanings of which are pretty straightforward. The flags are almost always accompanied by one or more horns or guns to make sure no one misses them. The following are a few of the more common flags you will encounter.

The race committee will hoist letters and numbers specifying the course to be sailed.

Answering pennant (AP)—postponement: The flag remains flying for the duration of the delay. When the postponement is over, the race committee will take the flag down, while sounding a horn or gun to signal one minute until the starting sequence begins again with the hoisting of a class flag. The long, tapered AP flag, with its bold red and white stripes, is affectionately known by many as the "Cat in the Hat" flag.

1st substitute (1st Sub)—general recall: So many yachts have crossed the line early the entire section has to start all over again. The race committee will also fire the gun twice or sound the horn twice to get everyone's attention. In most fleets the recalled section goes to the back of the line; i.e., the committee will continue starting the other sections in their regular order—tacking the recalled section on at the end. Look to see which class flag is used to continue the starting sequence. As is the case with the answering pennant, the class flag will be hoisted exactly one minute after the general recall flag is lowered.

X flag—individual recall: One or more yachts have started early. This flag is accompanied by a horn the race committee blows just moments after the starting horn. Again, the race committee does *not* have to specify verbally who was over early. If you think you're the guilty party, best do a restart to avoid being disqualified.

 C flag—change of course: If there is a dramatic windshift, the race committee sometimes will decide to change the heading of one or more marks. When this happens, the crash boat will fly the C flag at the last unmoved mark and display the compass heading to the next leg.

 S flag—shorten course: The race will finish at the end of the next leg.

 N flag—abandonment signal: This flag, which can be used to call off the race at any point, is accompanied by three horn blasts or three gunshots. When the race committee decides to begin the race again, it will lower the N flag and sound a horn, signaling that it will hoist a class flag in one minute. If the N flag is accompanied by an A flag immediately below it, racing has been abandoned for the rest of the day.

 Y flag—personal flotation devices must be worn. While on this subject, you should buy a comfortable life jacket and wear it all the time while sailing anyway.

THE RULES

Ah, the rules. Although they can be contained within the covers of a fairly small book, the rules of the game alone are enough to scare many sailors from sailboat racing for a lifetime. "A boat with an overlapped right-of-way must jibe at the mark or obstruction to sail her proper course. A boat clear astern must . . . " Huh? Vaguely biblical in tone and replete with legalese, they are enough to make a sadistic technical writer green with envy.

Still, for the novice racer there are three things to bear in mind when approaching the rule book before his or her first race.

1. The rules are universally based on common sense.
2. All the nuance and apparent gibberish stem from a few basic rules of the road.
3. If you play it safe and keep points one and two in mind, you will rarely if ever have to worry about the minutia.

(Here's a dirty little secret of sailing: many skippers aren't half as well-versed in the rules as an outsider might think. Why do you think protest committee meetings are so exciting?) Eventually, of course, you will want to study the rules in depth in order to begin sticking your bow into the thick of things, where all the shouting takes place. And they are easy to obtain: you can download them for free from the US Sailing Web site at www.ussailing.org or buy a book such as *Paul Elvström Explains the Racing Rules of Sailing, 2001–2004*. However, in the beginning, when in doubt, stay clear.

You're not necessarily looking to win your first race. The idea is to have fun, learn about your boat and yourself, and, with a little luck, still give at least a few boats a good look at your transom!

BASIC COMMON SENSE

Ultimately, the purpose of the rules, which are updated every four years by the International Sailing Federation, is a simple one: to ensure that the boats on the racecourse don't run into each other whenever two or more of them want to sail through the same piece of water at the same time. With that in mind, the vast majority of the rules are intended to establish which boat has right-of-way in a myriad of different meeting situations. It's true there are an infinite number of ways in which boats can approach one another, but a few basic ground rules cover 90 percent of those situations quite nicely. Specifically, if two boats are on separate tacks and there are no extenuating circumstances, a port-tack boat *always* gives way to a starboard-tack boat. If two boats are on the same tack and there are no extenuating circumstances, the windward boat *always* gives way to a leeward boat, and a boat clear astern *always* avoids a boat clear ahead. It's that simple.

Of course, there are complexities or variations of these rules that arise when there are obstructions in the area or a number of boats are approaching a mark. But again, the rules governing these extenuating circumstances, which will be covered where appropriate in the upcoming chapters, are largely based on

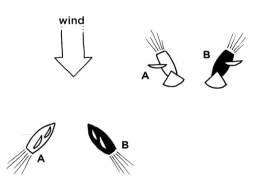

*Up- or downwind, port tack (boat **A**) gives way to starboard tack (boat **B**).*

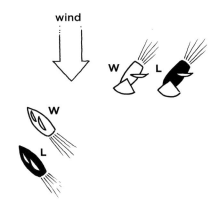

*Up- or downwind, the windward boat (**W**) stays clear of the leeward boat (**L**).*

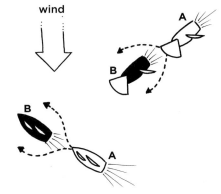

*Up- or downwind, the overtaking boat **A** stays clear of the lead boat **B**.*

common sense. And, although it's important to be familiar with the rules, playing it conservatively in the beginning of your racing career will help you avoid having to recite them in front of a panel of your peers when back on the shore.

A FEW MORE GENERAL RULES

Again, it's all about common sense. You're just starting out. This isn't the America's Cup, during which you are intentionally trying to draw fouls from your opponent. You can sail aggressively, but in the end it's much faster to sail a clean race.

Tacking. A boat in the act of tacking must keep clear of a boat on course. In other words, you can't just try to flop over onto starboard tack at the last moment in a starboard-port crossing situation and expect the original starboard-tack boat to keep clear while your sails are still luffing and you're passing through irons.

Avoiding Contact. To quote directly from Rule 14: "A boat shall avoid contact with another boat if reasonably possible." In other words, just because you're on starboard tack doesn't give you the right to cut the other guy in half. Bear in mind, however, that the right-of-way boat, "need not act to avoid contact until it is clear that the other boat is not keeping clear or giving room." What this means is, a boat with right-of-way can't just shy away because it's getting nervous, and then expect the other boat to be penalized when it still had an opportunity to yield right-of-way.

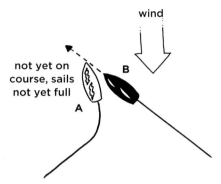

*A boat in the act of tacking (**A**) must keep clear of a boat on course (**B**).*

Obstructions. If there is an obstruction—the shore, a rock, a breakwall, or a floating log, for example—a boat having right-of-way is expected to change course or give way to a boat that doesn't have right-of-way, so the latter won't collide with the obstruction. When you think about it, this really is a very reasonable rule. This is, after all, just a game.

PROTESTING AND WHAT HAPPENS IF YOU BREAK THE RULES

Don't feel bad. It happens to everyone. Even Star-class champion Mark Reynolds was over the line early at the start of the last race of the 2000 Olympics in Sydney, Australia. (He recovered and went on to win the gold medal.) Still, the rules and race committee mean business. If you are found guilty of breaking a rule, you will be disqualified from the race.

Penalty Turns. After committing a foul, a boat can exonerate itself by doing a 720-degree turn at the first reasonable opportunity. But beware. Boats "taking a 720" lose all rights over other boats in the area, no matter what their respective positions or tacks.

Touching a Mark. Of course, touching a mark is a no-no. However, if you do touch the mark, you can redeem yourself by doing a 360-degree turn as soon as you get yourself clear of the other boats in the area. Note that if a boat is forced to touch a mark by another boat that didn't keep clear, the boat touching the mark does not have to do a penalty turn. If a boat commits a foul against another boat and touches a mark at the same time, it need only do a 720-degree turn (as opposed to a 1,080-degree turn, which would be brutal indeed!).

Protesting. If you are fouled by another boat, you must hail the other boat to let it know it's being protested and, if your boat is over 6 meters long, fly a red protest flag. Once you are ashore you must deliver your dispute to the protest committee—in writing—within two hours of the last boat's finishing. The committee will then set a time and place for a hearing, often later that same day, to decide what to do.

SOME FINAL THOUGHTS ON THE RULES AND PROTESTS

Good sailors are like good pool players. Good pool players rarely have to make difficult shots, although they can if necessary. Their real talent lies in setting up the game so they always have easy shots. The same is true with good sailors. You don't see them

The Protest Committee

If two or more boats are in dispute over an alleged infringement of the rules, they can take their case to the protest committee for a hearing back on shore when racing is finished for the day. During a protest hearing, a representative from each of the boats involved has the right to be in attendance while evidence is given—either by third parties or sailors from the two boats involved—and the committee makes its decision. The number of members in a protest committee, which is separate from the race committee, can vary depending on the size of the regatta, although it's not unusual to have three members. Protests will often be heard the same day as the race in question, especially during a major regatta. However, they can also be heard a few days afterward, as is often the case if the race in question was one in a season-long series.

thrashing it out in the crowd, yelling out rules and waving red flags. They avoid crowds and quietly work their way to the front of the fleet. Interestingly enough, you will find that as you move from club racing to higher levels, there are fewer protests. Good sailors stay away from protests.

Having said that, as you become more comfortable on the racecourse, it's important to learn the rules so you can stand up for your rights, especially in crowded areas such as the leeward mark. If you don't stand up for your rights, you will inevitably lose valuable boatlengths. As one of the authors of this book was told when his father gave him his first rule book: you don't actually have to read it *IF*—IF you can figure out how to start first at every race, and then increase your lead during each subsequent leg, so you still have the entire fleet safely behind you at the finish.

Q & A

Q. What are the three basic rules that form the foundation of 90 percent of the rest of the rules?
A. Port tack gives way to starboard tack; on the same tack, a windward boat gives way to a leeward boat, and a boat overtaking from astern stays clear of a boat ahead.

Q. What is the sequence of flags and horns used before the start?
A. Five minutes before the start, the race committee blows a horn and raises the class, or warning, flag to indicate the start of the sequence. Four minutes before the start, the race committee hoists a preparatory flag. One minute before the start, the race committee lowers the preparatory flag. A minute later the committee sounds a horn and lowers the class flag to signal the start.

Q. What does it mean if the race committee hoists a long, tapered flag with vertical red and white stripes? What does it mean when the race committee sounds a horn or fires a gun and takes the flag down?
A. The flag signals a postponement. When the committee takes down the flag, racing is about to resume; specifically, there is one minute until the race committee hoists the next class flag to restart the sequence.

Q. Adam is over the line early at the start. Although the race committee blows a horn and hoists the X flag, it doesn't say anything to him by bullhorn or radio. At the end of the race, it doesn't record Adam's finish and tells him he was disqualified, because he didn't restart. Adam protests the committee, saying it should have told him he was over early. Is he right?
A. Adam is wrong. The race committee verbally notifies competitors if they're over early only as a courtesy.

Q. Adam and Rich find themselves in a crossing situation when sailing to windward, with Adam on starboard tack and Rich on port. Rich thinks he can clear, but at the last moment realizes he can't and throws in a tack. At the very end of his tack, when he is almost on course but his sails are still luffing, Adam has to alter course to avoid a collision. Rich says he was on starboard tack, his bow having crossed through the eye of the wind and that Adam, as the overtaking boat, had to stay clear. Is he right?
A. No; until Rich gets his sails drawing, or full, on the new tack, he is considered in the middle of his tack and has no rights.

Chapter 2   STARTING

Having stated earlier that good sailors avoid crowds, there is one time in sailboat racing when it's pretty much impossible to avoid your fellow sailors, and that's at the start. Love it, hate it, or fear it, the start of a sailboat race is a pretty exciting time. Even when the air is light, there's a feeling of tension and anticipation. And when it's honking? Life is good!

Still, there is no reason for beginners to be in abject terror of the start, because like nearly everything else in sailboat racing, once you break it down into its constituent parts it's not half as confusing as it might first appear. Also, many sailors make starting much harder than it needs to be by trying to be the top boat off the line every time. Actually "winning" the start in a large, competitive fleet takes quite a bit of skill. But getting a good, competitive start in a moderate-sized fleet is very doable, even to a rank beginner. All you have to do is keep a few key things in mind.

BASIC TENETS OF STARTING

Air and Speed. Always bear in mind that, in addition to crossing the line as the gun sounds, your ultimate goal in starting is to do so with good boat speed and clear air. In fact, these two factors are closely interrelated. If you have boat speed when you hit the line, but there's a guy directly to windward blanketing, or gassing, you with the turbulent air coming off his sails, you're not going to have boat speed for long. If you've got clear air at the line, but you're sitting dead in the water, chances are some guy is going to run right over you; you won't be enjoying that clear air for long!

Timing. It is absolutely crucial that you get in sync with the horns, guns, and flags of the starting sequence. Otherwise, you will be in the dark as to exactly when you can cross the line, which can cost precious seconds. Worse yet, there are few things half as distracting or demoralizing as trying to figure out your starting strategy, knowing all the while that you've lost track of the time.

Most sailors set their watches to the sequence; in other words, they set their watches to five minutes, at which point the watch starts beeping until they turn it off. If you stop and think about it, though, this really doesn't make a whole lot of sense. For one thing, it's hard to believe sailboat racers need something beeping on their wrist at the same time a bunch of people are yelling at them, both aboard their own boat and the boats around them. Additionally, the last thing you want at the start is to have to stop concentrating on what you're doing to turn a beeper off. With this in mind, try setting your watch to the sequence *plus* the time limit; i.e., the time at which the race will be canceled if none of the boats has been able to finish. There are two reasons for this. The obvious one is you know when the race will expire. The second is, race committees very often set their clocks to the highly precise atomic clock; if

there is a general recall for your section, the committee will continue to use the top of each minute for the sequence. Therefore, even if you miss the next signal you can start the race with confidence, because your watch is already in sync.

Favored End. It's important to figure out which end of the starting line is the favored end, the end that is closest to the windward mark. Despite their best efforts, very few race committees are able to get their starting lines perfectly square. Even if they do, the wind is always shifting about, so they rarely stay that way. The easiest way to determine the favored end is to go head-to-wind somewhere on the line and see which way your bow is pointing. If your bow is pointing a little toward the committee boat, then that's the favored end. If your bow is pointing toward the pin end, you generally want to be there. Unfortunately,

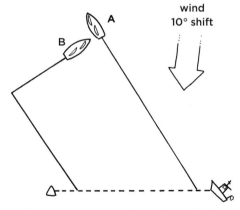

*Even if a starting line is skewed just 10 degrees, it can make a big difference. Despite the fact that both of these boats have sailed the same distance, boat **A**, which started near the favored end, is ahead.*

Finding the Favored End

The best way to determine the favored end is to keep track of your tacking angles when tuning up prior to the start, and then using that information to determine wind direction. For example, if your boat tacks through 90 degrees and you are able to sail a heading of 60 degrees on starboard tack and 150 degrees on port tack, then the wind direction is 105. In this case, if the line were square it would lie along a bearing of 15 degrees from the boat to the pin, or a reciprocal of 195. If in running the line on starboard you find that the bearing is higher than 15, say 25 degrees, the pin end is favored. If the bearing is less, say 5 degrees, the boat end is favored. Obviously this is a lot more complicated than simply going head-to-wind. But it saves your sails and forces you to get a feel for your tacking angles, which will help you play the windshifts once you are on the first beat.

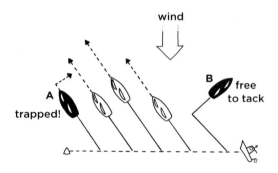

*If you want to tack soon after the start, stay toward the boat end of the line. Boat **A**, starting at the pin end of the line, has to sail across the entire fleet on port tack if it wants to head toward the right side of the beat. Boat **B**, on the other hand, can do as it pleases.*

flogging your sails by going head-to-wind is a sure way to shorten their useful lifespan. Therefore it is a better idea to determine the wind direction relative to the line by keeping track of your tacking angles when sailing up to the line prior to the start.

Freedom to Tack. You need to decide whether or not you want the option of tacking over onto port and sailing toward the right side of the course immediately after the start. If, for example, the wind is shifting around so that staying on starboard would mean sailing into a lull, you don't want to start at the pin end; that would mean sailing across the entire fleet on port tack when the other boats are still on starboard. The same would be true if there was an adverse current you wanted to avoid.

A FEW SPECIAL RULES

Not surprisingly, given the crowded nature of the starting area, there are a few special rules to help sailors figure out who has the right-of-way as they maneuver for position and go charging for the line in those last few moments before the gun. As is the case throughout the racecourse (and throughout this book), those basic rules outlined in chapter 1 still hold sway the majority of the time. It's just that in a few special cases there are other factors to keep in mind. Also, when thinking about the start always remember that, while it's important to check in with the race committee, you need to stay clear of the starting area until it is your turn to start. Specifically, stay a few boatlengths to leeward of the line and well away from the two ends where boats will be maneuvering just before the horn. The last thing the guys in the sections ahead of you want is a bunch of other boats milling around the committee boat at the same time they're struggling for position on the starting line.

Barging. Perhaps the most devilish of them all, Rule 18.1a states that in a starting situation a leeward boat need not give room to a windward boat at the mark, in contrast to much of the rest of the time when the inside boat has right-of-way. This situation often arises when a number of boats are crowding, or "barging," in toward the starboard or committee boat end of the line. In fact in this situation, the boat to leeward can luff up at will to cut off a boat to windward, provided it gives the boat to windward room and time to keep clear—no sandwiching the guy up against the committee boat or swerving up without warning to hit him amidships! An exception to this rule is when a boat establishes an overlap—its bow passing the aft-most point of another boat's stern—by sailing up from to

leeward and astern. In this case, although the leeward boat can sail as high, or as close to the wind, as it wants prior to the starting signal, once the race is underway it may not sail above proper course. Proper course is defined by the racing rules as the course a boat "would sail to finish as soon as possible in the absence of other boats." In other words, no luffing up to cut someone off at the committee boat. Another possible exception is when the mark is not surrounded by navigable water; for example, if one end of the line is a breakwall or the shore. In that case, the leeward boat has to stay clear. You can't just luff the poor guy up until he runs aground.

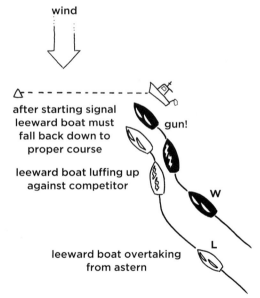

*When a leeward boat (**L**) establishes an overlap to leeward from astern, it cannot—after the starting signal—sail above proper course, the course a boat would sail to finish as soon as possible in the absence of other boats (in this case close-hauled), to pinch off another boat (**W**).*

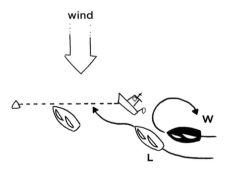

*Rule 18.1a: In a starting situation, a leeward boat (**L**) need not give room to a windward boat (**W**) at a mark. Boats that try to squeeze inside and around the committee boat are said to be "barging."*

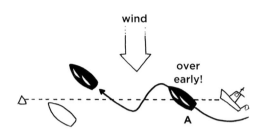

wind

over early!

A

*If a boat **A** crosses the line early, it must restart by returning to the proper side of the line.*

Hitting a Mark. As is the case with the rest of the course, if you hit a starting mark you can clear yourself by doing an immediate 360-degree turn once clear of the boats around you. Otherwise, you'll be disqualified. Pretty simple, and quite reasonable if you think about it.

Starting Early. If a boat crosses the line early, it must restart by returning to the proper side of the line, staying clear of all other boats as it does so. The exception to this is if the I flag is flying, prohibiting boats from crossing the line from the wrong direction within a minute of the starting gun. In this case, you must clear yourself by sailing around one end of the line or the other. Only then can you once again cross the line and begin racing.

STARTING STRATEGIES

What follows are four standard starting strategies. Don't feel like you're an inferior racer because you use them again and

again. The bottom line is that they work. In fact, if you were to sit back and watch the local fleet champion during the course of a season, there's a good chance you would see him or her using one of these strategies a good three-quarters of the time. Remember, you've already got plenty to worry about without trying to develop your own newfangled starting strategy. There's no reason to make sailboat racing any more complicated than it already appears to be.

REACHING OUT AND REACHING IN

This is probably the most commonly used start for the obvious reason that it is simple to execute and fairly straightforward. Basically, you note the time remaining to the start as you beam-reach by the committee boat on port tack. Then you tack or jibe when a little less than half the remaining time has elapsed and sail back toward the committee boat on starboard tack. In theory at least, you should hit the boat end of the line just in time for your start. If you are a little fast you can always luff your sails to slow down. Or you can just keep reaching along the line until you hear the horn, then harden up, sheeting in sails and steering a higher course to sail across. This can be good way to avoid barging at the committee boat end of the line.

Alas, but the very simplicity of this strategy contains the seeds of many a sailor's downfall. You will often see entire fleets of boats beam-reaching off on port

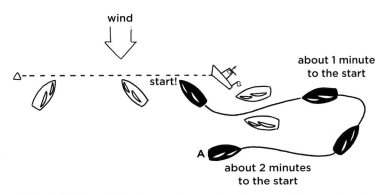

At about 2 minutes to the start, boat **A** begins reaching out and then reaching in, in order to cross the line at full speed at the starting signal.

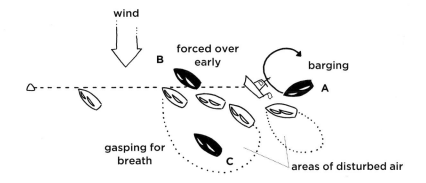

There are several dangers of starting at the boat end of the line with a reach-out, reach-in start. Here, boat **A** is caught barging; boat **B** is being forced over the line early by the boats to leeward; and boat **C** is sailing through the bad air coming off the sails of the boats to windward.

tack a couple of minutes before the start, only to come thundering back all at the same time, blocking each other's air, crowding the boat end of the line, and leaving at least a couple of poor fellows bobbing in their wake. As a result, you must be very careful not to be caught barging or in a position where someone to leeward can force you over the line early. And, oh yes, they'll do that, even to a wet-behind-the-ears beginner. Among other things, it's a hell of a satisfying feeling to knock out at least one

boat right at the beginning so you know it's securely behind you. It's also an excellent way to ensure you have clear air!

Let's say Adam, for example, sails past the committee boat on port tack with 2:32 to go to the start, and then tacks at 1:30, only to find himself with Rich ahead and to leeward as they approach the line. Rich, of course, not only wants clear air, he's miffed because Adam disagreed with him over the organization of one of the chapters of this book. As a result, he will try to do everything he can to catch Adam barging and make him go around. Fortunately, Adam foresees this dilemma and luffs his sails, slowing his boat so Rich will sail ahead. Unfortunately, the wind has picked up a bit, and they both sail past the committee boat a little early; in no time they find themselves reaching along the line on starboard tack, with various boats to leeward trying to make their lives difficult by forcing them over early. They flog their sails and bob and weave in the hope that the boats to leeward will either pass ahead or fall behind. But Adam is still caught out and has to recross the line. And remember, he has no rights over any of the other boats until he recrosses!

"Of course," you may be saying, "the obvious solution would have been to stay well below the line until the last few seconds before the gun, and then harden up." Unfortunately, this strategy can also result in problems, because it means there's a good chance there will be boats to windward stealing your air. Let's say Adam, having learned his lesson in the first race, stays well below the line for the second, with the express intent of giving back as good as he got. "Aha!" he cries as he jibes around and begins sailing back toward the committee boat on a course that will take him a few boatlengths to leeward. But there's a problem. Once he gets there he can't move. There's a solid wall of sails to windward, and he's trapped in their turbulence to leeward. Desperately, he tries to sail up to the line for a breath of air. Desperately, he strives to get his revenge on the guy that forced him over just an hour earlier. But it's

no use. He's barely moving. True, he's not going to be caught over early this time. But after the horn sounds, it's almost a full minute before he finally crosses the line, which is just as bad.

So what's a sailor to do? Is the reach-out, reach-in start any good after all?

The answer is yes, but you have to be careful. Don't get too close to the line, but don't let yourself get pushed down too far, either. Keep an eye out for other boats to leeward and try to anticipate their movements, so you can begin killing your speed in order to fall behind or dip below them. Note that, in addition to luffing your sails, a great way to slow down is to steer a zigzag course, carving a couple of dramatic turns to slow your forward progress. The advantages of this tactic are you don't have to mess up your nicely trimmed sails and you maintain much of your boat's momentum, leaving you in a much better position when it comes time to pour on the speed. Also, there are few things better for staking out your own private starting area than sailing up and down on a dramatic and erratic course. Luff up to scare away any boats behind and above, so they won't even think about trying to sail by to windward, stealing your air. Steer back down to let the guys to leeward know you're not giving anything away. In advanced racing texts this is called "defending your space." Follow the rules, of course. If someone is to leeward, they've got rights. But keep them guessing, and hopefully they will choose to avoid tangling with you at all.

Another simple solution to the barging

and over-the-line-early dilemma is to get ahead of the crowd—avoid the boat end of the line and go for a midline start. Again, as stated at the very beginning of this chapter, getting the absolute "best" start in the fleet can be a challenge, but getting an adequate start can be relatively simple. One of the best ways to do this is to stay away from the boat end of the line.

Let's say Adam, for example, is now getting ready for the third race in what, to this point at least, has been a pretty ill-started regatta. To hell with it, he thinks, and resolves to avoid the crowds, come what may. This time he passes the committee boat on port tack at around 2:50, and then at 1:50 he makes a nice easy jibe back toward the line, following a course some two or three boatlengths to leeward of the committee boat. Of course, at this point there are still all kinds of boats coming at him on port tack, but they are of no great concern because he is on starboard and has right-of-way. The same goes for the boats that are in the process of tacking or jibing over onto starboard. At one point he sees Rich pinching up toward the committee boat, sails flapping as he tries to kill his speed. But Adam just ducks below him, maintaining speed all the time and continuing his quest for an open stretch of line. Eventually, he finds himself a bit ahead of schedule—not being used to all this clear air!—so he executes a few sharp turns to slow himself down. At 10 seconds before the horn, he is two boatlengths below the line and moving fast. Just as the yelling begins in earnest back by the committee boat, he hardens up and begins sailing upwind. When the horn sounds, he is crossing the line with clear air and at full speed.

And Rich? Poor fellow. He paid the price for being greedy by getting run over by all those windward boats; he was left wallowing in their turbulent air. It appears Adam was right about that chapter after all!

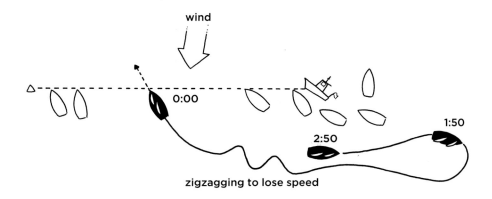

A midline start can prevent problems with barging and bad air. Note that while the committee boat end is favored because the wind direction is not quite perpendicular to the line, there is enough traffic there that some boats are in big trouble; at least two of them are in danger of being caught barging.

The Midline Start

Although many sailors try to "win" the start by shooting off the line right at the boat end or the pin, it is often best to start toward the middle of the line, where there is less traffic and you can concentrate on hitting the line with boat speed right at the gun. Remember, if you fail to beat out the rest of the crowd at the ends, you may find yourself barging, being taken over the line early, or choking on another boat's bad air.

APPROACHING ON PORT TACK

The Tartan Ten (T-Ten) fleet in the Upper Midwest is a thing to behold, with scads of boats and hundreds of gung ho sailors. Imagine anywhere from forty to forty-five boats, each of them over thirty-three feet long, all taking part in the national championship or the Detroit or Chicago National Offshore One-Design (NOOD) regattas. Of course, the starts are more than a little crazy, even with starting lines over two thousand feet long. Think solid walls of fiberglass and sailcloth hemming you in from every direction; boats careening about with only a few feet or even inches of water between them. It's a good thing most T-Ten sailors know their stuff; otherwise, there would be a heck of a lot of work afterward for repairmen and insurance adjusters.

Still, a funny thing happened one year on the first day of the Chicago NOOD regatta. Acclaimed sailing photographer Walter Cooper was there, taking pictures of one of the starts from a helicopter, and when the films were developed, there they were: holes!

Great holes in the middle of the fleet, with all the clear air a sailor would ever need. Of course, most of the line was crowded with boats, all battling for space. And if you had asked the average sailor (there were well over three hundred of them in that fleet alone!), they would have said there was barely room for all of them to fit. Still, there they were—the holes. Anyone hitting them would have been off and running in a prime position to win the whole shebang.

It is with these holes in mind that we move on to the second starting technique—approaching on port tack—since it is a flexible style designed to take advantage of any gaps in the fleet. This time when there are two or three minutes left before the start, you will reach off on starboard tack away from the buoy end of the line, and then come back in on port tack on a course parallel to the line and two to three boatlengths below it. As you sail along on port, watch the boats ahead and to windward coming at you on starboard tack and keep an eye out for gaps. Then, when you see one—a gap, that is—flop over onto starboard tack and go for it, preferably aiming for the windward, or weather end of the opening. That will leave you room to foot off, sailing a slightly lower course to pick up some extra speed if necessary. (For more about footing off, see chapter 7, Basic Tactics and a Few Tips.) The beauty of this technique is it allows you to avoid bunches of boats, and you therefore avoid the problem of being taken over the line early. One disadvantage is that while on port tack, you have to keep an eye out for starboard-tack boats. In addition, when you find your hole you have to be able to accelerate effectively after your tack. However, neither of these challenges is beyond the ability of any competent skipper or crew. And, again, developing skills like these is one of the reasons we go racing in the first place.

To help illustrate this style, let's imagine that Rich, still shaken from that last start, decides to try a port-tack approach to the line, while Adam goes back to the old reach-out, reach-in. At 2:50 before the horn, Rich is sailing away from the pin end of the line on starboard. Then at 1:50 he tacks back, sailing a course just below the buoy, so that he will be three boatlengths to leeward. Notice that, as was the case when Adam did his midline reach-out, reach-in start, Rich didn't just divide the time in two while adding a few seconds for a tack. Instead he left himself plenty of time to sail a portion of the line before flopping over onto starboard and powering up to develop some speed as he's driving for the start.

Coming back in on port, he passes the buoy end of the line with 45 seconds to go and begins checking out the fleet to see what kinds of opportunities are out there. Of course, off in the distance a whole herd is coming in on starboard tack from beyond the committee boat, but Rich and his crew are more concerned with the boats in the immediate area; the situation doesn't look too bad. Among other things, he and his crew have once again decided on a midline start, which means they will avoid much of the traffic. And, although being on port tack is in many ways a disadvantage, it has one huge advantage: you are not yet committed to a single approach to the line and can ultimately pick whatever course you think is best.

Eventually, after a couple of boats on starboard tack rush by on their way to their own midline starts, Rich flops over onto starboard to take advantage of a gap he's been eyeing for a few seconds. Once on starboard he begins to power up, first sailing a close reach to get some boat speed, then hardening up to hit the line.

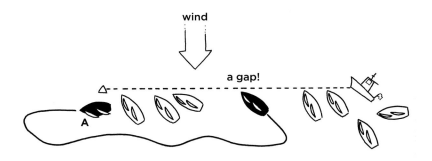

*Approaching the starting line on port tack: Note how boat **A** has lots of room to sail a slightly lower course to pick up speed if it wants.*

But what about all those boats on starboard, you ask? Ah! Remember, Rich is not only on starboard tack, he is also the leeward boat, so they have to stay out of *his* way. Say, for example, Adam manages to claw his way ahead of the crowd. Rich can now luff up to pinch him off or make him bear away and either eat his bad air or continue down the line. In fact, if Rich has played his cards right, he is now in the catbird seat: he can control the boats to windward and he has a wide-open space to leeward, where he can foot off to accelerate and be content with the fact that there's no one around to force him over the line early. Before you know it, he's got a couple of boats stacked up to windward, and he cracks off his sheets to get a bit more boat speed. When the horn blows, he's in a perfect position as he goes powering off the line, much like those lucky crews in the Tartan Ten fleet. Actually, come to think of it, maybe those T-Ten sailors weren't just "lucky" after all.

To the savvy sailor, even the biggest fleet has its opportunities. A port-tack approach might seem dangerous at first. But it can be leveraged into a position of great power when boats start bunching up as they close with the line.

THE VANDERBILT START

The Vanderbilt start (named for the wealthy yachtsman Harold Vanderbilt, who skippered the three America's Cup J boats *Enterprise*, *Rainbow*, and *Ranger*), is a simple and reliable start that works well, as long as you aren't in a fleet that's too large or competitive. Basically the strategy consists of reaching away from the line on port tack, on the reciprocal of a close-hauled starboard-tack

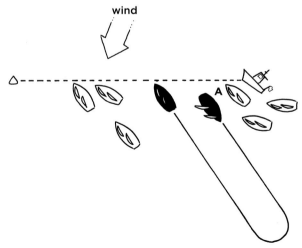

*In the Vanderbilt start, boat **A** initially sails away from the starting line on a broad reach. At a little less than half the time between the time it sailed away from the line and the start, it will tack or jibe around and begin driving for the line, theoretically hitting it at full speed just as the gun is sounding.*

course. At first glance this might appear to be the same as the reach-out, reach-in start. But it is in fact quite different, because you are sailing away from the line on a broad reach, instead of a beam reach, which takes you to leeward of the reach-in, reach-out crowd. Then, at the appropriate time, you tack or jibe around and begin driving for the line, theoretically hitting it at full speed just as the gun is sounding.

Of course, the advantage of this plan of attack is that, assuming you've got your timing down, there's little chance of being caught over early. Granted, if someone else is following the same strategy to leeward, he can luff you up in an effort to defend his space. But you'll never know the terror of that poor guy beam-reaching down the line with a good 20 seconds to go with seemingly the entire fleet coming up from leeward. There's also the added perk of having a nice view of the boats to windward; much like the port-tack approach strategy, you can pick your spots. If one part of the line, for example, is beginning to look a little crowded, you can foot off to a spot where there's a bit more space. If someone is just sitting on the line flogging his sails, with all kinds of open space to windward, and you've got your timing down and plenty of boat speed, this might be a good time to pinch up a little (sail slightly higher) and roll right over him off the line.

Of course, as is the case with nearly everything in sailing, there's no such thing as a free lunch, and the Vanderbilt start is rife with hazards in the form of bad air. If you have decided to make your racing debut at the Optimist National Championship regatta, for example, where the boats number—quite literally—in the hundreds, a Vanderbilt start will likely leave you wallowing in the back row, waiting patiently for the rest of the fleet to get halfway to the windward mark before you start moving again.

Still, if it's just a handful of racer-cruisers mixing it up on a Wednesday night and you are unwinding from a long day at the office, there's no harm in giving it a try.

Let's say Rich, for instance, is out with some friends on a new J/109 racing boat, with eight other boats in a Performance Handicap Racing Fleet, or PHRF, class out of Waukegan Harbor. The wind is steady out of the southwest at around 18 knots, the water is flat, and there isn't a cloud in the sky. With 2:15 to go before the horn, he starts sailing away from the boat end of the line on a broad reach. Then, at 1:15 to the horn, he jibes, allowing a few extra seconds to come back up to speed. At this point, the better part of the fleet is also coming toward the line to windward on a reach-out, reach-in pattern. But Rich, having jibed so that he is on a heading to cross the line a little downwind of the committee boat, has clear air and is moving well. In fact, Rich is moving a bit too well and is afraid of getting to the line too soon. Therefore he throws in a couple of dramatic zigzags to slow himself down and work his way a little farther away from the committee boat, ensuring he won't get caught in anybody else's bad air. One of the boats that mistimed the start is now roaring past up ahead.

But Rich lets him go, and the other fellow is relieved not to have to tangle with a competitor to leeward when he is so close to the line. With 20 seconds to go, Rich hardens up and drives for the line. There is no one below and, even if there were, Rich now has the speed to roll him or her. The boats to windward are busy playing their boat-end games, all the while giving Rich a wide berth and eyeing him like a herd of gazelles keeping tabs on the Lion King at a watering hole. At this point Rich's only concern is hitting the line at full speed, just as the horn sounds. When it does, the crew of the J/109 is off and running.

DINGHY START

The fourth starting technique works for dinghies, small centerboard boats, and catamarans—basically those boats that are quick to accelerate. With this approach, you sail up to the starting line a few seconds early, luff your sails to park your boat in a good position, and wait. Then just before it's time to go, you trim in to build up boat speed, so you'll be ready to take off from the line at the gun. The idea here is, if you're not moving, you're not barging either. True, you don't have rights, but at the same time, the boats coming up from behind have to give you the opportunity to get out of the way. Of course, if you aren't moving you can argue that you *can't* get out of the way.

Obviously, this strategy won't work for a heavy cruiser that takes a day and an age to get up to speed. But it can be quite effective if your boat is a nimble one, especially in larger fleets where space at the starting line is at a premium. In fact, in some large centerboarder fleets, it's not at all uncom-

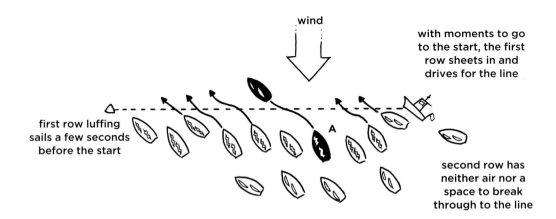

wind

with moments to go to the start, the first row sheets in and drives for the line

first row luffing sails a few seconds before the start

A

second row has neither air nor a space to break through to the line

*Racers who use the dinghy start sail up to the starting line a few seconds early, park, and wait for the gun. In this illustration, boat **A** is one of a number of boats in a large, crowded fleet using this strategy to secure a space on the line. The boats that didn't get to the line early have been relegated to the "second row" and have no choice but to cross the line late.*

The Four Types of Starts

Reach-out, reach-in: Simple to execute, but there is the danger of getting caught in a crowd. Often works especially well when setting up a midline start.

Port-tack approach: Offers a lot of flexibility in finding holes in the starting line, but requires heads-up crew work and good sail handling.

Vanderbilt start: Another simple start to execute, this has the advantage of being a good way to avoid being taken over the line early. On the downside, there is the danger of finding yourself to leeward of the competition and choking on their bad air.

Dinghy start: Good if you have a boat that accelerates quickly, especially in larger fleets, because it assures a place at the starting line and you don't have to worry about being taken over early. However, take care not to be overrun by boats coming up from astern, especially in larger fleets.

mon to see the entire "front row" of boats just below the line, luffing their sails a few moments before the start. However, in large fleets in particular, you don't want to be overtaken by a boat coming up from astern and to windward. If you can't get up to speed quickly enough, you might find yourself getting rolled over by a number of boats and wallowing in their bad air.

A WORD ABOUT BOAT HANDLING

As you may have noticed in the previous four sections, the start is one of those times when you have to be pretty comfortable with your boat handling. The person at the helm has to be confident about throwing in a quick tack or jibe or steering an irregular course to slow down. The sail trimmers have to be ready to do their part when changing tacks or speeds, and the rest of the crew has to be confident about calling out the time to the start and keeping an eye out for other boats—all pretty tall orders for a bunch of casual sailors. But then again, isn't that what this whole racing exercise is about: to become better sailors?

If you're at all nervous about your abilities, practice with your crew. Practice tacks and jibes, accelerating, and slowing down. Try steering your boat with the sails as opposed to the rudder to see how it behaves. Practice different approaches to the starting line. Maybe even pretend that you've been caught barging and have to make a quick tack out of there and do it again.

Sound like a lot of work? Well, it is. But again that's all part of the fun. There are plenty of nonsailors and non-racers out there who think sailboat racing is a sedentary sport requiring little more exertion than a video game. How wrong they are! Still, after all the work, what a great feeling you will have when you get back on shore. You've earned that beer!

While we're at it, here's another dirty little secret of sailboat racing: almost nobody actually practices. Granted, some of those saltier dogs have a good bit of experience under their belts. But plenty of crews just make it up as they go. In fact, it's amazing how little time some sailors actually spend on the water. Take your crew out for a couple of well-planned practice sessions and you might be surprised at how things turn out on the racecourse.

Boat Handling Practice for the Start

To hone the sailing skills necessary for confident starting, go out on a sunny day with your regular crew and practice your tacks and jibes, swerving about to kill speed, accelerating from a near standstill, and luffing sails to slow down. The idea is to become comfortable with how your boat responds to this kind of maneuvering. Find a navigational buoy with plenty of water around it and imagine it's the committee boat. Use it to practice hitting the line at a certain time and at full speed. Try coming around ahead of schedule to practice killing speed while making sure you still hit the line at full speed just before the horn. Finally, try steering with your sails as opposed to just using the rudder: strap in your mainsail to induce some weather helm and bring the bow up; then strap in the jib and ease the main to bring the bow back down. These practices will give you a much better idea of how your boat performs. The more you know about how your boat handles, the better you'll do on the racecourse.

FINAL THOUGHTS ON STARTING

The astute reader will have noticed that although we said at the beginning it's important to determine the favored end of the line, there has not been a lot of talk about how to take advantage of that information. The reason is that, at this stage of the game, it doesn't make that much difference. If the line is dramatically skewed, you will want to modify one of your four strategies to move you a bit to one side or the other. But it is still a good idea to go for a midline start, away from the crowds. Your goal should be to position yourself a little left or right of center.

Some readers might also be wondering about port-tack starts, those near-mythic situations in which some gutsy sailor hits the pin end on port tack at full speed, and then sails with impunity across the bows of the starboard-tacked fleet. The answer is that the beginner (and most veterans, for that matter) has absolutely no business even *contemplating* such lunacy. Granted, you'll be the talk of the fleet if you pull it off. But there are so many things that can go wrong—other boats trying the same thing slowing you down, a starboard-tack boat getting in your way when you should be thundering across the line—that you stand a much better chance of getting a good look at all their transoms. Remember, your goal at this point is not necessarily to get the best start in the fleet, just a darn good one. If you do find yourself in a situation in which the pin end is heavily favored and you want to take advantage of that, fine. You can always set up your reach-out, reach-in or your port-tack approach so you'll be over toward that end, without running the risk of total disaster. Let some other maniac start on port tack. Even if he succeeds, your start will still have been a good enough one that, with a little luck and some fast sailing, you should be able to reel him in on the way to the windward mark.

Along these same lines, it sometimes makes sense to actually aim for the *unfavored* end in an effort to stay out of traffic. This is especially the case in larger fleets where the issue of clear air can be truly daunting. One year at the Soling World Championship regatta, for example, renowned sailor and author Stuart Walker decided to start every race at the pin end, even though with seventy boats taking part on a line that was over twenty-eight hundred feet long he sometimes had to sail ten boatlengths farther than the guys starting toward the other side. Oddly enough, it didn't seem to matter. Even when the committee boat end was dramatically favored, he had clear air and was going fast enough to quickly make up the difference. Not only that, he became so proficient at starting toward the pin end that, when it *was* favored, he had little trouble beating the boats in the area. Once again, the rest of the fleet found itself playing follow the leader.

Granted, the idea of intentionally avoiding the favored end might seem a little extreme at first. But remember: during any given race in this regatta, there were probably fifty boats all trying to start at the favored end at the same time. Of those, five may have had good starts, the next twenty may have taken off in somewhat bad air, and the rest would have been left in the dust. As the regatta continued, Stuart found more and more boats joining him at the pin end, just trying to get a halfway decent start so they could be among the top twenty at the first mark. From 20th place you can work your way up. If you're in 60th place at the end of the first leg, you're in trouble.

While on the subject of disasters, it's always good to keep in mind that everyone has starts that go to pieces—even veterans. Everyone also has been caught barging or been forced over the line early at some point. So don't be too hard on yourself if the gun goes off and you find yourself at the very back of the fleet, spinning about without any steerage. The start of a sailboat race can already be a little scary and more than a little unnerving, so don't make it any worse by taking the attitude that the world will end if you can't squeeze your way in at the committee boat. This is only a game after all, and despite what some may say, the start alone does not predetermine the finish. In fact, it's often just the opposite. Good sailors don't just do things right, they don't give up when they've done things wrong.

So, if you're caught barging or find yourself getting pushed over the line early with no escape, accept your fate and allow the guy to leeward to rain on your parade. That's life. Your turn will come. Whatever you do, don't ruin the other competitors' day by continuing to barge or just holding your course and sailing down the line, and the rules be damned. Among other things, doing those things can be quite dangerous.

One time during a major regatta on Lake Michigan, the owner of a brand-new 40-footer persisted in sailing down the line, despite the fact that a number of boats were trying to force him up to a higher course that would push him over early. Everyone else in the fleet couldn't help but stop and watch; there was that much yelling as this boat continued on its way, oblivious to everyone else in the area. Finally, with about three seconds to go, another new boat, trimmed in for the beat, appeared from out of the confusion to leeward and crashed into the barging boat at full speed. Over $700,000 worth of hulls and hardware crunched. What happened was that the boat to leeward couldn't see the barger because there were so many boats in the area going slow and bunched up along the line. To make matters worse, the barging boat protested. So, not only did that skipper ruin the day for the crews involved, he also ruined the night.

The lesson here is simple: if things start going wrong, bail out and live to sail the next race. If you do somehow foul one of your competitors, be a good sport and do your penalty turns. When the race is over it probably wouldn't hurt to also buy the other skipper a beer, just to make sure there are no hard feelings and everybody stays friends.

Q & A

Q. With 15 seconds to go to the start, Rich is luffing up toward the committee boat and Adam is reaching across toward the line. Adam calls out for room at the mark. Rich tells him to go stuff himself. Who has the right-of-way?
A. According to Rule 18.1a, Adam has to stay clear of Rich. This is a classic case of Adam being caught barging.

Q. With 30 seconds to go to the start, Rich luffs his sails to kill speed, and Adam sails up alongside and to leeward. With 20 sec-

onds to go, both sheet in and start driving for the line. Both are late, and 5 seconds after the starting signal, but before they have crossed the line, Adam starts luffing up to pinch Rich off at the committee boat and make him go back around. Rich tells him to go back down to his proper course. Should Adam give way or keep luffing?
A. Adam needs to go back down to a beat, because he established his overlap from behind and to leeward.

Q. What is the best way to kill time if you are running a bit ahead of schedule on your final approach to the line? Why?
A. Steer an erratic course by making some dramatic turns—if there's room to do so. This way you will not have to get your boat up to speed again, and you will be able to carve out an area of clear air and maneuvering room for your own start.

Q. What is the primary down side to the reach-out, reach-in start?
A. You run the risk of being caught barging.

Q. Why is the favored end not always the best place to start a sailboat race?
A. Because it is generally very crowded, especially with larger fleets. Only a handful of those boats at the favored end will get good starts. The rest will be left behind as they struggle through bad air or get caught barging.

Chapter 3

THE
WINDWARD
LEG

Congratulations! You've survived the start. That wasn't so bad now, was it? Now you're off, and really racing.

Before you get too complacent, though, make sure you're sailing fast and going in the right direction. The best start in the world can be for naught if you get run over by a bunch of boats to windward mere moments after the horn. It would also be a shame if you threw away that lovely position by sailing into a spot on the course where there's no wind.

While you're at it, be sure and get into a comfortable position where you can feel the boat. Don't hunch over or sit in a spot where you have to cock your head at strange angles to see the sails. Relax and sit or stand in a stable position. Sailboat races last longer than most other sporting events, and there's no real way to ever take a break. Don't be a "one-lap Louie" and tire yourself out.

Back in the 1960s, in the Chicago area, there was a kid named Ritchie Stearns who used to sail a Soling. Because it was the hot new Olympic class at the time, the fleet was filled with good sailors who were also good family friends; on race day it was like having a half-dozen dads out on the water. All of a sudden, while sailing upwind in a race, he would hear, "Ritchie! Sit up straight!" And there would be Buddy Melges yelling, "You can't win all slumped over like that!" Needless to say, this was more than a little mortifying for a kid in the throes of adolescence. But it was good advice, especially for those longer regattas.

SAILING SMART ON THE WINDWARD LEG

The good news is there are no special rules. You've left the starting line behind and the windward mark is still off in the distance. It's just you and the rest of the fleet hammering away to windward—may the best crew win.

The bad news is you are now in a situation in which boat speed is paramount, especially in those first few moments of the race. It's amazing how, within minutes of the horn, so much distance can separate the front from the back of an otherwise evenly matched fleet.

In terms of sail trim, the details of upwind sail theory and boat speed are covered in chapters 9–11. Still there are a few basic principles you and your crew should follow by way of preparation and boat handling to ensure you wring the most performance possible out of your boat.

Trim Your Sails in Advance. If you wait until after the gun or horn to figure out things such as your jib lead angle and headstay tension, you're already dead meat. This all should be done prior to your section's starting sequence, while you're sailing around getting ready for the race. That way, when the horn sounds, all you have to do is sheet in sails and you're on your way. Granted, the conditions may have changed during the battle at the line, and as soon as you're racing you may have to reevaluate

how your sails are set for the wind and waves. But at least you'll have a good baseline from which to get started.

Not only that, by having your basic trim set before the start, you can concentrate on fine-tuning for any tactical situations you may face as you blast off the line. For instance, if you need to speed up a bit to keep your air clear, all you have to do is ease your sheets ever so slightly and steer down just a touch. If, on the other hand, you need to pinch up to get rid of a boat to windward and astern, trim in hard and maybe let the boat heel a little to help bring the bow up a few degrees. Whatever the case, have your sail adjustments set. You don't want people fumbling about, tweaking the outhaul or cunningham at the same time you're dealing with the tactical situation.

Never Be Satisfied. Whether the conditions are fairly constant or variable, you should always be thinking about your sails, your boat's angle of heel, the waves, the wind, the competition, the weather, and the helm to make sure your boat is going as fast as possible. Don't just set your sails and enjoy the ride.

Small adjustments are what we're looking for here. Remember that optimum speed for different boats requires different trim settings (for more information about sail trim, see chapter 9, Boat Speed, Part 1: Sail Controls and Concepts). Spending time on the water will make it feel like second nature. Eventually, as you get comfortable with your boat and sails you will know what a half-inch of ease looks like in the sail.

Concentrate on your steering. You want to "feel" the boat. Next time you are out practicing, try sailing with your eyes closed (with one of your crew keeping an eye out for hazards, of course). Well-designed boats will tell you when you're going fast or slow. In fact, good steering can make up for deficiencies in other areas. Years ago during a major Star boat regatta, North American champion Peter Wright seemed to have better boat speed than the rest of the fleet, causing a number of his competitors to take a closer look at the set of his sails. In fact, his trim wasn't very good at all. But he was concentrating and steering so well, he ended up winning the race anyway.

If you are sailing parallel to one of the other boats in your class, use it as a "trial horse." Constantly adjust your sails and helm in an effort to sail faster and higher, or closer to the wind, than the other guy. If you are in gusting winds, the mainsheet trimmer should be in continual communication with the helmsman to make sure the sail isn't overpowering the boat, causing it to heel over too far, making it harder to steer, and slowing it down. The rest of the crew should be hiking out on the windward rail and keeping an eye out for gusts or puffs, so they can warn their comrades at the helm and at the main to be ready. In light air, however, the crew should position itself so the boat has the right angle of heel and isn't too far down in either the bow or the stern.

Know before you start racing how your boat handles, but always be ready to learn a new lesson. Back in 1986, there was a race in which the *Heart of America* America's Cup contender won the start against Tom Blackaller and the San Francisco syndicate's *USA*, but then had a hell of a time fending off the other boat's counterattacks. It was windy and choppy, and while sailing in a straight line the San Francisco boat kept drawing closer and closer. It was pure boat speed, and there didn't seem to be anything the *Heart of America* crew could do about it. Using a few choice words, helmsman Buddy Melges proclaimed he was "not going to steer this damn boat anymore." He then gripped the wheel hard and just sailed her straight. Within moments, *Heart of America* started to gain on *USA* and, lo and behold, at the end of the day *Heart of America* won the race. Afterward, the general consensus was, because Melges held the wheel firmly, the rudder was able to act more effectively as an additional lifting surface, almost like a second keel. The additional lifting action more than overcame the extra resistance that resulted from hitting the waves head on after Melges stopped steering around them. The lesson here: never stop looking for ways to make your boat go a little bit faster.

Tack Intelligently. Think before tacking, and then tack to maintain maximum speed. Whenever possible, this should include trying to gain a bit of speed before the tack or, at the very least, finding a smooth spot in the water in which to make your turn. Keep in mind that on most boats, for every tenth of a knot you've lost going into a tack, you will come out at least two-tenths of a knot slower than if you'd tacked at the optimum speed.

In terms of the actual process of tacking, all too often neophyte crews will cast off the old jib sheet too early or be too slow in taking up on the new sheet, so the headsail billows out to leeward after the bow has come through the eye of the wind. This, of course, makes it that much harder to sheet in and drags the boat to a screeching halt. To prevent this, make sure the crew casting off the old sheet and taking in on the new one are working together. If your boat has a large overlapping jib, be sure the trimmer has a couple of wraps around the winch in advance, so he can begin sheeting in as soon as the jib comes across the foredeck. You might also need to position a crewmember at the mast to make sure the sail gets across cleanly. Aboard boats with small non-overlapping headsails, like a Thistle or a Mumm 30, the jib should snap across cleanly, with the new sheet following so quickly there is absolutely no need to haul it in under load or resort to the use of a winch handle. In fact, the rule of thumb on this kind of boat is, if you have to crank in after a tack, someone is doing something wrong. To tack a boat with a large overlapping genoa, the helmsman begins the tack by easing the boat into the wind until the genoa begins to luff about a third of the way aft. At this point, the trimmer releases the sheet. After that, the helmsman guides the boat through the wind a bit faster, until the genoa blows through the foretriangle. Once it has, he should steer the boat back up toward the wind again, so the genoa

won't luff out too far as the crew is taking it in. Many helmsmen make the mistake of immediately steering down for speed, filling the sail so that the poor crew has to crank it all of the way in under load. This is both slow and hard on the arms. Only when the sail is most of the way in should the helmsman steer down for speed, making the crew work as it pulls in the final trim.

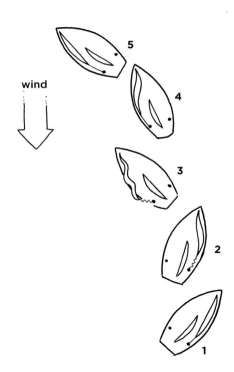

*When tacking an overlapping genoa, the helmsman begins the tack (**1**), and when the genoa starts to luff, the trimmer releases the sheet (**2**). The helmsman steers around until the jib blows through the foretriangle, at which point the crew tails in the jib without using the winch handle (**3**). Next, the helmsman sails high to backwind the genoa, until it is most of the way in (**4**). After that he steers down to course, while the crew cranks in the final jib trim, using the winch handle (**5**).*

No matter the size of the jib, when sailing in heavy air, try to keep the crew on the windward rail for as long as possible, instead of having everyone tumble inboard as soon as you make the decision to tack. Otherwise, you may suddenly find the boat on its ear, slowing it at precisely the same time you want all the boat speed possible for sailing through the eye of the wind.

Maintain Clear Air. Don't sail in other boats' disturbed air. When sailing to windward, a sailboat leaves a wind "shadow" of turbulent air at an angle to leeward and astern that is about ten times as long as the mast is high. Making a habit of sailing in this kind of bad air is a sure way to end up at the back of the fleet.

It also is a generally bad idea to sail directly behind another boat, although the difficulty here is more psychological than physical. Specifically, whenever you are trailing a competitor, the boat in front usually gets the air first, which means it can sail the windshifts, whereas you have to decide between sailing your optimal course and reacting to what's going on in front of you. For example, if the boat in front heads up in a lift, your first reaction might be to change course as well, so you won't fall any closer to the other guy's bad air. Unfortunately, because you aren't yet in that new air you might have to pinch, which means you will slow down and end up farther behind. The key then is to try to ignore the guy ahead and play your window of clear air for as long as you can. Unfortunately, this is often easier said than done.

Along these same lines, don't allow other boats to lee-bow you by sailing ahead and to leeward. Contrary to popular belief, unless you are trailing a boat with a *huge* main, such as that aboard a modern America's Cup racer, the boat to leeward and ahead will not actually be hurting you by deflecting the wind. Still it's a bad idea to be in this position for two reasons. First, because the other guy has the right-of-way, he can steer wherever he wants—down for acceleration and speed or up to pinch you off—while you can only steer a fine line to stay away from him. Second, although he's not necessarily hurting you, you are definitely helping him; specifically, the air in front of your boat is being bent to leeward before it hits your sails, then accelerating over the leeward side of your jib as it creates the force that makes your boat go. The result is you provide a boat ahead and to

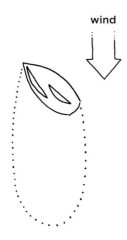

wind

A boat's wind shadow is an area of disturbed, turbulent air stretching about ten mast lengths to leeward and astern.

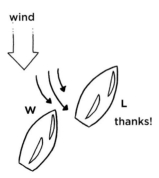

wind

W

L

thanks!

*In a lee-bow situation, the windward boat's (**W**) sails accelerate the wind and deflect it forward, giving the leeward boat (**L**)—the competition—a lift and more wind.*

leeward with both a lift and more wind, which is very generous of you, but not in your own best interest, to say the very least. (For more information about lift, see chapter 9, Boat Speed, Part 1: Sail Controls and Concepts.) Ultimately, whether you think there is bad air to windward and astern of the guy in front or good air to leeward and ahead of the guy in back, they amount to the same thing: you can't sail long with someone off your lee-bow.

Don't Be Taken by Surprise. As you sail to windward, always be on the lookout for

Smart Sailing to Windward

- Adjust your sails for the conditions prior to the start, so you will be sailing fast right off the line.
- Tack efficiently, making sure the helmsman and crew work together to maintain boat speed.
- Maintain clear air at all times.
- Be aware of other boats on the course—don't be taken by surprise!

other boats, especially to leeward on a windy day where the view is obstructed by your sails. This holds true for boats on both port and starboard tacks. It's amazing how even a boat as large as a 45-foot racer-cruiser can sneak up on you if you aren't paying attention. There have been countless instances in which two boats on opposite tacks have sailed right into one another on a clear sunny day, simply because neither was looking where it was going. Furthermore, even if you manage to avoid a collision, few things will kill boat speed as fast as a panic-stricken crash tack thrown in at the last moment to avoid hitting another boat. Sails flog in the wind, sheets thrash out of control, and the boat stops dead in the water. By the time you're up and going again you may have lost a dozen boatlengths on the competition.

PLAYING THE SHIFTS

In addition to boat speed, the other key to sailing quickly to windward is playing the shifts, doing your utmost to harness different slants of wind in order to sail the shortest distance possible to the mark. Contrary to appearances, even the steadiest of breezes has some variation in it, often swinging 5 degrees or more around an average. This in turn means a 10-degree variation in terms of the direction in which your boat is sailing on a given tack. Not only that, in the event of a dramatic change in wind direction, getting yourself on the wrong side of

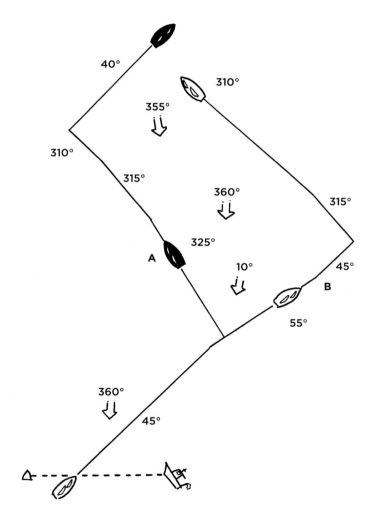

△ windward mark

*The distances for courses **A** and **B** are the same, but by taking advantage of the windshifts—tacking when it finds itself headed so that it will sail on the lifted tack—the boat following course **A** ends up closer to the mark.*

a shift can mean sailing much farther than necessary. Remember, when sailing to windward, pointing ability is as important as flat-out speed.

Let's say, for example, that the upwind leg of the racecourse is bearing 360 degrees with the wind out of the north. Your boat tacks through 90 degrees, so on port tack you are sailing a heading of 45 degrees, while on starboard tack your heading is 315. A few minutes after the start, you're on port tack when the wind in your area veers, or shifts clockwise, 10 degrees to the east, so that it's coming from 010 degrees. Immediately, you find you have to fall off—or sail a lower course—to maintain boat speed; now you are on a heading of 55 degrees. This is obviously not good; you have been headed, or knocked, on this tack, so the course you're steering is at a greater angle from where you want to go, namely the mark. Your progress is impeded.

Fortunately, this situation is easy to fix: simply flop over onto starboard tack. Now things are suddenly looking much brighter. Whereas moments earlier you would have only been able to sail a heading of 315 degrees, you are now sailing a heading of 325, which is taking you more directly toward the windward mark. Put another way, you have now been "lifted" 10 degrees. Your crew looks at you with a whole new kind of respect (see illustration previous page).

Of course, nothing this good lasts forever. A few minutes later, the wind backs, or shifts counterclockwise, 10 degrees to its original heading, so that it's blowing out of the north once again. But you're not overly concerned, because this is the average wind direction you have come to expect anyway. A few minutes after that, when the wind decides to continue backing until the direction is 355 and your starboard-tack heading is 310, you simply flop back over onto port tack. Now you are sailing a heading of 40 degrees, lifted toward the mark on a course that is 5 degrees higher than when the wind was blowing from due north.

By comparison, imagine what would have happened if you had maintained your original course after discovering that first windshift, and then tacked just before the appearance of that second shift to the west. The whole time you could have been sailing a lifted starboard tack, you would have been sailing farther and farther from where you wanted to be. It would, of course, have come as a great relief when wind direction returned to 360. But then again, by that time you probably would have begun to notice that the competition on the other side of the course seemed to be slowly pulling ahead. Hoping to get whatever it was they were getting, you might have gone over onto starboard—only to have the wind shift into the west so that you were once again on a headed tack. Before long those boats that tacked away on starboard at the first shift and then came back onto port with the second would be crossing your bow a good half-dozen boatlengths ahead. It would have been all too apparent that something had gone terribly wrong.

Welcome to the agony and the ecstasy of windshifts!

WHERE TO GO

Of course, actually getting "in phase" with the windshifts, as in the example above, is much harder in reality than in theory. The wind can be an incredibly fickle creature, and woe betide the sailor who isn't paying attention when the water on the horizon darkens with ripples, under the influence of a fresh breeze. In addition to oscillating windshifts, in which the wind direction swings back and forth around an average, there are also persistent shifts, in which the average direction shifts completely, and combinations of the two. In fact, this latter, hybrid type is actually the most common. Unless you are in the trade winds or in the throes of a stationary and powerful weather system, the wind is constantly twisting about, bouncing back and forth around an ever-changing mean. Furthermore, few races are set up completely beyond the meteorological influence of the surrounding land. During the course of the day the sailing conditions will often change quite dramatically until the winds in the morning bear little resemblance to those in the afternoon or evening.

In order to determine what the wind is doing and where it will go, it's important to both have a basic understanding of weather and how winds are generated (see chapter 8, Weather) and carefully monitor what the wind is doing on land and as you sail about in the minutes preceding the race. Many sailors will do this by periodically luffing up into the wind and then taking a reading on its direction. But again, this technique is both sloppy and plays hell on your sails—flogging them unnecessarily is a sure way to break down the fibers that give them their strength. A better way to monitor wind is to keep track of your close-hauled headings, paying particular attention to any changes in wind direction, and then use this information to determine what you think the wind will do after the start.

Let's say, for example, it's 30 minutes before the start and you are heading out toward the committee boat in a fresh northerly breeze. Instead of just powering the entire way, you hoist your sails and begin sailing. As you sail, you record a close-hauled heading on port tack of 70 degrees and a starboard-tack heading of 340, giving you a wind direction of 25. A couple of minutes later, while close-hauled again on port tack, you find yourself sailing on a heading of 75 degrees and, flopping over on starboard tack, you find you can now hold a heading of 345. Clearly the wind has veered a few degrees to where it is now blowing from a heading of 30 degrees. Flopping back on port, you continue sailing on 75 for a while. Then you find yourself on 70 again, and even 65. Extrapolating from this latter number, you write down that the wind direction is 20.

After that you find yourself occupied for a few minutes reaching around the committee boat, letting them know you're there and that you intend to race. Then it's back to windward for a few tacks, tuning up the sails, getting the feel of the boat, and taking another look at the wind.

This time, you start out on starboard

Calculating Wind Direction

Instead of periodically turning head-to-wind in order to find wind direction, it's a better idea to calculate where the wind is coming from by keeping track of your close-hauled headings: recording the compass headings on the two tacks and calculating the wind direction as a heading midway between the two. For example, if you're sailing a port-tack heading of 25 and a starboard-tack heading of 295, the wind direction would be 340. Bear in mind that keeping track of course headings and wind directions can get confusing, especially in the heat of competition. So get in the habit of paying attention to your close-hauled headings while out daysailing or cruising, so it becomes second nature.

tack on a heading of 335, which tells you the wind direction is 20 and that on port tack you should be able to manage a heading of 65. Sure enough, tacking over to check the jib lead, you find that this is now exactly what you can do. However, it isn't long before you find that the inside telltales on your jib are lifting, and you're back on a heading of 70, and then 75.

After that it's back to the line, because you don't want to get too far away in case the wind fades. Then a little later, while maneuvering around the committee boat, you harden up on starboard tack for a few moments and find that you are once again sailing a course of 335. By this time your course is clear. It appears to be an oscillating wind, and you have the necessary information to know when and if either tack is favored. A couple of minutes later, the race committee sets a good, square line and signals that the heading to the first mark will be 25. Six

minutes after that, you've managed a decent reach-out, reach-in start at the middle of the line and are powering along on a heading of 340 to 345, confident that you are on the lifted tack. Slowly the other boats in your division begin splitting tacks in search of clear air, but you hold your course, even hitting 347 for a few moments before falling back down to 343. Eventually, you find yourself sailing a heading of 335 and know that, on this tack, you're sailing in a header; in other words, the wind has shifted so it's coming from a direction closer to the bow. After waiting a moment to make sure the shift is the real thing, not just a fluky bit of air, and that there are no other boats in the way, you tack over on port and power up to a course of 65.

From that point on you continue to play the shifts, keeping track of the changes in wind direction as indicated by your different headings, and always remaining on the alert for new extremes, as these might be the precursor to a whole new wind. For example, are you suddenly able to hold a heading of 55 or even 50 on port tack in freshening conditions? Then it's possible you might be experiencing the beginning of a new wind. Be careful though: no matter what tack you're on, the lulls will initially seem like headers and the puffs will feel like lifts—thanks to the effect of wind velocity on apparent wind. Apparent wind is the wind you feel as you are moving across the water, as opposed to the true wind that you would feel if you were standing still. While you're at it, keep an eye out for clouds, patches of dark water, or even flags or smokestacks on shore. This is an area in which a heads-up crew can be invaluable. Many times on an upwind leg, the crew thinks it has nothing to do but hike, when in fact it should be looking for wind and other telltale signs on the horizon. However, be careful not to overload your tactician and skipper with too much information, because that can also cause problems.

To help keep track of all the data when sailing to windward, many skippers simply write the various headings and courses in pencil on the deck by their side. During the 1972 Soling Olympic trials in San Francisco, for example, it was interesting to see that, while guys like Lightning champion Bruce Goldsmith and Bob Johnstone of J-Boats fame kept their boats scrupulously clean, Lowell North's boat was covered with writing in marker and grease pencil. There were notes on everything, from windshifts to work that had to be done on the boat after the race. The best note, which was on the hull since there was no room left on the deck, was "buy more markers."

No matter how you decide to keep track of the wind, be sure to get out on the water far enough in advance of the race to get a good feel for what the wind is doing. It's shocking how many sailors will go roaring up to the line under power just moments before the race, or drift around between races, not paying the least bit of attention to the wind and the waves. If you don't pay attention to the wind and the waves, you give the advantage to your competition before the race even starts. You're basically guaranteeing you will be sailing off the line blind.

Along these same lines, keeping a log of races you compete in is something that few people do, but is a great idea. It helps you get a feel for both the local shifts and your boat's performance in different conditions. East Coast boatbuilder Mark Lindsey, for example, keeps detailed notes of every race he sails. Therefore, if you sail with him in, say,

Writing things down will make it easier to keep track of what's going on in terms of windshifts and sail settings. (DAVE GENDELL)

Keeping Track of Data

If you're squeamish about writing on your pristine white fiberglass, you can buy special Velcro-backed dry-erase boards and markers, although in reality, pencil will come off your deck just fine. If you are sailing a larger boat and have the luxury of a crewmember who can devote his or her time to graphing windshifts on a separate handheld board, by all means have the crewmember do it. Many digital compasses also come with features that indicate whether you are being lifted or headed off a preset course. However, for the beginner in particular, these can be confusing. And for all their precision, these silicon wonders are not as good as the tried-and-true pencil for highlighting trends.

California he will already have notes from the last three or four times he was there, which can give you a real edge on the rest of the fleet.

Also, don't be afraid to ask questions, and not just of sailors. Fishermen are a great source of local knowledge when it comes to current and wind. Although confusing at first glance, the conditions in many sailing areas are often both predictable and heralded by easily recognized signs. On San Francisco Bay, for example, if a little cloud forms over the Golden Gate Bridge, hold on to your hat. Similarly, on Lake Michigan, if the air temperature off Chicago Harbor climbs to 78°F in the spring, expect the breeze to shift to 123 degrees; there's now enough heat to start up the local thermal.

This kind of local knowledge can make all the difference on race day.

PERSISTENT SHIFTS

At this point, the astute reader may be wondering what happens after you've been sailing the lifted tack in a persistent shift for a while and suddenly find you have no choice but to come around onto a horribly headed tack just to make the mark.

The answer is you don't get yourself in this position. Basically, if you believe that a persistent shift is in the offing, the goal is to sail what will be the headed tack first, so it can be avoided further down the road. In racing circles this has been summed up in the adage, "sail to the shift." In other words, choose the tack that takes you toward where you believe the wind will be coming from.

Let's say for example, that the beat has been set on a heading of 15 degrees, and you are sailing about a mile east of a north-south shore. It's a hot, sunny day, and you are sure that as the land heats up there's going to be a sea breeze coming in from the east. Before the start, you find that your port-tack heading is varying between 55 and 70 degrees; and a few minutes after the start when you are sailing on port you notice your compass is pretty much stuck on 70. Clearly, on this tack you are in a header. Instead of flopping over onto the lifted tack, however, you stick to your guns, convinced this is just the beginning of more to come. Sure enough, despite some light, fluky moments when the wind backs and you find yourself sailing as high as 60 degrees again, the wind not only continues to veer, it builds. Now you're feeling better and better about yourself and wondering why every race doesn't go this way. Eventually, after sailing a heading of 80 degrees for a few minutes, you flop over onto starboard where you can now maintain a heading of 350 degrees (as opposed to 330 at the start of the race!). After that the wind continues to shift until you are sailing a heading of 005 degrees; you have reached a point where you can nearly make the mark. Meanwhile the part of the fleet that flopped over to starboard at the beginning of the shift is now back on port, dramatically headed and comfortably behind.

Note that this is an example of when you would want to begin your race at the starboard end of the starting line. That way you could sail as quickly as possible toward the favored side of the course. If you allowed yourself to slip down to the pin end, you might find yourself, after the horn, with a solid wall of starboard-tack boats to windward, making it impossible for you to tack over onto port without ducking beneath every single one of their transoms. Not good! In the event you expected the winds to back to the west, a middle or port-end start would be fine. In fact, the latter might even get you to the new wind that much sooner.

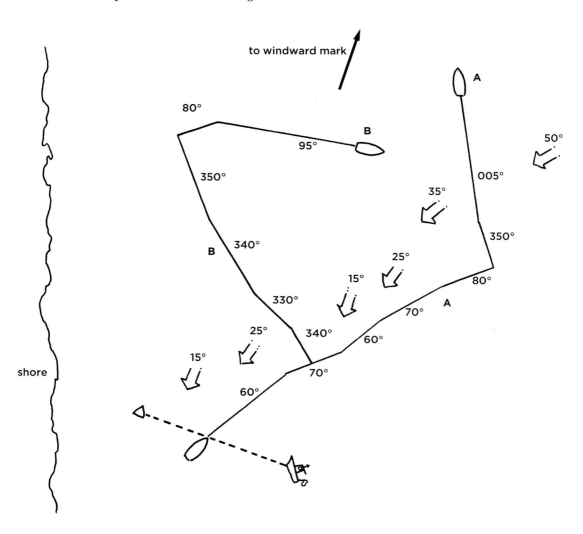

*The distances for courses **A** and **B** are the same. Anticipating a persistent shift, boat **A** doesn't tack when it first experiences a header, but continues to sail in the direction of the anticipated shift. When the shift comes, boat **A** tacks onto a dramatically lifted heading. Meanwhile, boat **B**, which didn't "sail to the shift," finds itself dramatically headed and crossing tacks far astern of the competition.*

Needless to say, intentionally sailing into a header in hopes of gaining something further down the line can take nerves of steel. But then again, it's not like you have to take a flier, splitting with the rest of the fleet and sailing off into the middle of nowhere to take advantage of changing conditions. In fact, your goal is merely to leverage the changing conditions so they'll put you in front of the rest of the fleet; in other words, sail to the anticipated shift just enough to put yourself between it and everybody else. Keep playing the oscillations. Keep your eyes open for any unexpected developments in the weather. But all the while, work yourself slowly and cleverly to the favored side of the course. Don't be greedy. Remember, at the end of the day, you don't have to humiliate the competition. Just make sure they're a few boatlengths behind when you get to the finish line.

MORE TIPS/RULES FOR THE BEAT

While the basic idea is to sail on the lifted tack for as much of the beat as possible, there are a few other general rules for ensuring that you make the most of the windward leg.

Avoid the Corners. True, every time you tack the boat you slow down. But that doesn't mean it's a good idea to allow your beat to consist of just two long tacks with a

single change of course between the two. This is because once you end up on the layline—the point at which you can weather the windward mark—you are pretty much locked into a single course of action; any additional moves will simply hurt you (see chapter 4, Windward Mark Roundings, for more information about laylines). For example, if other boats get in the way or steal

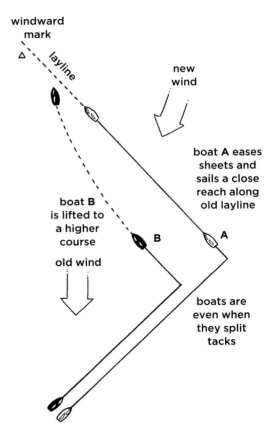

*Once you are on the layline and weathering the windward mark, you no longer benefit from a lift, while the rest of the fleet still can. In this case, when the new wind comes in, boat **A** finds that it is overstanding the mark and sailing a longer distance than boat **B**.*

your wind, you either have to grin and bear it or take a pair of quick tacks to clear your air, slowing the boat and overstanding the mark—sailing farther than you need by going beyond the layline. Of course, you will

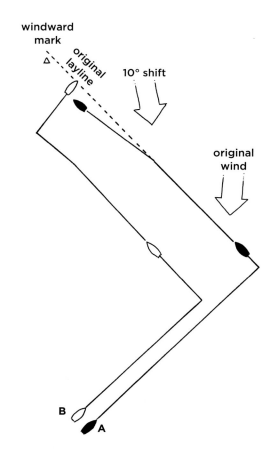

*Even a header can hurt if you are on the layline. Here, boat **A** sails on port tack to the layline, while boat **B** flops over early to starboard. A 10-degree windshift knocks both. Now boat **A** has to throw in a couple of quick tacks to avoid missing the mark. Boat **B**, on the other hand, which planned on making two more tacks all along, will have time to get back up to speed before tacking from port back to starboard. Not only that, when boat **B** is on port it will be on the lifted tack, giving it just enough of an edge to cross in front of boat **A**.*

also be overstanding the mark if you get a lift at this point, whereas tacking a little earlier could have meant reaching the mark while sailing a shorter distance. Overstanding might seem like a good thing in terms of boat speed, because you can crack off, or ease the sheets, and sail a slightly lower course. But because you are sailing farther than necessary to get to the top of the beat, the result is a net loss.

As if that wasn't enough, even a header will hurt you at this point, because you are no longer in a position to take full advantage of it. Imagine, for example, that Adam and Rich are sailing neck and neck on port tack near the end of a beat. Rich carries the tack all the way to layline, while Adam flops over onto starboard a little ways short. Moments later the wind backs a few degrees, giving them both a knock. Rich will now just miss making the mark, so he will have to throw in a couple of quick tacks. Adam, on the other hand, knew all along that he would be tacking again, and because he's carrying that first tack longer, he will be able to get his boat back up to speed before throwing in the second tack. Not only that, when he goes over onto port it will be the lifted tack, giving him just the edge he needs to put himself in front of Rich.

The bottom line is, although you might want to stay to the right or left side of the course, don't go all the way to the edge. In a corner, you lose all chances of being lucky. Don't bang the corners!

Long Leg First. If the wind shifts dramatically and creates a skewed beat, the general

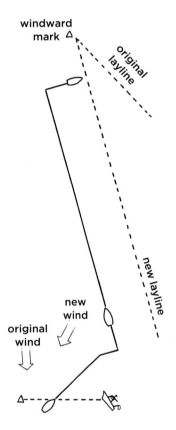

If a shift skews the beat, sail the long tack first. Otherwise you will find yourself on the layline with a long way to go to the mark.

rule is to sail the long tack first for the simple reason that by sailing the short tack first, you can end up on the layline before the beat is half over. Not a good thing. If that long tack were to become lifted with you on the layline at the beginning of the leg, you could find yourself overstanding the mark by a mile.

Don't Give Up. The windward leg can be a brutal one, especially in fluky conditions when you find yourself on the wrong side of a major shift. No matter what happens though, stay cool! Again, everyone gets burned on occasion. It's not the end of the world. Keep tracking those windshifts, watch what's happening to the competition, and make sure that the next time around it's you who gets that lucky break. Persistence is as much a part of sailboat racing as brilliance, if not more. It's amazing how with a little hard work you can snatch, if not victory, then at least a respectable finish from the jaws of defeat.

By the same token, don't try to win the whole thing back in one fell swoop and end up doing something stupid. One day one of the authors of this book (here's a hint: he's the one with the initials RS) was competing in a Star boat regatta, when he went the wrong way on the first beat and ended up mid-fleet. On the next beat, he split with the fleet in an effort to get a whole pile of places back. Instead, he dropped even more boats. By the next run he was near the back of the fleet, so he took yet another flier in search of a miracle and ended up second to last. As if that wasn't bad enough his brother-in-law from Texas was in town, so although he could make the race his throw-out for the regatta, it's still immortalized in family history.

More Smart Sailing to Windward

- Be sure to note how the wind is shifting **before** the start.
- If you are expecting a persistent shift, "sail to the shift."
- Avoid the layline until the very end of the windward leg.
- If a windshift skews the beat, sail the "long" leg first.

Q & A

Q. Why is it important to figure out your sail control settings *before* you begin sailing the first beat?

A. So the boat will be ready to sail off the line as fast as possible in the first few moments after the start.

Q. Sailing out to the starting line, Rich is able to sail a close-hauled heading of 15 degrees on starboard tack and 105 degrees on port tack. What is the wind direction?

A. 60 degrees.

Q. Why is steering head-to-wind a bad way to gauge wind direction?

A. Because it flogs the sails unnecessarily, a sure way to break them down. It's better to keep track of your headings when sailing to windward, and then use them to derive the wind direction.

Q. Shortly after the start, Adam is on port tack, and finds the wind direction has shifted dramatically from 20 degrees to 65 degrees. He thinks it's a persistent shift and realizes he's closing in on the new layline. What should he do?

A. Tack! Not only is he being headed, if this is in fact a persistent shift, he is sailing the "short" tack on a skewed beat. He needs to sail the "long" tack first, so he doesn't find himself on the layline too early.

Q. Why is it best to tack short of the layline when you are still a good distance away from the mark?

A. Once you are on the layline your hands are tied tactically and strategically; any kind of tack or course change will be detrimental. Also, if you get a lift while sailing on the layline you will overstand the mark.

Chapter 4

WINDWARD MARK ROUNDINGS

As is the case with the start, mark roundings can be a time of great excitement and more than a little stress, with a number of different boats trying to sail through the same piece of water at the same time. Boats may be coming in on both port and starboard tack; various boats may be to windward or leeward of one another; like moths approaching a flame, everybody wants to cut the corner as close as possible without getting burned. Back in the early 1980s, when the J/24 was considered a cutting-edge racing boat, there was a good-size fleet of them in Cleveland, Ohio, crewed by various ex-Ensign, Highlander, and Flying Scot skippers, all ready to make the big time. The first mark rounding of every race was a thing of chaotic beauty as the fleet began inventing various new rules, and then variations on those new rules, to see who would be first to pop out on the

next reach. It was always a source of wonder how they all managed to get around without leaving a debris field of broken spars and shattered hulls behind.

Ultimately, there are three main aspects to making the turn around the windward mark in one piece:

1. understanding the rules, so you will know when to give way and when to press on in a crowd;
2. judging the layline—in other words, knowing exactly when to tack so you can weather the mark without over-standing;
3. handling your boat, so you'll be up and going on the next leg as quickly as possible.

There are also a couple of strategies you can use to stay out of trouble, so you can concentrate on sailing fast instead of having

52

bad thoughts about that guy blocking your air to windward or agonizing over whether or not you can pinch up to make the mark. In the vast majority of cases, when sailing an inshore course you leave marks to port; i.e., you go to the right of the mark when going around. In fact, races in which you leave windward marks to starboard are so rare they won't really be discussed here, beyond the way they are regulated by the rules.

THE RULES
AT THE MARK

For all the hubbub, the rules at the windward mark are fairly straightforward. Once again, starboard tack has right-of-way over port tack; on the same tack, boats to windward must keep clear of boats to leeward, and—with one important exception—an overtaking boat astern must keep clear of a boat ahead. Note that when leaving marks to port, a starboard-tack boat closest to the mark is also the leeward boat, and therefore has the right to pinch as high as it wants to squeeze around, leaving very little room for ambiguity. When coming in on port tack, there are a couple of rules that must be kept in mind. But they are fairly straightforward, and in the beginning especially, you'll want to avoid coming in close to the mark on port tack anyway.

Tacking Close to the Mark. Not convinced that sneaking in on port tack is a bad idea?

How about trying on Rule 18.3a for size? Basically, this little gem says that if you tack within two boatlengths of the mark, you cannot cause a starboard-tack boat to sail above close-hauled to avoid a collision. Therefore, if a competitor is on the layline, you have to sail beyond this point in order to tack, unless you're absolutely sure you'll be able to get up to speed or out of the way without impeding his progress. True, this will very likely put him ahead going into the next leg. But better that than being protested.

Of course, if the other boat has overstood, you are free to tack in front of him; he shouldn't have to sail above close-hauled to avoid you. Be aware, however, that it can be a bit tricky proving your point in the protest room since, if a dispute ensues, the burden of proof is on the port-tacker. If the other guy's jib or genoa backs or begins to luff, you better be ready to prove it was eased and could have been trimmed to

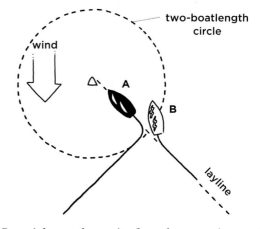

*Boat **A** has to do a pair of penalty turns; it caused boat **B** to sail above close-hauled after boat **A** tacked within two boatlengths of the windward mark.*

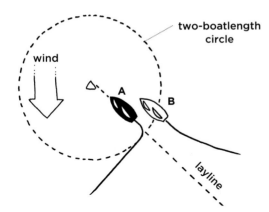

*No foul: Although boat **A** tacked within two boat-lengths of the windward mark, boat **B** never had to sail above close-hauled to avoid it; it had overstood the mark and was coming in on a close reach.*

close-hauled if you don't want your finish voided.

Hitting a Mark. As is the case at the start, if a boat hits a mark even lightly with the tip of its boom or the edge of a sail, it must immediately do a 360-degree turn to exonerate itself, all the while keeping clear of the competition. (Bear in mind that "immediately" means as soon as it is safe to do so. If you hit a mark and start doing your circle right there, you will likely hit a bunch of other boats rounding. Instead, sail a bit beyond the mark and off to one side before paying your dues.) If a boat has the right-of-way and is pushed into the mark by another, it does not have to do a penalty turn, but must protest the offending boat.

In case you are thinking maybe you can work this 360 thing to your advantage, you may not intentionally hit a mark in order to gain a competitive advantage. For instance, let's say Rich sails in on port tack, only to find that there are 20 boats lined up on the layline, leaving him with two options: he can either dip his competitors by dropping behind and sailing around all 20 of them, or try to tack in front of the first boat and hope for the best. (For more information about dipping, see chapter 7, Basic Tactics and a Few Tips.) While attempting to carry off the latter, he touches the mark and has to do a 360-degree turn. When he is done, he finds that he's in 10th place. Not bad!, he thinks, especially compared to the prospect of rounding the mark in 21st place. Unfortunately, it's not allowed either. Rich should be protested for gaining this advantage.

Room at the Mark. In the event that two port-tack boats are approaching a mark to be left to port, the buoy rules apply, which temporarily suspend the basic dictum that a windward boat always gives way to a boat to leeward. Specifically, these rules state that if a boat to windward has an inside overlap on a boat to leeward at the moment the leading boat is two boatlengths away from the mark, the leeward boat must give the windward boat room to round the mark, including room to tack. Note that the windward boat gets right-of-way even if the tip of its bow just barely overlaps the leeward boat's stern. And it retains that right-of-way, even if the overlap is broken moments after the leading boat crosses the theoretical two-boatlength circle surrounding the mark. Obviously, this is a rule that does not get a lot of use when going to windward, especially in big fleets; regardless of which of the two boats has right-of-way, both are entirely at the mercy of any boat coming in on starboard. Still, it's a good rule to be aware of, because anything is possible in sailboat racing.

The room-at-the-mark rules can also come into play on occasion when leaving marks to starboard. For example, there are times when two boats might be coming in close on starboard with the aim of tacking around the mark at the last moment. In this case, the inside boat would be entitled to room if it has an overlap, even though it is to windward and would normally have to stay clear. Note that the rules do *not* apply between two boats on opposite tacks at the windward mark. For instance, when leaving marks to port, a port-tack boat does *not* have the right to room at the mark just because it has an overlap with a starboard-tack boat when one or the other crosses the two-boat-length circle.

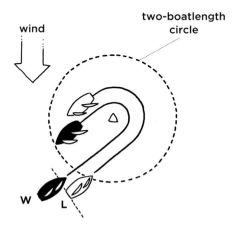

As these boats pass the two-boatlength circle at the mark, the windward boat (**W**) is entitled to room to round because its bow overlaps the leeward boat's (**L**) stern.

APPROACHING THE MARK

Ah! The agony and the ecstasy that is weathering the mark at the top of the beat! Because starboard tack is so clearly favored, the typical sailboat race will see pretty much the entire fleet flopping over onto the starboard layline in the last few minutes of the beat, then charging up on starboard tack, all the while setting up spinnaker gear in preparation for the next leg. The obvious question is, how do you know when to tack, especially when you are still a fair distance away from the mark? True, if you've been keeping track of your windshifts since

Sea State at the Windward Mark

Remember, the wind and other boats aren't the only things you have to be aware of when deciding when to tack for the mark. You also have to consider the waves and any currents in the area. In lumpy seas especially, you won't be able to point the same as when things are calm. If there's a tide or some other kind of current working against you, be sure to factor that in. Conversely, if a current is working in your favor, you may be able to tack a little earlier than you might otherwise. Unfortunately, there is no hard and fast method for determining how exactly the sea state will affect your boat in any particular situation. The best thing to do is spend time on the water getting to know your boat and how it performs in different situations. Try to think like a racer, even when you're out for a relaxing day sail.

before the start, you should know the headings you can sail on starboard. But there's a big difference between sailing a heading and actually weathering a fixed point. How, for example, do you account for drift? Changes in wind direction? Current? The effect of waves on your true heading? Then there's the matter of all those other pesky boats in the area, disturbing the air in general and occasionally tacking on your bow, just when you were thinking this damn beat was almost over!

LAYLINES

Ultimately, judging the layline is a combination of art, science, and luck; one of those timeless indicators of seamanship that separates the true sailors from the wannabes in the yachting caps. For centuries, a mariner's ability to determine whether a vessel was capable of weathering a reef, island, or other obstacle often meant the difference between smooth sailing and catastrophe. Developing your own ability to both judge a layline and then make that windward mark will result in your being that much better a sailor in general.

Unfortunately, judging the layline can be very hard to actually practice because the angle changes with every fluctuation in wind velocity, making each rounding situation unique. Still, get in the habit of watching how your boat performs whenever you're sailing to windward, especially if there are any points of reference, such as buoys or breakwalls, in the area. On nonrace days, practice pinching up to make a

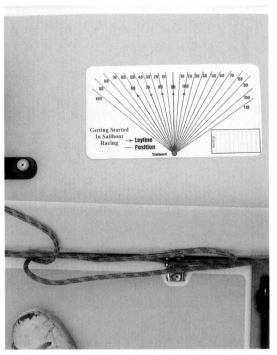

Tacking lines on deck will make it easier to judge the layline.

navigation buoy to become familiar with how your boat responds in this kind of situation. (See chapter 7, Basic Tactics and a Few Tips, for more about pinching up.)

Out on the racecourse, make a mental note of the angles at which the other boats are sailing whenever you cross them or they cross you. You don't have to figure out the exact angle in degrees, but at least be aware of whether they are sailing a course above or below 90 degrees compared to your heading. Some sailors will put tacking lines on their boats; after they take the bearings of the other boats on a leg, they can sight down these lines to judge where to tack once they reach the layline.

When judging laylines, it's also important to consider what the rest of the fleet is doing, and whether or not tacking onto what appears to be the layline will actually get you to the mark. One year during a light-air race at the Soling World Championship regatta, for example, there were a number of boats that tacked on the layline about a quarter mile from the mark, only to find a bunch of other boats camping on their wind. So they were forced to tack again and again in order to clear their air. Early

on, one lone competitor had sailed out to a point some one hundred yards high of the other boats. In a smaller fleet he would have been shooting himself in the foot by overstanding so dramatically, but here he ended up in 5th place around the mark, while those who'd tacked on the layline wallowed far behind. With a bit more wind the situation might have been very different. But in the right conditions this kind of forward thinking can earn big gains.

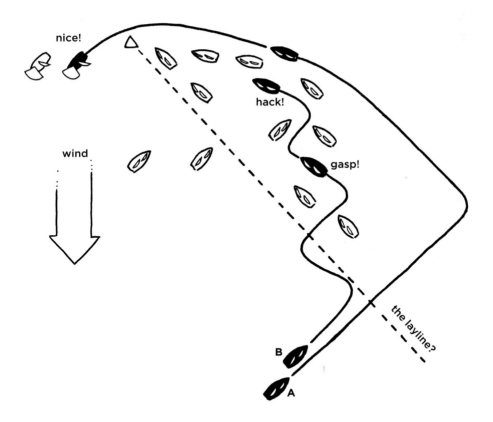

*Be sure to look at what the other boats in the area are doing before tacking for the mark, especially in a large, crowded fleet. Here, although boat **B** is on the "layline" when it tacks, the bad air from the other boats in the area slows it down and hurts its pointing ability, forcing it to tack again and again. In contrast, by sailing beyond the crowd, boat **A** rounds well ahead.*

BOAT HANDLING AT THE WINDWARD MARK

As stated in the beginning, this book assumes the reader knows how to handle his or her boat, and that assumption applies to spinnakers as much as any other sail in the inventory. Still, there are a few things you can do to make your mark roundings a little faster and easier as you make the transition to the next leg. Even if you are using a jib and main only—not a bad place to start your racing career, since forgoing a spinnaker can simplify the process greatly—paying attention to your sails and boat trim can make a huge difference in performance. As you will see once you get out on the racecourse, marks are one of those places where you can gain or lose boatlengths in an amazingly short period of time.

For starters, as is the case when tacking, try to keep as much crew as possible to windward for as long as possible, both when setting up your spinnaker gear—when raising the pole and attaching the sheet, guy, and halyard to the spinnaker—and when making the actual rounding. Allowing the crew to come bounding in off the rail will result in excessive heel and make the boat want to round up into the wind—precisely what you *don't* want to have happen when getting ready to crack off to leeward.

Also, when executing your actual rounding, be sure to ease off the main as you fall off; keeping it strapped in, especially in heavy air, can make it difficult—if not impossible—to steer down to a lower course. This is particularly important aboard boats with larger mainsails, such as Thistles, Mumm 30s, and scows. In fact, if the wind is up and the main is strapped in, some of these boats will barely respond to the helm at all. Along these same lines, once you are around, don't forget to change your various sail controls for optimum efficiency on what is now a very different angle of sail. For the main trimmer this might mean easing off the backstay, cunningham, and outhaul to give the sail more curvature, or camber, and power. If you are carrying your jib for the entire downwind leg, you'll want to move the lead forward to help keep the leech from twisting off to leeward. You'll also want to ease the halyard in order to induce a little more leeward sag in the forestay to make the sail a bit fuller. (For more information about forestay sag, see chapter 9, Boat Speed, Part 1: Sail Controls and Concepts.)

In terms of spinnakers, the important thing is to make sure everything is ready for the hoist before you actually begin to execute your mark rounding. Also make sure everyone on board knows what to do to hoist the chute and get it drawing. In the last couple of minutes before going around, have a crewmember attach the halyard, sheet, and guy to the spinnaker (which was, of course, packed before the start!). Then, just before the rounding, have the foredeck crew either extend the bowsprit if the boat flies an asymmetrical spinnaker or, with the help of one of the cockpit crew, raise the pole if you are using a conventional chute. After that prefeed the guy, sneaking out the spinnaker by trimming in on the guy, until it's most of the way out to the end of the bowsprit or to where the pole is resting on the forestay. This is important; keeping the spinnaker clews separated will prevent the sail from twisting around itself in a dreaded hourglass shape—a state of affairs that can sometimes lead to taking the entire thing down again. If you've got the clew up near the pole and have taken the slack out of the sheet before you even begin heaving on the halyard, there should be very little additional trimming to do to fill the sail after it has been raised. With this goal in mind, you might want to consider marking your spinnaker sheet with a permanent felt-tip pen for the approximate trim downwind. Put a tick or band on the sheet where it exits the spinnaker lead when the sail is full on a reach or run. This will keep your trimmer from grossly overtrimming the sail as he's getting it to fill.

The spinnaker won't fill properly until the genoa is either radically eased or down, so make getting the old headsail out of the way a priority as soon as the chute is up. It's generally best to ease the genoa only slightly at the weather mark. This will both help pull the bow down to a reach and keep the sail inboard when you dump it after the spinnaker hoist. Once the spinnaker is up, blow the jib halyard—in other words, let it run free so the sail will fall onto the foredeck as quickly as possible. On larger boats in particular the foredeck crew should help

Sneaking out the spinnaker clew before the hoist will help the spinnaker fill and keep it from wrapping around itself into a dreaded "hourglass."

speed up the hoisting process by jumping the spinnaker halyard at the mast—hauling the sail up as quickly as possible from where the line exits the mast, while a member of the cockpit crew gathers in the slack. Ideally, the foredeck crew should be able to get the sail all or nearly all the way up before it starts to fill, leaving very little grinding work for his shipmates aft. After that the foredeck crew should immediately work with the cockpit crew to bring down the jib, bunching it up on the foredeck. He can secure it with a sail tie or two in heavy weather, so it won't interfere with the

A crewmember begins to "jump" the spinnaker halyard as his boat rounds the windward mark. Note how the main has been eased out dramatically, while the jib has only been eased a little. This helps bring the bow down as the boat falls off onto a reach.

spinnaker in the event that you need to make a jibe.

Throughout this process (which is known as a bear-away set), the members of the crew should be communicating with one another as calmly and clearly as possible and watching the sail, not just grinding in on their own little piece of rope, oblivious to everyone else on board while all hell breaks loose around them. If, for example, you're trimming the guy and the sheet is so tight it's stretching the foot of the sail to the breaking point, don't just scream, "Ease! Ease! Ease!" like an enraged kamikaze in a grade-B war movie. Address your shipmate by name and clearly say, "Ease the sheet a

couple of feet." Maybe even say "please" every now and then, just for the fun of it.

Obviously, you should practice the maneuver in advance on a warm, sunny day, hoisting and dousing your spinnaker over and over again until it becomes automatic. It's also a good idea to have your crew alternate jobs, so they can get a better understanding of the entire process and how, exactly, what they do affects the well-being of the other people on board. There's nothing like putting a sheet trimmer up on the foredeck a couple of times to make him sensitive to the plight of those up at the pointy end. Then again, having your foredeck crew tend the guy a couple of times might actually convince him or her that the folks aft are doing more than just mindlessly pulling strings.

As was the case when practicing for the start, find a navigational buoy and do a few practice roundings, starting from a short distance away so you can judge the layline and prepare the spinnaker the same way you would in a race situation. If there is traffic in the area, so much the better. You're certainly not going to have the ocean or lake to yourself on race day, so you may as well get used to keeping an eye out for boats when things get busy, as well as when you're just sailing along in a straight line.

While you're at it, you might want to practice a maneuver known as a jibe set, in which you don't just fall off from a beat to a reach, staying on starboard the whole time, but actually jibe the boat around the mark and then hoist the spinnaker on port tack. Obviously, if you are sailing a triangle or the first leg of an Olympic course, this maneuver would be irrelevant and you would simply go with the bear-away set described above. But if the next leg is dead downwind, going with a jibe set can yield big gains for various tactical and strategic

Crew Assignments

Crew assignments depend on the number of sailors on board. With a crew of three, for example, the helmsman steers, controls the mainsail, and calls tactics; the middle crew helps with the main and tactics and trims the spinnaker; and the front crew trims the jib and works the foredeck, setting and jibing the spinnaker pole during the downwind legs.

In a crew of four, the helmsman steers, calls tactics, and might still trim the main. But for the most part, the mainsail is now the responsibility of the next crew forward, since on a larger boat it will take that much more strength to handle the larger sail. The third crewmember will trim the headsail and spinnaker, while the fourth crew works the foredeck.

In a crew of five, the helmsman steers and calls tactics; the second crew trims the main and helps call tactics; and the third crew trims the genoa and spinnaker. The fourth crew works the pit—handling the halyards and sail controls like the cunningham and spinnaker-pole topping lift—and usually comes back to fly the spinnaker. The fifth crewmember works the foredeck.

In a crew of six, the delegation of responsibilities is pretty much the same as in a crew of five, except you have an additional sail trimmer to help crewmember number three with the genoa and spinnaker. No matter how many sailors you have on board, everybody should know everybody else's job and be ready to lend a hand when things get busy. Everyone also should be aware of how crew weight is affecting trim and, whenever possible, hike out on the windward rail, during heavy-air beats in particular.

reasons, such as avoiding other boats' bad air or taking advantage of a windshift.

In terms of the actual hoist, the major difference between a jibe set and a bear-away set when approaching the windward mark is you hook up the spinnaker on the starboard side, as opposed to the port side. Also, you don't raise the pole until after you have rounded the mark. Otherwise during the jibe it will foul the jib as it comes around to the other side. You can attach the inboard end of the pole to the mast, and even raise that side to its proper height. But leave the outboard end resting on the deck. It might sound awkward, but the jib will still be able to sweep across cleanly, provided all your lines have been run properly so that everything is clear. Obviously, if your boat is equipped with a bowsprit you simply extend it as you normally would.

Once you have rounded the mark, or even *as* you are rounding the mark, you should jibe the boat and then hoist the spinnaker as soon as both the jib and main have been brought over to the other side. Note that, on all but the very biggest boats, your primary concern here is hoisting the spinnaker and getting it to fly, *not* raising the pole. If the crew and helmsman work together, the chute will be just fine on its own. In fact, it can be "free flown" without a pole indefinitely. Only after the jib is down and the spinnaker up and full should you worry about raising the outboard end of the pole and attaching the guy. (If necessary, the foredeck crew can act as a kind of human spinnaker pole while he or she is getting the outboard end of the pole

Rounding the Windward Mark

- Keep crew weight to windward as long as possible.
- Prefeed the spinnaker to help separate the clews.
- Ease the main, but only ease the genoa a little, so it will help pull the bow down and be easy to drop on the foredeck.
- During a jibe set get the spinnaker drawing first, and then worry about the pole.

attached with the help of comrades in the cockpit.) On larger boats you might need to have the outboard end set before the actual hoist, due to the increased forces at work as a result of having a larger rig. But, of course, there will be a lot more people on board to handle these kinds of extra tasks, so raising the pole shouldn't slow the process down too much. Also note that when doing a jibe set aboard a larger boat, the foredeck crew should go forward to help lift up the pole, maybe even resting it temporarily on his or her shoulder. Because of the downward angle of the pole when the outboard end is on the deck, the outboard end can be difficult to raise with the topping lift alone. Giving it this little boost on the shoulder will make raising the pole a breeze.

CLEAN ROUNDINGS

Windward mark roundings are fairly straightforward in theory, but in practice they can be a bit tricky. On the one hand, there's the option of sailing for the layline early, tacking over onto starboard while you're still a good distance from the mark, and then plowing through the crowd with the right-of-way. Unfortunately, this approach leaves you vulnerable to the possibility of a competitor tacking on top of you, taking your wind, and putting you in a position where you can no longer make the mark. The other option, of course, is to avoid the layline until the last moment and tack over onto starboard only a short distance from the mark. That way it will be easy to judge the layline, and you can tack on top of that guy who gave you such a bad time back at the start. Unfortunately, this strategy also has its downside: as you come in on port, you might find yourself faced with an impassable "picket fence" of sailboats on starboard, forcing you to duck a half dozen transoms before you can find a hole to windward. Obviously, tacking short—to leeward of this wall of Dacron—would be suicide, because you'd be left wallowing in a world of bad air.

The solution, then, is to be flexible and get yourself in a position where you can tack for the layline at the time and place of your choosing, while keeping your air clear so the rest of the fleet doesn't roll over you to windward. You may also have to face reality and throw in another tack when it becomes obvious you're not going to make the mark, as opposed to hoping against hope for a miracle when your poor sails are gasping for breath. It may hurt, but in the long run, tacking sooner rather than later will get you around with a minimum of trouble. Wait until the last minute and you might find yourself meeting with bad-air disaster.

Let's say Adam, for example, finds himself on port tack about halfway up the beat and heading out toward the right side of the course. He's fast approaching the layline, but is still a good distance from the mark; to avoid banging the corner, he tacks over onto starboard, which will bring him back toward the mark and to where the rest of the fleet is approaching on port tack. Moments later when he sees that things are going to get crowded, he decides to flop back over onto port tack. This way he can reach the layline early, avoid having to find an open spot later on, and have plenty of time to set up his spinnaker gear. Unfortunately, a couple of hundred yards from the mark, Rich crosses his bow and tacks over onto starboard. Adam is now in a wind shadow and beginning to wonder if he's going to make the mark after all. Tough luck!

Alas, already in a tough position, Adam does the worst thing possible—nothing—and keeps pressing on, pinching up and strapping in his sails in an effort to sail as close to the wind as possible. Eventually, he realizes this just won't do. But by now he is in a tough spot, for he has lost boat speed. This will make it that much harder to tack over onto port quick enough to cross the bows of that menacing crowd of boats smoking up from behind and to windward on starboard. Putting the helm down he manages to get his bow around, but the boat is slow to accelerate and he has to fall off and

duck transom after transom. Finally he finds a spot where he can slip through to some clear air and once again sail for the mark. In the process he has lost a dozen boatlengths—just like that—so he is at the tail end of the fleet. And he has actually been one of the lucky ones. If he had carried that starboard tack much closer, to within, say, a couple of boatlengths of the mark, he could have been left wallowing forever, watching as boat after boat went plowing by, ruining what had otherwise been a pretty decent beat (see illustration next page).

For his part, Rich, after doing poor Adam wrong, also had a competitor tack on top of him. But instead of sailing into a hole, he immediately tacked over onto port to clear his air. It cost him a couple of boatlengths in the short run, but meant he had plenty of air for a clean mark rounding. Of course, with a little more boat speed he might have been able to pinch up to escape the other guy's wind shadow. Then again, if he was confident he could make the mark he might have footed off, sailing a slightly lower course to power ahead into clear air. The main thing is he didn't just sit there and take it. He recognized that doing nothing would lead to problems and fixed the situation before it got any worse.

Again, in larger fleets or in situations where a number of boats are approaching the layline en masse, it may make sense to sail slightly beyond the layline, giving yourself a little cushion so you will have room to maneuver. And whatever you do, don't tack into somebody else's bad air just

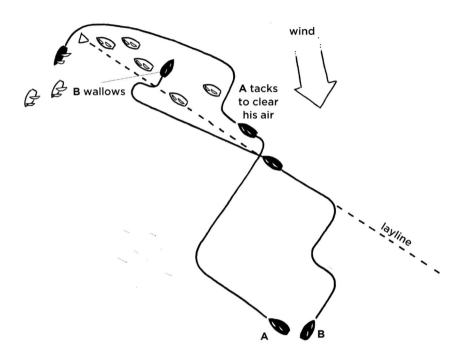

*If you get in trouble while approaching the windward mark, don't wait to remedy the situation. Take action. In this case, when boat **A** tacks on top of boat **B** on the layline, putting boat **B** in its wind shadow, boat **B** tries to push on without improving the situation. It loses speed and ends up wallowing, while other boats come up from behind. When another competitor tacks on top of boat **A**, **A** immediately tacks over onto port to clear its air. As a result, boat **A** has plenty of air for a clean mark rounding.*

because you've reached the layline. Otherwise you will soon find yourself going slowly and missing the mark. Similarly, when you are still a fair distance away, beware of pinching in the hope of weathering the mark, even though it looks like you've tacked short. The smart thing to do is keep sailing fast and deal with the situation as it comes. If you need to throw in another tack, just do it—at a time and place of your choosing. If a windshift comes along to lift you around, so much the better. The main thing is don't give away speed and boatlengths early in an effort to rectify an iffy situation.

Ultimately, when it comes to windward mark roundings, you have to be quick on your feet, creative in your thinking, and aware of your surroundings. Try to visualize what the situation at the mark will be and plan accordingly. As you draw near, be ready to revise that plan if things get crowded. You want to find holes and clear air, like you did at the start. Keep your eyes open for possibilities and threats, stay calm, and before you know it you'll be off on the next leg and sailing well.

Q & A

Q. At the end of the beat, Rich approaches the mark on port tack, and then flops over onto starboard tack one-and-a-half boatlengths from the mark. He gets his sails trimmed in, but is slow to accelerate. As a result Adam, who's coming in from astern on starboard, has to swerve to windward to avoid him, luffing his sails in the process. Adam protests. Rich says he was on course on starboard and Adam had to avoid him as the boat clear astern. Who's correct?

A. Adam has right-of-way; any boat tacking onto starboard within two boatlengths of the windward mark cannot cause another boat on starboard to sail above close-hauled to stay clear.

Q. Adam brushes against the mark while trying to pinch around in light air. Immediately he does a 360-degree penalty turn. During the turn, Rich has to swerve to avoid Adam, who is on starboard tack and hardening up prior to a tack. Rich protests. Adam says he was on starboard tack and was the leeward boat as well. Who's correct?

A. Adam has no rights, because he is in the middle of doing a penalty turn. Now he gets to do two more!

Q. When rounding the mark for a bear-away set, is it more important to ease the jib or the main first?

A. It's important to ease the main, which will make falling off onto a lower course easier. In heavy air it might actually be impossible to fall off with the main strapped in.

Q. When doing a jibe set, is it more important to raise the pole or hoist the spinnaker first after the jibe?

A. On all but the largest boats the chute goes up first, since it can fly perfectly well without a pole. If necessary, the foredeck crew can be a "human spinnaker pole" and hold out the guy until the pole is put in place.

Q. You're sailing in on the starboard layline two hundred yards from the mark, and are just barely making the layline when a competitor tacks two boatlengths ahead and to windward. Your boat speed drops. A number of other boats are converging from below on port and astern on starboard. What do you do?

A. Tack! And do it quickly while you've still got enough boat speed. You were already just barely making the mark, so don't kid yourself; there's no way you're going to pinch up and make it now. You might even want to take your port tack a little beyond the starboard layline, so you will have some extra room to play with when those other boats eventually converge.

Chapter 5

DOWNWIND LEGS/ REACHES

All too often sailors round the windward mark, hoist the chute, and then crack open a beer, relieved to have survived the beat and gotten the spinnaker flying with a minimum of trouble. They reason that, because they no longer have to struggle to make every inch possible to windward, they no longer have to try so hard. The truth is, when you're on a run, you can make some of your biggest gains or experience your biggest losses. Granted, you no longer have to hike out, the sun is warm, and it's good to be alive. But you still have to keep your wits about you and sail as fast as you can. Remember, it's even better to be alive with lots of boats admiring your transom!

There are three normal ways to make big gains downwind. The first is to know your boat. The second is to look back and play the wind. And the third is to get lucky.

Of these three the first is the one you want to really work on. Knowing your boat is what wins races time and time again in the absence of wind shifts and luck. Olympic veteran and boatbuilder Bill Abbott, for example, knows the Soling as well as just about anyone, which makes him especially effective on the reaching and running legs. When he gets around the windward mark in the lead, the rest of the fleet is stuck playing follow the leader. If he gets around in the middle of the fleet, where many of the boats will harden up as they fight for clear air, Bill knows better and stays low. He dodges other boats' wind shadows, plays the shifts, and picks off countless competitors in the process. The key is having a feel for the boat and knowing how it performs at different sailing angles, something that only comes from spending *time on the water*. You might be interested to know that Bill does all of this without the help of fancy instruments. In fact, instruments can be a hindrance, especially aboard larger boats. Even the best instruments have a lag time built into them, so relying on them can slow a boat down more than it helps.

When looking behind you for puffs and shifts, take comfort from the fact that it is much easier to do when sailing off the wind as opposed to on a beat. For one thing, on the windward leg, all that zigzagging back and forth across the course makes it harder to see which way the puffs are moving. Also, because you are sailing into the wind, the puffs are coming at you that much more quickly. On the downwind leg you will still be doing some zigging and zagging, but it's generally not as dramatic. And because you are moving in the same direction as the puffs, they will come at you more slowly, giving you ample time to change your heading or even jibe to catch a gust that otherwise would miss you.

Thanks to their different configurations, getting down to the leeward mark is a far different matter on a triangle course than on a course in which you are sailing straight up- and downwind. And, not surprisingly, the tactical and strategic concerns also are markedly different. As stated in the first chapter, a leg going dead downwind is more complicated than a pair of reaching legs with a turning mark. But that doesn't mean you can't get into trouble on the latter.

Because they constitute two completely different types of legs, they will be treated as such in this chapter.

Instruments for Reading the Wind

Although it's best to develop a feel for the wind and windshifts, there are plenty of precision instruments on the market to help sailors read the wind in a number of different ways. Various sailing "computers," for example, not only show true wind speed and direction (as opposed to the apparent wind readings shown by conventional wind meters), they can also calculate windshifts and log things such as boat speed, average speed, and distance traveled. For smaller boats there is also the Tacktick brand of solar powered compasses and sailing computers, which are portable and can be easily attached to a mast or bulkhead without a separate power source or any kind of fancy wires. However, be aware that these little miracle workers are banned by some one-design class associations.

SAILING DEAD DOWNWIND

Again, to a non-racer, a running leg seems to be the easiest thing in the world: simply hoist the chute, aim straight for the leeward mark, and enjoy the ride.

In fact, nothing could be further from the truth. Among other things, unless you're sailing in heavy air you *never* want to sail in a straight line directly downwind. If you do, you will also be sailing in a straight line to the back of the fleet. This is especially true if your boat is rigged with an asymmetrical spinnaker; because it lacks a moveable spinnaker pole, its wind is easily blocked, or blanketed, by the main. Never forget: DEAD DOWNWIND IS SLOW! Instead, a good downwind leg consists of a number of jibes; you want to sail a zigzag course so you're always on a broad reach, either on port or starboard. It's much like a beat without all that hiking out. The reason for this is the phenomenon of apparent wind.

APPARENT WIND

Because of apparent wind, a boat will always sail much faster on a reach than a run; so much so that, despite the fact you're actually sailing a longer route, you will get from point A to point B in a shorter period of time. Imagine, for example, that you're sailing on a newly refitted 35-foot sloop in about 10 knots of breeze. The bottom is clean and the sails and lines are new; you can take full advantage of the wind, and immediately accelerate to a speed of 3.5 knots. Beyond that point, however, you can go no faster: as you increase speed when you sail downwind, there is less pressure on your sails. This is because your boat speed is subtracted from the true wind speed, giving you less wind to work with. In the case of our 35-footer, for example, when sailing at 3.5 knots downwind, the apparent wind on board is a mere 6.5 knots. Let's say you manage to eke out another knot of boat speed to make 4.5 knots. The apparent wind on board will drop to 5.5 knots, yielding even less pressure on the sails. Chances are you won't be going 4.5 knots for long.

Now imagine changing course so that you are on a broad reach with the wind 45 degrees forward of dead astern. Once

again you accelerate to a speed of 3.5 knots, but this time the situation on board vis-à-vis your apparent wind is much different. For one thing, each knot of boat speed is no longer subtracted in its entirety from the true wind speed, because you are no longer sailing directly away from the wind. Not only that, each knot of boat speed is both creating wind on board and changing its direction, because the boat is moving at an angle to the true wind direction instead of being pushed directly before it. Specifically, the apparent wind speed on board is now 8.5 knots and its direction has moved a few degrees forward, so that it's coming from an angle closer to the bow. It's almost beginning to feel a bit like a beam reach. Best of all, there is still good pressure on the sails, which means your boat continues to accelerate. This time, when the knotmeter reads 4.5 knots, you are still experiencing 8.5 knots of breeze at an angle of about 20 degrees aft of abeam. The foredeck crew is smiling and the sail trimmers are tweaking the sheet and guy, hoping to get that reading higher still. This is sailing! Granted, you aren't going directly toward the mark anymore. But in a little while you will jibe around and bring that same boat speed in on the opposite tack, or jibe, as the different tacks are often called when sailing downwind. When once again you cross the rhumbline—the imaginary straight line drawn from point A to point B, in this case from the windward mark to the leeward mark—you will be crossing well ahead of that fellow wallowing along on a run at a paltry 3.5 knots.

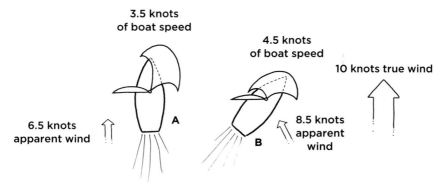

Two identical boats on different angles of sail experience very different winds in the same conditions. By sailing on a higher angle of sail—in this case a broad reach—boat B generates enough apparent wind to travel a full knot faster than boat A.

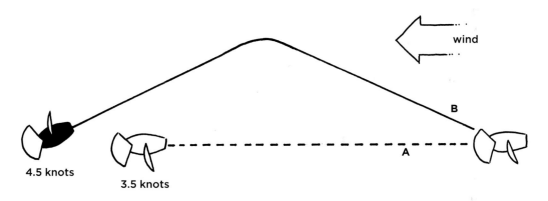

Sailing on higher, or "hotter," jibe angles that take advantage of apparent wind means you will get to the mark faster, even though you are sailing a longer distance. In this case, the boat following course B has to travel farther, but it still comes out ahead because of its boat speed.

For those still having trouble understanding apparent wind, think about it in the extreme. There is a class of iceboat called a Nite, for example, that has two seats and is relatively slow for an iceboat, going a mere 50 knots in 12 knots of wind. If you let the sail out and go directly downwind in 10 knots of wind, slightly less than 10 knots of boat speed is the best you will get. (There is still a bit of friction where the blades con-

tact the ice, although *far* less resistance than a conventional boat sailing through the water experiences.) If, however, you turn the boat to a beam reach, the wind will not only be hitting the sail from the side, you will also be generating a forward component to the wind equal to the boat's speed across the ice. As the boat accelerates to 20 knots, the wind it experiences is now made up of 10 knots from the beam plus 20 knots from the direction in which it is going. The result is, the apparent wind—the wind on your face—feels more like you are on a very tight reach. It's also coming with far more force than if you were standing motionless on the ice. The boat continues to accelerate and, by the time it's going 40 knots, the apparent wind resembles a beat.

One of the best things about the phenomenon of apparent wind is, in some situations, it can be harnessed to generate a breeze where there seemingly is none. One day the Peterson 43 *Pied Piper*, for example, was sailing against two other Peterson 43s in a 30-mile port-to-port race on Lake Michigan that was almost directly downwind. For an hour after the start the three boats sailed side by side. Then the crew on *Pied Piper* decided to heat it up to a broad reach. It was light, blowing around 4 knots, but as the boat headed up the speed increased by nearly 2 knots. On the downside, this left the boat pointing about 15 degrees in the wrong direction. But once the boat was up to speed, the crew found it could slowly—meaning about 2 degrees every 15 seconds—bring the boat back down without losing what it had gained, thanks to its new apparent wind. A few minutes later the boat was actually sailing on its original course, but going 1.5 to 2 knots faster! Meanwhile, the other two boats were still barely moving. Later, after winning the race by over an hour, everyone had a great laugh about how lucky *Pied Piper* had been to catch that little sliver of air—especially the crew that had caught the puff.

WINDSHIFTS

The advantages of jibing downwind can be further enhanced by playing the windshifts and puffs, trying to find more pressure and advantageous changes in wind direction in much the same way you did when sailing upwind. Again, puffs are actually easier to see and easier to use downwind than upwind; when the crew (which is hopefully looking *back* at the competition!) sees a dark spot, it should let the helmsman know where it is and where it seems to be going, so that he can position the boat to sail through it. For example, if you're on starboard tack and a dark spot is behind you and passing to leeward, jibe to it as it gets close. After that, try to position your boat so you will sail in the puff as long as you can. In contrast to the beat, where the puffs come and go, you are now sailing with the wind, which means you can stay with them a good deal longer.

In terms of shifts, on the downwind leg you're looking for headers that will enable you to sail at a higher or hotter angle of sail, while steering a course as close to the rhumbline as possible.

Let's say, for example, that Rich has just rounded the windward mark aboard his LS-Ten on the second downwind leg of a windward-leeward course. The wind is blowing at a mere 8 knots and oscillating through some 15 degrees of arc, while the bearing to the leeward mark is due south at 180 degrees. From past experience, Rich knows that in these conditions he should be able

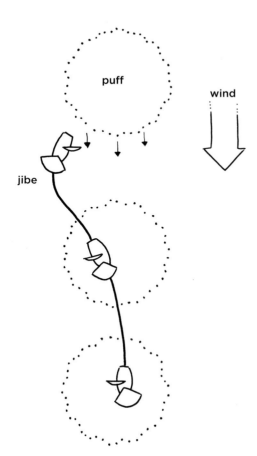

Steer for puffs and try to stay in them as long as possible. Puffs are evident from patches of dark ripples on the water.

to do about 4 knots, with the wind around 40 degrees forward of dead astern—in this case sailing on a heading of 220 degrees on the starboard jibe and 140 on port. Beating up to the windward mark on starboard, he is able to maintain a heading of 315, which means the wind is coming directly from the north and is at the midpoint of the current series of oscillations. Therefore he decides that, after rounding the mark, he will sim-

ply fall off onto a starboard reach and hoist the spinnaker in bear-away set.

Once the spinnaker is up and he is on a course of 220, however, he doesn't just steer a straight line. Instead he works with the spinnaker trimmers to make the most of the light breeze and keep an eye out for the windshifts that he knows are coming. If the wind goes light and the apparent wind shifts aft a few degrees, he might sail a slightly higher course to keep up both the boat speed and apparent wind. In puffs he might sail a slightly lower course, because more pressure on the sails will enable him to maintain boat speed while sailing a more direct course to the mark.

Eventually, Rich notices that he has to sail a heading of 230 to maintain both his apparent wind angle and boat speed; clearly he is now on the lifted tack, and it's time to jibe over onto port in order to maintain a hot angle while sailing a more direct course to the mark. Sure enough, after getting his main and spinnaker drawing on the headed tack, he finds he can sail along quite nicely on a course of 150 and still maintain boat speed. This heading is, of course, 10 degrees closer to the rhumbline than what he could have sailed with the wind coming directly out of the north. Life is once again good, and he and his spinnaker trimmers get back to the job of wringing as much boat speed as possible out of the breeze. When the wind backs 10 degrees to 360, he holds his course because the wind is at the midpoint in its oscillations. But when the wind backs another 10 degrees, he jibes over to starboard, which

Spotting New Wind

When looking for windshifts and puffs, go with any kind of evidence you can find. Obviously, patches of dark rippled water or whitecaps are signs. But also keep an eye on the other boats in the area and wind indicators on shore, such as flags, trees, or smokestacks. Always be on the lookout for a new wind, whether you're in the middle of a race or just out for an afternoon sail.

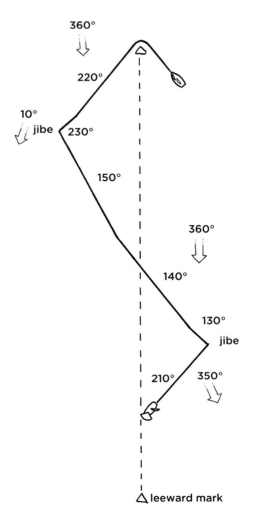

has become the headed tack. Now he is sailing a course of 210 and still maintaining speed.

When thinking about jibing downwind, bear in mind that in contrast to a tack, a well-executed jibe during which the spinnaker keeps drawing results in little or no loss in boat speed. There's little penalty for going over to the other tack—and everything to be gained. The main thing is to stay on your toes and keep a weather eye out for puffs and windshifts that you can turn to your advantage.

Also note that Rich didn't wait until he had the spinnaker up to begin worrying about windshifts. Instead he started formulating his downwind strategy before he reached the windward mark, using the data he had gathered while sailing on the beat to make sure he started off the next leg on the right foot, so to speak.

With this in mind, let's say that after a less than stellar beat, Adam is approaching the same mark on starboard a minute or two later. He's in a lift, sailing a course of 325 as he speeds along the starboard layline. This, of course, is great when sailing to

Play the shifts on a run. Jibe to sail a more direct course to the leeward mark, while maintaining a higher angle of sail to take advantage of apparent wind. Here, the wind veers 10 degrees, forcing the crew to steer a less direct heading of 230 in order to maintain a fast angle of sail. The crew then jibes so it can sail its desired angle of sail, albeit on the opposite tack, and achieve a more direct heading. When the wind eventually backs to 350, the crew jibes yet again. Notice how the boat is now sailing a course that is 20 degrees closer to the leeward mark than the course it sailed when the first shift came near the beginning of the leg.

windward. But it means he will be on the lifted jibe if he opts to go for a bear-away set; he will have to sail at a heading of 230 on starboard to maintain any kind of boat speed. Realizing this is most definitely not a good thing, and wanting desperately to

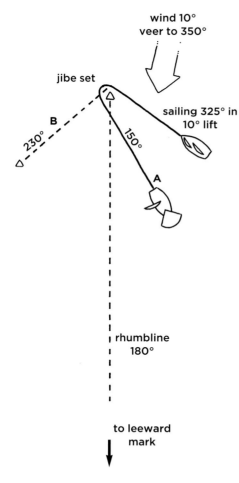

wind 10°
veer to 350°

jibe set

sailing 325° in
10° lift

B

230°

150°

A

rhumbline
180°

to leeward
mark

*If the wind has veered, a jibe set makes it possible to start the run on the headed tack. Here, the crew noted the wind direction by paying attention to its close-hauled heading on the last tack of the beat. Courses **A** and **B** represent the same angle of sail on opposite tacks, but course **A** is at a heading that is 20 degrees closer to the rhumbline to the leeward mark.*

catch up to Rich and the other hotshots at the front of the fleet, he decides to do a jibe set at the windward mark, so he can start his downwind leg on the headed tack (port).

As he approaches the mark, he has his crew shift the spinnaker halyard and sheets around to the starboard side—making sure the crew stays to windward as much as possible as they come around. Then the foredeck crew prepares the pole, attaching the inboard end to the mast, but leaving the outboard end on deck. Sailing around the mark Adam throws in a quick jibe and calls for the spinnaker hoist, reminding the crew to get the sail up all the way and drawing before worrying about the pole. In no time they are sailing along on a heading of 150 with 4 knots of boat speed. Upon rounding the mark, the main trimmer was quick to ease his backstay and other sail controls. Now Adam and his trimmers are working together, exchanging information on things like heading and pressure, while the foredeck crew tucks away the jib and gets himself aft. Everybody settles down for the run ahead and begins working on catching up to Rich.

THE MECHANICS
OF SPEED AND SHIFTS

Of course, as is the case with playing the shifts to windward, the actual process of sailing a good downwind leg can be a lot more confusing in practice than in theory. Among other things, subtle shifts can be tougher to detect, because you don't have the obvious feedback that comes when sailing to windward: the sails won't immediately luff in a header or the leeward telltales start dancing in a lift. You also have less opportunity to encounter shifts on a run since you are sailing away from them, which makes it harder for them to catch up.

Ultimately, it takes time on the water and concentration to understand what's going on in terms of apparent wind angle and speed. But like everything else in sailboat racing, it ain't rocket science. And again, the gains can be huge. Keep an eye on your sailing instruments and masthead wind indicator, and stay in constant communication with your sail trimmers. As the ones with their hands on the sheet and guy, they can be your most sensitive wind indicators of all. Know in advance what your target speeds should be in different winds and at different sailing angles, and take immediate action, whether it be to change your course or tack, when those numbers fall out of place. Be aware that in a lull the apparent wind angle will initially swing forward as the boat's momentum carries it through the still air. But immediately afterward, boat speed will begin to drop and the apparent wind will swing back aft. This obviously is not good, and something needs to be done. In other words it's time to jibe. In a true header the apparent wind angle will not only swing forward, the crew on the sheet will feel an increase in pressure, while the wind speed indicator remains constant or even climbs.

If you are the owner of a common production boat, especially one designed in the past few years, there may be a polar diagram

available that will provide you with a detailed analysis of how your boat should perform at all angles of sail and in all kinds of winds. This can be invaluable in terms of knowing just how your boat is performing relative to its potential. Study the diagram carefully, and take it out with you on prac-

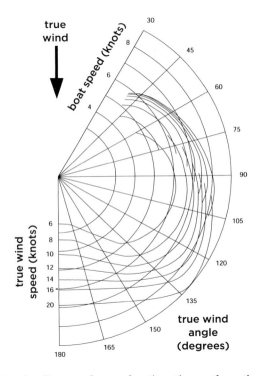

A polar diagram shows a boat's optimum theoretical speed as a function of true wind velocity and angle. In this example for the J/80 one-design racer, there is a crossing and overlap between the lines for jibs and spinnakers. The curved lines represent wind speed. The point on the graph where a line is located represents boat speed. For example, when sailing in 8 knots of wind with a spinnaker up, a J/80 should go 6 knots when sailing 135 degrees off the wind. When close-hauled at 45 degrees off the wind in the same conditions, the boat should go a little under 5.5 knots. Note how slow the boat goes dead downwind, when it would manage just over 3 knots in 8 knots of wind.

tice sessions and during races so you will become conversant with how your boat should perform in different conditions.

If on the other hand a polar diagram isn't available for your boat, and you don't feel like plunking down hundreds of dollars for your own personal VPP (Velocity Prediction Program) analysis, you will just have to discover for yourself how your boat sails. You can do this by observing and keeping records of how your boat performs in different winds and at different apparent wind angles. Again, time in the boat makes all the difference in the world. Olympic sailors don't spend hundreds of hours practicing aboard their dinghies just because they want to work on their tans.

As a general rule, in winds of 8 knots or less, you have to sail at an angle about 40 degrees higher than dead downwind. That's right, 40 degrees; your jibing angles will be nearly as great as your tacking angles were on the upwind leg. In these conditions, your main concern is boat speed, not the distance you have sailed. It's critical to keep the boat moving. Sailing a shorter distance doesn't mean a thing if you're sitting dead in the water. As the wind edges up toward the higher end of the range you can try sailing a slightly lower angle in the puffs. But for the most part you will want to maintain as hot a sailing angle as possible. Otherwise, you will find your boat speed falling away dramatically.

In contrast, as the wind builds to 9 knots and higher, you have to be more sensitive to changes in wind velocity and the trade-offs in speed and apparent wind angles. A 1-knot

increase in true wind speed, for example, can give you the ability to sail at a slightly lower wind angle, say 5 degrees lower, while still maintaining boat speed. It is in these conditions—between 9 and 15 knots—that

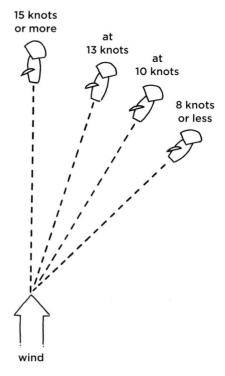

In 8 knots of wind or less you need to sail at a jibing angle about 40 degrees higher than dead downwind to maximize your VMG (see pages 136–37) with the help of apparent wind. As the wind speed builds from 9 to 14 knots, start steering a course that brings you closer to the rhumbline. Notice wind changes, steering down in the puffs and a little higher in the lulls. Only with a breeze of approximately 15 knots or more will you be able to steer a course dead downwind toward the leeward mark. As always, the exact jibing angle for each boat is unique, so you need to experiment to see what works best for you. Be aware that with an asymmetrical spinnaker you generally will be sailing higher jibing angles than you would with a symmetrical spinnaker, since asymmetricals tend to become blanketed by the main on a broad reach or run.

you especially want to play the puffs, sailing higher when there's a decrease in pressure and slightly lower if the wind builds. Be aware, however, that if your boat flies an asymmetrical chute, you're still going to be maintaining a fairly high jibing angle; it's impossible to rotate a bowsprit aft the way you can a conventional spinnaker pole, which means it's prone to blanketing by the main.

If your onboard instruments include a true wind indicator, use it to keep track of whether you are in a header or a lift. If they don't, pay close attention to speed, heading, apparent wind angles, and the pressure on the sheet and guy, until the breeze climbs to a point where you can maintain speed at a course just a few degrees high of a true run. Usually, this happens in around 15 or 16 knots of true wind. From this point on you can pretty much sail dead downwind. Your main considerations now are keeping clear air and, especially in high winds, controlling the spinnaker to avoid a broach (a situation when the force of the wind on the spinnaker pins the boat on its side so the boat is out of control and simply dragging sideways through the water). You can do this by trimming the sail carefully and sailing at an angle at which you won't be adversely affected by waves.

Note that in moderate conditions many boats experience steps, speeds at which you can feel the boat take off. If your boat experiences these, try steering a scallop course: sail up until you feel the boat start to accelerate, then keep pointing the boat in that direction until you get the full benefit of the

Downwind Sailing Tips

- Be sure to keep looking astern for shifts and more breeze.
- In light or moderate air, always jibe downwind to take advantage of apparent wind.
- Remember: in less than 15 knots of wind, dead downwind is slow.
- Play the shifts so you're sailing in headers whenever possible. This way you can sail a hot, more direct angle to the leeward mark.
- Boats with asymmetrical spinnakers need to sail higher and hotter jibing angles in order to get the spinnaker out from behind the mainsail.

acceleration and your apparent wind. After that, slowly burn off your speed by pointing down just a few degrees at a time. When you feel the boat drop off the step, turn back up to the acceleration course and do it all over again. The winner will be the skipper who understands exactly where the best course for acceleration is without pointing the boat too high. Instruments can help, but again all instruments have a lag time due to the dampening built into the system; you could be 5 to 20 seconds late picking up the subtle difference. Try to be a "seat-of-the-pants" sailor. Concentrate on the pull of the sails and the feel of the boat.

GOOD AIR

Finally, when sailing downwind you not only want to be on the lookout for the shifts in your immediate area, you also want to keep an eye on the "big picture," so you can anticipate where a new wind might be coming from and ensure that you don't end up sailing in another boat's dirty air.

For example, if you noticed that there was more air on one side of the course than the other when you were sailing the beat, then by all means head that way when you are going downwind. (The same advice goes for current: if you found an advantageous current on one side of the course going upwind, be sure to avoid that area on the run, because that current will push against you when going downwind.) In near-calm, or "ghosting," conditions especially, look for the dark bands on the water that signify a puff of breeze and watch the other boats in your area, whether they are in your class, another class, or non-racers just out enjoying a sunny day. If your competitors off to one side of the course are struggling to keep their spinnakers full, there's no reason to go over and join them. If you see a lot of boats carrying a good breeze down the other side of the course, maybe position yourself so you can join the party. In contrast to sailing on a beat, where it's a bad idea to try to tack out of a hole and risk bringing the boat to a stop, jibing out of a hole when sailing downwind usually helps. There are two reasons for this. First, as mentioned earlier, you don't slow down as much in a jibe as you do in a tack. Second, often what seems like a hole is, in fact, a lift with the wind shifting more behind you, reducing your apparent wind. If you jibe in this case you will find the other tack is favored.

Remember that a new breeze will generally come in from windward, which means the tail end of the fleet will get it first, providing valuable clues as to what is coming. Whatever you do, don't ignore the boats behind you! Running legs are the one place where fleets tend to get bunched up again— as opposed to beats and reaches, where boats generally get stretched out—which is why windward-leeward courses are so popular; they make for more exciting racing. If you are at the tail end of the fleet at the windward mark, don't despair—your turn may soon come. If you are up front, be aware of what the boats behind you are experiencing, or you may soon be trading places with them.

Along these same lines, be aware of other boats' wind shadows; they can hurt you as surely on the run as they did on the

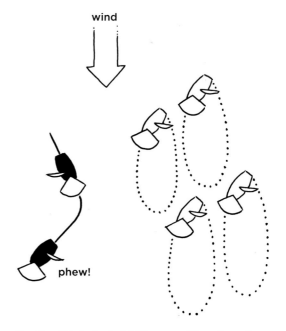

Don't sail into bad air! Jibe away if you have to.

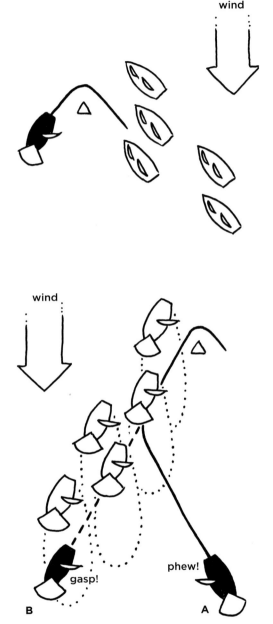

wind

wind

gasp!

phew!

B

A

*The lead boat has clear air as it rounds the windward mark, but boats are stacked up on the layline behind it (top). The lead boat should jibe early to maintain clear air (bottom, **A**). Otherwise, it will be left gasping in the other boats' wind shadows (bottom, **B**).*

beat. As is the case when sailing to windward, the area of disturbed air stretches some ten mast lengths to leeward of a boat sailing before the wind. They should be avoided at all cost—there is no surer way of losing your lead downwind than to be gassed by the competition. Watch for boats approaching from astern or on the opposite jibe. Try to anticipate whether they will affect you and respond accordingly, either by modifying your own course slightly or even jibing away. This is especially true if you see clumps of boats.

Clear air can also be problematic at the beginning of the leg, so execute your rounding accordingly. If, for example, you have a clump of boats behind you stacked up on the windward layline, consider jibing early so they won't hurt you when they get their spinnakers up. Remember, well-executed jibes cost you very little.

REACHING LEGS

In many ways reaching legs are the picture of simplicity. All you do is bear away during your mark rounding and follow the rhumbline to the next mark. Because you're no longer beating, the world is your oyster in terms of heading. Also, because you're already on a broad reach, there are no worries in terms of jibing downwind or being on the alert for windshifts. In fact, all you really need to do is two things: sail the shortest distance possible—the rhumbline—and sail as fast as possible.

Alas, actually accomplishing these two

things can be a little more complicated than it looks on paper, thanks to that pesky phenomenon of the racecourse known as "competitors." In big fleets in particular it seems they are forever trying to pass to windward when you would much prefer they not sully your air. Then there are those times when you want to sneak by to windward—heck, it should only take a few seconds!—and yet they get it in their heads that *they* deserve to have air that is clear and unsullied as well. Hmmm . . .

Finally, as if that wasn't already enough, you can't be completely cavalier with regard to windshifts, because even small changes in wind can result in substantial differences in terms of boat speed. In fluky conditions in particular, you need to be aware and take advantage of the changes in wind velocity and direction to maximize boat speed. If you expect a new breeze to come in at some point during the reaching leg, you will definitely want to factor this into your overall strategy.

Clearly, a reaching leg is nothing to be taken for granted.

CLEAR AIR

In many ways, the time to ensure that you have clear air on a reach is before you even get to the windward mark; to anticipate if you're going to have trouble, and then take that into account as you approach your rounding. If, for instance, you are all by yourself, you can simply make your rounding and sail the rhumbline. But if you are surrounded by other boats as you beat along

the starboard layline, you'll want to do something about all that traffic. This is especially the case if you're in a PHRF division that includes boats with markedly different boat speeds (see chapter 12, Getting Involved, for more information about PHRF ratings), or if you're sailing on a course with a number of other sections and some of the boats that started behind you are beginning to catch up. The thing you want to avoid above all else is sailing way above the rhumbline in an effort to maintain clear air and boat speed. Sailing high of the rhumbline not only means sailing a longer distance, it also means you will be sailing at a lower apparent wind angle during the second half of the leg. The most extreme instances of sailing high of the rhumbline occur as a result of luffing matches, in which a boat to leeward all of a sudden hardens up onto a close reach to try to block a competitor attempting to pass to windward. Even without luffing matches, fleets have a tendency to work their way to windward as they jockey for clear air, and try to maintain boat speed in the context of a reaching-leg spinnaker parade.

In order to avoid this tendency, the best thing to do is put yourself in a position a couple of boatlengths to windward of the rhumbline—and by extension your competitors—as soon as you've turned the windward mark. That way they won't be tempted to pass you to windward, because it will require a dramatic change in heading. Furthermore, if there are boats ahead that are slower than you, you'll have a better chance to pass them, because again, they will have to go well out of their way if they want to tangle with you. Make this move right away to separate yourself from the fleet. Don't just slowly ease your way up. That might tempt others to join you. Make your move a dramatic and sudden one. In light air this will also get the boat up to speed faster. To reiterate, the idea is to get away from those other boats so they will leave you alone and let you sail your race.

Of course, if for some reason one of your competitors decides to join you, you have to stay on your toes and decide how to best minimize the impact of his company. If the other boat is bigger and clearly faster, by all means let it by, preferably to leeward, but to windward as well if there's nothing you can do about it. In the latter case, one

thing to watch for is whether this big bully has a bunch of friends coming up from behind. Remember, when a competitor gasses you, it not only slows you down, it also takes a while to get back up to speed after he's gone—especially in light air. In the meantime, if you're not careful, another boat could be in an overtaking position to windward, and you will find yourself sailing through a whole bunch of turbulence all over again.

On the other hand, let's say you're in a closely matched one-design fleet in which the competitor in question has about the same boat speed as you. In this case the situation is slightly more complicated. Not only does letting a competitor by mean you're falling back a position, but because the two of you are so closely matched, you

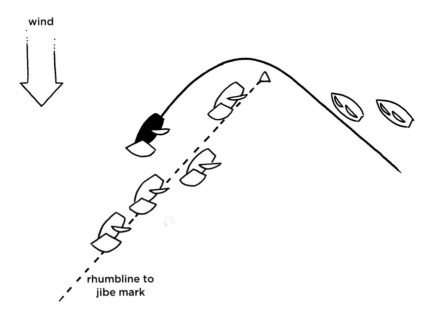

On a reaching leg put yourself a boatlength or two above the rhumbline to avoid tangling with the other boats.

will be in his bad air for an awfully long time.

The answer here is to defend your position by staying between him and the jibe mark, the mark separating the two reaching legs of a triangle course. In doing so, however, don't overreact and try to match his new course. Instead, ease your way to windward just a touch. The idea here is that, despite the fact that he might be building up a little more boat speed in the short term, he is now sailing a longer leg and will have to come back down to the rhumbline eventually. More importantly, if you go up to where he is, your sailing angle back to the mark will actually be lower and *slower* than his; because you're ahead, your competitor doesn't have to alter course quite so dramatically to sail down to the mark. That

could really get you into trouble; by sailing the rest of the leg on a hotter angle, your competitor might be able to sneak inside and establish an overlap by the time you reach the jibe mark. That would be all he needs to pass you while rounding the mark.

If you do find yourself in a position where you have to harden up to fend the other guy off—for example, if your competitor has a few feet more waterline length and is therefore inherently faster—your goal should be to do it so the price you pay isn't exorbitant. That means making your move hard and fast. Don't just change course a few degrees to get your boat speed up and prevent him from passing. Wait until he gets close or actually tries to pass, and then make a dramatic change of course. Sail into him so he isn't just trying to match your

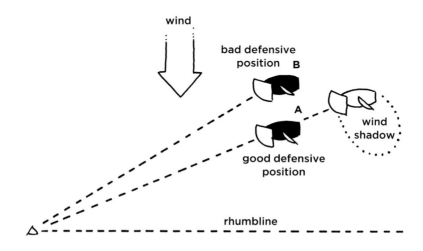

*To defend against an overtaking boat, position yourself between the competition and the mark (boat **A**). Note how the poorly positioned boat (**B**) must sail a lower and slower angle to the mark than the boat it is defending itself against.*

boat speed, but is also trying to avoid running into you. (However, remember that, while the leeward boat has right-of-way, you have to permit the windward boat room to get clear.) Put the fear of God in him so he won't try it again.

When sailing a crowded reaching leg try positioning a crewmember where he or she can always keep track of the boats behind you. If there's eye contact the other boats will be less likely to attack. If a competitor does try going up a bit, make sure your "watch dog" tells you about the move loud enough for the other crew to hear. That will negate any idea they may have that the element of surprise is on their side. Another, less exciting but *very* effective option is to try talking to the other skipper. Courteously point out that, if he dares try to go over the top of you, you would be more than happy to lose the race in order to start a luffing match that will take him to Mexico. No one in their right mind really wants to get in-volved in a luffing match. The threat alone might persuade him not to attack.

On those occasions when the shoe is on the other foot and it's you who is causing all the problems by coming up from behind, it again pays to be decisive. Select a strategy and execute it skillfully, so you don't end up getting caught in a luffing match that has you sailing to the moon. Once again, a good way to avoid problems is to pop up to a position two or three boat-lengths to windward of the boat in question, in order to obtain some separation. If that doesn't look like it's going to work, but you think you're moving fast enough to get by to leeward, then do it. First, sail right up to your competitor's transom. Then, when you see you have a surge of speed, steer a dramatically lower course, *diving* below him and sailing through his shadow. Because his shadow is smaller (albeit more intense) close by, your momentum may be sufficient enough to carry you through—although you may have to dive down two or more boatlengths to do it. Let the other skipper know what you're doing, so he won't get too spooked. If his is a smaller boat and he's not in your section, he may even feel so re-lieved that you're not going to spoil his reach that he will head up a bit as you sail by; that way neither of you will be hurt too much. Unfortunately, this kind of maneu-ver is nearly impossible to do if your boat speeds are roughly equal.

Of course, just as you expected that other faster guy to be reasonable with you, it only makes sense that you should be rea-sonable in return. How much slower than

Staying Cool on a Reach

Luffing matches, or even the prospect of a luffing match, can be pretty stressful. Fortunately, as was the case with cross-ing situations on the beat, just being aware—keeping an eye on the competition so you aren't taken by surprise—can make all the difference in the world. Is another competitor creeping up from behind? Don't panic. Think through your options and decide how you'll deal with the threat. Try to an-ticipate the tactical situation you'll face, and then act deci-sively ahead of time. If the other guy realizes you're fully aware of his presence, he might decide not to tangle with you at all.

you is he, really? How much will you lose to the competition if you don't actually get around him? Is it really worth a luffing match? Pick your battles and your wars. Sailing, like chess, involves a sequence of decisions that, when combined, lead to the outcome of the race. A small battle between you and a competitor can cost both of you precious time and distance—maybe even the war. Ultimately, because it is so hard to pass on reaches, it often makes more sense to concentrate on positioning yourself to pass at the mark, where you can gain (or lose!) boats much more quickly and easily. On the first of the two reaching legs this means working your way low, so you will be able to establish an inside overlap at the jibe mark. On the second reaching leg you need to make sure you don't let any of your competitors go over you to windward. You can do this by defending your position intelligently, while establishing your own inside overlap with any nearby competitors to leeward as you approach the leeward mark.

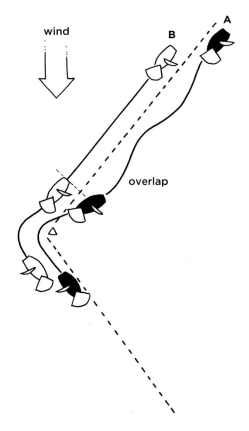

*Actually passing on a downwind leg is difficult. Instead, set yourself up to pass a slower competitor at the jibe mark. Here, boat **A** establishes an inside overlap at the jibe mark and passes boat **B** as they go around.*

SAILING FAST

As the saying goes, there's nothing like good boat speed to make you look like a tactical genius, and nowhere is this truer than on a reaching leg. All the talk of luffing matches is irrelevant if your competitors can't catch you in the first place or if you're blowing by the other guys like they're standing still.

In terms of the reaching legs, the basic rule is to bear off in the puffs and harden up in the lulls in order to maintain boat speed, without wandering too far from the rhumb-line. The same goes for oscillating shifts; if the breeze was shifting back and forth on the beat, be prepared to modify your heading on the reaching leg as well, so that you will always be sailing on a hot angle of sail.

Likewise, if the breeze is dying or building or if you're anticipating a large shift, factor that into your thinking. For example, if the breeze is building, you might want to begin the leg sailing a course high of the rhumbline to maintain boat speed on a

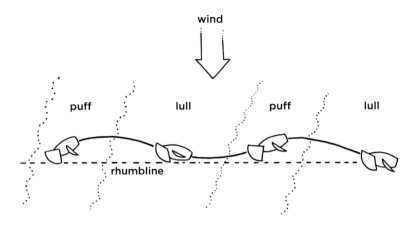

To maintain boat speed in reaching legs, bear off in the puffs and harden up in the lulls without straying too far from the rhumbline.

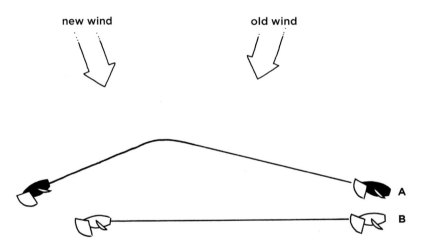

*Steer a higher course early if you're anticipating a knock, especially in light air. Here, although boat **A** has to sail a greater distance, the boat speed it gained by harnessing apparent wind with a higher angle of sail put it in front of boat **B**.*

hotter angle of sail. Later on, as the new breeze comes in, you can steer down for the mark on a lower apparent wind angle. Obviously, if the wind is dying, your best approach is the exact opposite: sail low of the rhumbline early, while there's still good pressure, and then harden up as the wind begins to fade. If you're dealing with a header, sail high first, then lower later on as the wind moves forward. If you're anticipating a lift, sail low early so you can steer a higher course as you near the mark; the lift won't affect you quite as severely.

Obviously, these latter strategies in par-

Reaching Leg Tips

- When there is a lot of traffic heading into the windward mark, pop up to windward a couple of boatlengths at the beginning of the reach to separate yourself from the competition and maintain clear air.
- If a competitor tries to pass to windward, defend your position by staying between the other boat and the mark. But don't sail as high a course as your competitor astern.
- Sometimes it makes sense **not** to pass a competitor, if doing so will slow you down.

ticular carry an element of risk; if the wind doesn't do as you'd hoped, you may be left steaming. But then again, if you aren't paying attention and miss this kind of opportunity, you may find yourself going backward relative to the skippers who made it to the correct side of the shift ahead of you. When in doubt, sail the rhumbline and play the puffs and shifts. But don't get so fixated on boat speed that you miss the big picture. Watch the competition, the water, any other daysailers that might be in the area, and the wind indicators on shore. And if you do get burned once in a while, big deal. At least no one can say that you didn't try.

RULES FOR SAILING DOWNWIND

When it comes to rules, the downwind leg is fairly straightforward, at least until you get to the marks (more on that in chap-

ter 6). Starboard always has right-of-way, even if a starboard-tack boat is approaching from astern; on the same tack a leeward boat always has right-of-way over a windward boat; and, unless the boats are on opposite tacks and the boat ahead is on port, an overtaking boat must always keep clear of the boat ahead.

The one situation in which things can get a bit complicated is when a leeward boat establishes its overlap by coming up from behind and within two boatlengths of a competitor. (However, it's much better than in the bad old days of "mast abeam," when sailors had to judge where the mast of one boat was in relation to the helm of another to establish rights.) Basically, according to Rule 17.1, if an overlapping boat establishes its overlap from astern by sailing up to leeward and within two boatlengths of a competitor, it cannot sail above proper course in an effort to tangle with that competitor, even though it has right-of-way. In other words, it cannot sail above the course that would take it most efficiently to the next mark in the absence of any other competitors. By the same token, the windward boat cannot sail below proper course in order to hamper the leeward boat's efforts to get past.

Bear in mind that in mixed-boat fleets or in situations in which different fleets are sailing on the same course, the idea of "proper" course can become problematic. One time, for example, an LS-10 and Melges 24 found themselves dealing with this issue during a Chicago NOOD regatta, in which both boats were sailing in separate one-design fleets around the same set of buoys. When sailing against each other in a PHRF fleet they rate about the same. However, because a Melges flies an asymmetrical spinnaker on a bowsprit, as opposed to a symmetrical spinnaker on a standard pole, it has to sail along much higher and hotter jibe angles than the LS-10 to get downwind in the same amount of time. This means the two boats have to sail far different headings when on a run. In this instance, the Melges 24 came up from behind and to leeward, where it promptly hailed to the LS-10 to sail up to proper course. The LS-10's skipper, however, responded by saying he *was* sailing the proper course for his kind of boat and that he was under no obligation to sail any higher just for the sake of the other guy's polars. As bad luck would have it for the Melges, the LS-10 was entirely in the right. Because it couldn't sail through the LS-10's wind shadow, the Melges had to slow down and go astern of the LS-10.

Of course, these kinds of niceties become totally irrelevant if the overtaking boat is trying to get by to windward. In that case, the leeward boat can sail as high as it wants, while the overtaking boat must do everything in its power to keep clear. Again, when hardening up during a luffing match, the leeward boat must give the windward boat room to keep clear. But at the same time, the overtaking boat cannot put itself in a position where the slightest change in the leeward boat's course will immediately result in contact.

Q & A

Q. As Adam approaches the windward mark in light air on the starboard-tack layline, he notices that he is sailing in a 10-degree lift. Explain any effect this might have on his choice of spinnaker hoists at the start of the next leg, which is dead downwind.
A. He will want to do a jibe set in order to start the leg out on port. That way he will be sailing on the headed tack, which will allow him to sail closer to the wind, while sailing a more direct course for the mark.

Q. Where is it best to pass a competitor on a reaching or running leg?
A. Trick question! It's often best not to pass him at all. Instead, focus on establishing an inside overlap as you approach the next mark, in order to pass him during the rounding. Trying to pass a competitor downwind will often result in a mutually damaging luffing match.

Q. Adam is approaching the windward mark with a crowd of other boats on the first leg of a triangle course. How should he approach the beginning of the next leg?
A. Once he is around the mark, he should quickly establish a position two or three boatlengths to windward of the rhumbline. This separation will discourage the other boats from trying to pass to windward or engage in a luffing match, if and when he decides to pass them.

Q. Rich comes up from astern of Adam, only two boatlengths to leeward. When the two of them are sailing neck and neck, he suddenly hardens up, saying he has rights as the leeward boat and Adam has to stay clear. Adam cries foul. Who is in the right?

A. Because Rich established a leeward overlap from astern and within two boatlengths of Adam, Rich cannot sail above proper course.

Q. Rich is sailing on a reaching leg in a fluky breeze. How should he handle his boat to get the most out of the conditions?

A. He should sail high in the light spots and low in the puffs, in order to maintain boat speed without straying too far from the rhumbline.

Chapter 6

LEEWARD MARK ROUNDINGS AND FINISHING

The windward mark can be a pretty stressful place, thanks to the problems of judging the layline and avoiding other boats' bad air. The leeward mark, however, should be the picture of simplicity, because you're sailing off the wind. Actually "making" the mark is never really in doubt, so there shouldn't be a problem, right?

Wrong!

For one thing, although the rules situation at the end of a reaching or running leg is simple in theory, it can become a bit complicated as clumps of boats all try to go around at the same time or when someone decides to get "creative" with the law. Beyond that, although you don't have to worry about pointing ability, avoiding other boats' wind shadows is still very important, both to maintain boat speed and facilitate sail handling. This is especially true when

the air is light on a busy racecourse. One year during the first day of a NOOD regatta in Chicago, for example, the wind oscillated wildly throughout the morning as a front came through out of the west. It alternately whipped up whitecaps and left the dozens of boats from all around the Midwest gasping for breath. On the "B" course, where things were especially congested, the various divisions of S2s, Tartan Tens, and mid-size PHRF boats inevitably clumped up by the score at the end of each downwind leg, and heaven help the crews that got caught in the middle. The boats in front went slower and slower, trapped by multiple wind shadows behind them, while the boats with clear air and better boat speed came plowing into the melee from behind like cars in a chain-reaction crash on a foggy freeway. The sounds of slatting sails, clanging halyards, and frustrated cries for room

HOW TO GUIDE for

Outdoor
living

DESIGN YOUR PROJECTS · CHOOSE THE RIGHT PRODUCTS · INSTALL WITH PROFESSIONAL RESULTS

Oldcastle®
Designer style. Professional grade. DIY price.

PRODUCT/**Four Cobble Paver**
This unique, new paver resembles traditional
cobble stones but is much easier to install.

A panoramic aerial shot showing plenty of action at the leeward mark. (The mark is just astern of the third of the three boats sailing close-hauled.) Note how the fourth boat is coming in to the mark wide in order to make a tactical rounding. The three leading boats still on the run are dropping their spinnakers so they will be able to maneuver more easily.

slowly crescendoed into a kind of "perfect storm" of leeward mark chaos.

Sound like fun? Then let's try to make some sense of the mess!

RULES AT THE LEEWARD MARK

With the exception of the start, an understanding of the rules is more critical at the leeward mark than anywhere else. This is because the nature of the leeward mark is such that boats can approach from different directions and attitudes of sail. Also, the general rules regarding port-starboard crossings and windward-leeward right-of-way don't always apply. Still, the rules are not half as complicated or mysterious as some sailors would have you believe. Basically, as explained in Rule 18.2, when two boats are approaching the leeward mark and the inside boat—the boat closest to the mark—has an overlap with the outside boat at the moment the first of the two boats reaches a point two boatlengths from the mark, the outside boat will give the inside boat room to go around. Note that when the Rule says "at the moment," it means it. For example, if the inside boat's overlap is broken mere seconds after the leading boat touches the two-boatlength circle, the outside boat still has to allow it room at the mark. If, on the other hand, an inside boat establishes an overlap mere seconds after the outside boat has crossed the two-boatlength threshold, the inside boat is out of luck, *even if it would normally have right-of-way.* In other words, the rule governing room at the leeward mark takes precedence over the rules governing the rest of the course, a situation that can be critically important when rounding marks to starboard, or when sailing through a gate instead of simply leaving a single mark to port.

As an example, let's say that Rich and Adam are both approaching the right side of a gate. Adam is on starboard and Rich is closest to the mark on port. Two boatlengths or more away from the mark, Adam can sail wherever he wants and Rich has to stay out of his way. If, however, Rich has an overlap at the moment one or the other of them crosses the two-boatlength threshold, Adam (the starboard boat) has to allow Rich whatever room he needs to get around.

Not surprisingly, the situation can get a bit confusing when you're dealing with more than two boats. But if you keep your wits about you and start thinking about overlaps before you reach that magical two-

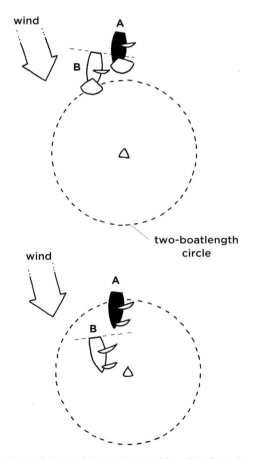

*Even though boat **A** loses its overlap after boat **B** reaches the two-boatlength circle, it is still entitled to room at the mark.*

When It's the Starboard-Tacker Who Stays Clear

Remember: when rounding a downwind mark, there are times when a starboard-tack boat has to give way to a port-tack boat and a boat to leeward has to yield to a boat to windward. If an inside boat has an overlap with a boat on the outside at the moment one or the other crosses a point two boatlengths from the mark, the boat on the outside has to give the inside boat room to make a rounding, regardless of its angle of sail or position in relation to the inside boat.

boatlength point, it should never be that difficult to sort out.

There are a couple of other things to keep in mind. First, when the rules say an inside boat is entitled to room at the mark, they do not mean all the room in the world; just room to go around. In other words, unless the inside boat is also to leeward and on starboard tack—a situation in which it is said to have double rights—it has to make a nice tight circle often referred to as a seamanlike rounding (something you will often hear yelled out as a clump of boats goes wheeling around together). Second, an outside boat must give room only if it is able to.

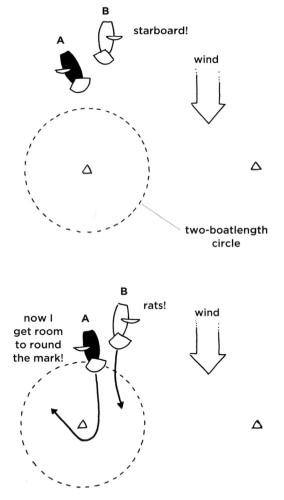

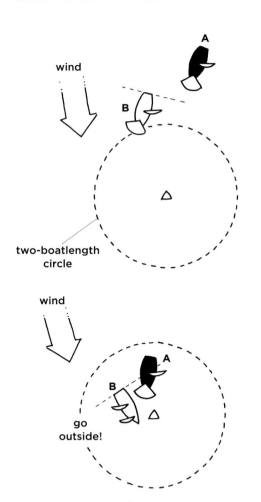

*Because boat **A** did not have an overlap when boat **B** crossed the two-boatlength circle, it is not entitled to room, even though it is on starboard.*

*As boats **A** and **B** approach the leeward mark, boat **B** on starboard has right-of-way over boat **A**. However, once boat **A** crosses into the two-boatlength circle boat **B** must give it room to round since boat **A** has an inside overlap and the rule governing room at the mark takes precedence over port-starboard.*

Establishing Rights at the Leeward Mark

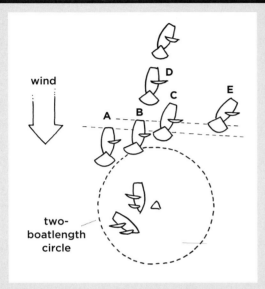

wind

A   B

D

C

E

two-
boatlength
circle

Boat **B** has just reached a point two boatlengths from the mark, which means it has now established its own personal pecking order there. Specifically, boat **A** needs to give it room while **B** has to give room to both **C** and the distant **E**. The fact that **D** has an overlap with **C** means nothing as far as **B** is concerned. **B** is clear ahead, and if **D** tries to stick his bow in, he will be breaking the rules.

Note that, although the situation has been established for **B**, the other boats have yet to work things out between themselves and some of the other boats, as none of them have reached the two-boatlength point. For example, it **appears** that **C** will have to give **E** room at the mark, but it's by no means certain. If **C** were to surge ahead so that **E** no longer has an overlap at the moment **C** reaches the two-boatlength point, then **C** can cut the corner as close as it wants. Then again, while **A** is clear ahead of **E** for now, that could very easily change by the time **A** reaches the two-boatlength circle, in which case it will have to give **E** room to round. **E** may also be able to slip inside by default, because it has an overlap with **B**, who in turn has an overlap with **A**. Part of **B**'s rights and obligations include providing room for **E**, whether **A** likes it or not!

If, for example, an outside boat is being overlapped by an inside boat, but the outside boat has a whole herd of competitors right on its hip—where falling off would result in a collision—the inside boat can't force its way in. Of course, the outside boat can only get away with this kind of excuse if the inside boat establishes its overlap at the last moment. If the two boats have been overlapped for some time, the outside boat has to take the inside boat into account to ensure that there will be room when it's time to round. Because of the potential for confusion, it's often a good idea to start communicating with your competitors to establish a pecking order well before the first of you reaches the two-boatlength circle, especially if you are in a fleet made up of boats of varying speeds. For example, if a faster boat is coming up from behind when you are three lengths from the mark, clearly state, "I am a boatlength from the circle. You will not have room, so stay clear." Then, when you reach the two-boatlength circle, clearly state the situation once more, making sure any other boats in the area are aware of what is going on as well: "Boat astern, you will not have room. I am at the two-boatlength circle now, so stay clear. Boat to leeward, do you hear what I am telling boat astern?" Note that, because you put the situation into words out on the water, if you do find yourself in the protest room you can explain a time line and call a witness, which will make your case that much stronger. Hashing things out ahead of time is also a good idea if you are the boat trying to establish an overlap from astern; it's up to you to prove that an overlap exists before you start demanding room at the mark. According to Rule 18.2e, if there is a reasonable doubt that an overlap existed, it didn't. Race committees tend to look with more than a little disfavor upon sailors who just stick their noses in at the leeward mark and then hope for the best.

STRATEGIES AT THE MARK

As if the rules alone weren't enough, the leeward mark can also be a tricky place in terms of tactics and strategy. In a big fleet especially, picking the right spot and executing a good rounding can make a huge difference in the number of boatlengths gained or lost. In fact, in a competitive fleet, the boats in your immediate vicinity will have been sailing the entire previous leg with this very goal in mind.

No matter how you choose to approach the rounding, always set yourself up to come into the leeward mark with speed. Don't get fooled into thinking you can "deadhead" run the last 100 yards by going

directly downwind. Keep to your normal sailing angles. Otherwise, your speed will drop precipitously and you will be easy pickings for the competition.

ALL BY YOURSELF

To begin with, let's look at what to do in the best of situations, when you are all alone and can round the mark however you want. The basic principle to follow here is one of wide-in and tight-out, allowing yourself some extra room on the approach to the mark, then cutting in close as you go around. This is true whether it's a leeward mark at the end of a run or a jibe mark separating the two reaching legs on a triangle course. When coming in under spinnaker or with your jib sheets cracked at the end of the reach or run, give yourself a couple of extra boatlengths as you approach the mark, so you can make a nice easy turn. Then cut in close as you steer onto the next leg. Using this approach will make it that much easier to bring the spinnaker around at a jibe mark. It will also allow you to retain boat speed without losing anything to windward when going from a run to a beat.

In the latter case, when you're coming up onto a beat, be sure to bring the main in as you're going around, while letting the jib lag behind so the bow isn't forced down. Then, as you're coming around through the end of your turn, steer a couple of degrees above close-hauled in order to position yourself to windward a bit and allow the crew a second or two of easy trimming before you bear off for speed. This kind of "tactical" rounding will leave you in a good position and with plenty of speed at the start of the next leg. If, on the other hand, you come in tight and cut the mark as close as possible at the very beginning, you will either have to put the helm over hard to pivot around the buoy—immediately killing boat speed—or lose a valuable boatlength or two to windward as you maintain your way through a nice easy turn. Always remember: just getting around to the next leg is only part of what you want to accomplish in a mark rounding. You want to be able to slingshot your way around, carrying your speed with you so your boat is spit onto the next leg like a melon seed on a hot summer's day.

Mark rounding is yet another maneuver it pays to practice on those days off, as op-posed to figuring out how best to proceed in the thick of competition. Find a convenient bell buoy or some other navigational mark and throw in a few roundings: both reach-to-reach and run-to-beat. When practicing a run-to-beat rounding, determine exactly how much time your crew needs to get the jib up and the spinnaker down. That way you can avoid playing the "when-exactly-should-we-drop-the-chute" game on race day. Remember to set your sail controls, such as backstay tension, cunningham, and outhaul, *before* you reach the mark, so you can get up to speed right away on the next leg. When doing a reach-to-reach rounding, practice the jibe so the helmsman and crew work as one, with the boat and sail coming around at the same speed. While you're at

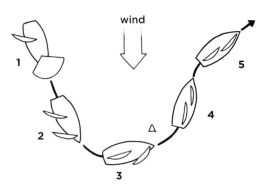

*Come in wide and go out tight at the leeward mark. As you approach the mark, be ready to drop the spinnaker (**1**). When you are close and have just enough time to do so before reaching the mark, run up the jib and bring down the spinnaker (**2**). Pull the main in as you round the mark and let the jib lag behind (**3**). Once you round the mark, steer slightly high of close-hauled for position and to help the jib trimmer (**4**). Then bear off for speed (**5**).*

Using Your Sails While Rounding the Leeward Mark

When practicing reach-to-reach and run-to-beat mark roundings, try to use as little rudder as possible. If you are at the helm this will involve working with your mainsail trimmer, or trimming in the main yourself, so the sail will help turn the boat into the wind. At the same time the jib trimmers should take in the headsail a little more slowly, so it won't try to bring the bow back down. As you become increasingly proficient, try rounding a mark a few times using no helm at all, trimming in the main to bring the boat up to a beat, and then trimming in the jib to stop the turn. Obviously you would never want to actually race without using the rudder, but this kind of drill can give you a real edge in terms of your feel for the boat.

it, practice jamming in a few tight turns. Then you'll be ready for those times when you have to make your rounding under less than optimal circumstances.

TWO'S A CROWD

Of course, the point of this book is to go sailboat *racing*, and it would hardly be a race if you were the only boat on the course. Inevitably you will find yourself overlapped by a competitor either to the inside or the outside or both, so you may as well be prepared.

If you are the one on the inside, your goal is to maintain boat speed and make sure you are still ahead and in clear air when the two of you pop out on the other side of the mark. Not surprisingly, this is easiest to do when you have double rights, since you have every right to execute a wide-in, tight-out turn, the same as you would when sailing alone. With this in mind, if you are the inside boat approaching the jibe mark on a triangle or Olympic course, don't hesitate to steer a slightly higher heading just before the rounding. This will ensure that you come out of the turn as tight as possible and that the overlapped boat can't work to windward and steal your air on the next leg. The same technique works if you are on starboard tack at the end of a run. (However, note that in both cases you will have your hands tied if you established the overlap by coming up from behind and to leeward by less than two boatlengths, as per Rule 17.1.) The main thing is don't let the boat on the outside sneak inside so that it's gassing you on the next leg. Also be careful, when steering high, to set up your tactical rounding so that you don't let another competitor duck inside and establish an inside overlap of his own (see illustrations page 96 and left illustration page 97).

Of course, the situation is much trickier if you do not have these double rights. In this case, the outside boat only has to give you enough room at the mark for a seamanlike rounding, which means he can force you to come in as tight as he wants. At the very least, this can result in the loss of valuable boat speed. At worst, if you don't come out of the rounding tight enough, it can allow the other boat to sneak inside to windward. This can be especially devastating when going from a run to a beat.

Of course, if you're the trailing boat you want to do exactly that: force the boat on the inside to sail as close to the mark as possible, while making your own tactical rounding in an effort to come out on top at the start of the next leg. While you are coming in to the mark, tell the inside boat to keep it tight, and convince 'em that they have no choice in the matter by staying right with them. Then at the last moment, swerve out a boatlength or two in order to both separate from the other boat and set yourself up for a tactical rounding. At this point the other crew will probably be paying more attention to boat handling and less attention to you, so your attack may come as a complete surprise. If you're going from a run to a beat you might also want to drop the spinnaker a bit early. The loss of a little boat speed will help you separate even

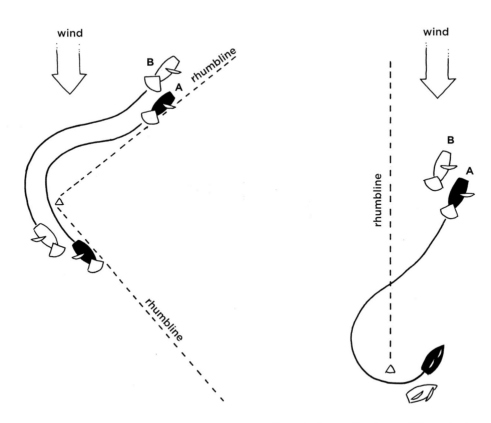

When you have double rights—when you are both on starboard and to leeward—at the jibe mark, you should always try to make a tactical rounding. Here, boat A steers a higher heading just before making a tight rounding at the mark, preventing boat B from sneaking in to windward and stealing its air on the next leg.

A tactical rounding is possible at the leeward mark as well, if you have double rights.

farther, giving you more room to sneak inside. It will also give you more time to think about getting the boat up to speed on the beat (see right illustration opposite).

If you can't sneak inside, take your competitor around as tight as possible, and may the best crew win! This is one of those situations when practicing your mark roundings during a day off can make all the difference in the world. Make a clean jibe

and/or spinnaker drop and try to get your competitor into a lee-bow position by trimming in your sails smoothly and cleanly as you power up onto the next leg. Keep in mind, especially on those occasions when you're trying to sneak inside, that no matter what you do you have to make sure you don't run into your competition from behind. Even the nimblest of keelboats can slow down in an amazingly short period of time when carving tight turns, and the boat clear ahead always has rights over the boat clear astern.

Still, for those who are willing and able

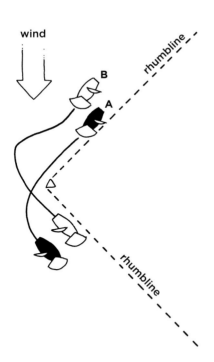

*Here, the trailing boat (**B**) makes a tactical rounding and sneaks inside boat **A** at the jibe mark, which came in tight and went out wide.*

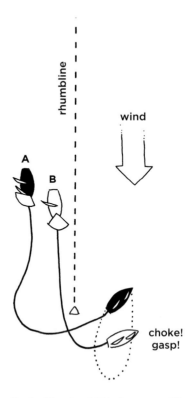

*If you are the trailing boat (**A**), have your jib up and be ready to drop your spinnaker. Force the leading boat (**B**) to come in tight. Then swing out wide for your own tactical rounding in order to make a pass at the leeward mark. By doing so you will leave boat **B** gasping for air in your wind shadow.*

to cut to the inside, the gains can be quite impressive. Tartan Ten sailor Ken Quant, the advertising director for *SAILING* magazine, has an incredible knack for sneaking his bow inside at the last moment and making the competition pay. During those same fluky races at the NOOD regatta in Chicago, there were a couple of instances when cutting to the inside meant not only getting ahead of his immediate competition, but having the clear air to escape from the melee as a clump of boats came bearing down with their spinnakers up. In one case, simply putting down the helm and making a tight turn yielded a gain of a dozen boat-lengths on the competition, if not more.

CROWDS: WHEN SLOWER IS SOMETIMES BETTER

Even beginners will occasionally find themselves facing crowds like the one mentioned at the beginning of this chapter. Granted, you might be in a small section of, say, half a dozen casual PHRF boats. But there will almost always be at least one or two other sections out on your racecourse, and these disparate groups will often clump up at the marks because of contrasting boat speeds.

Alas, it doesn't take many sailboats to make for a complete mess at the leeward mark!

In this situation, the best thing to do is slow down a little and look for a way to sneak inside. Douse the spinnaker well before you might otherwise, in order to both kill boat speed and increase your maneuverability. Then, with that little chore out of the way, look for an opening. True, it can be difficult emotionally to ease off the gas in the heat of competition. But giving up a boatlength or two early on can mean gaining multiple boatlengths farther down the road (or, at the very least, not losing multiple boatlengths by sailing into a hole). Remember, no matter how crowded things get, if you can sneak in tight at the mark, you're pretty much guaranteed clear air and the freedom to either tack or harden up when you come out on the other side. If, on the other hand, you try to make an end run, sailing around the outside of the mass of sailboats as it makes a giant pinwheel around the buoy, you could find yourself gasping for air for what will seem like an eternity as, on the inside, boat after boat rolls over you. This, of course, is something you want to avoid if at all possible. So when you see things beginning to stack up, drop that spinnaker early, slow down, and wait for the mess to clear.

Note that this is a situation in which you have to be especially careful not to bump into anybody from astern. To reiterate, sailboats have an uncanny ability to slow down when you take away their wind or ask them to turn on a dime. And as the boat coming up from astern, it's your job to stay clear. Luckily, if there's enough wind for you to be coming in at a decent pace, there will also be enough wind to help the fellows ahead of you on their way. If, on the other hand, the boats ahead are absolutely parked, it's highly unlikely that your boat is thundering along with a bone in its teeth anyway.

Whenever you see a problem in the making up ahead, be sure to warn any boats to windward or leeward that you might need to take evasive action. For example, let them know they might not be able to take you up as high as they might otherwise, because doing so could force you into another competitor. Then again, this might be a situation in which granting room at the mark to a boat with an overlap is impossible. Hopefully, you and your competition will have already been figuring out your various right-of-way positions, and they won't be shocked if you inform them they can't just do whatever they want.

Leeward Mark Tips

- When rounding the jibe mark or leeward mark, always go in wide and come out tight.
- When coming up onto a beat at the leeward mark, sheet in the main first and let the jib lag behind to help bring the bow up.
- If you are the trailing boat, try to force your competitor to make a tight-in, wide-out turn so you can sneak inside to windward and steal his air.
- When there is a crowd at the leeward mark, it sometimes makes sense to drop the spinnaker early, slow down, and look for a way to sneak inside.

ROUNDING GATES

In the beginning you will rarely find yourself having to deal with gates. They are typically used only in races involving large fleets; situations in which congestion would be just too damn awful to contemplate if there was a single leeward mark.

For the most part, the techniques for rounding the gates are the same as those for rounding a single buoy. The main difference is you have to figure out whether to round the buoy on the left or the buoy on the right. There are three things you have to ask yourself when deciding: 1) which mark is closer, 2) which mark is less crowded, and 3) which mark gets you closer to the favored side of the course? When choosing how to round, keep in mind that you will have to sail *twice* the extra distance if you go to the

unfavored side, because you have to cover that distance going downwind and upwind. Therefore, whichever is the shortest distance will almost always be your primary consideration when choosing.

Of course, because this is sailboat racing, the situation is often complicated by the presence of other boats; your rounding objectives might then contradict each other. For example, let's say you really want to get to the right side of the course on the next beat, but the buoy to the left is a seething mass of boats. Then again, imagine you are coming in on starboard tack and the left-side buoy is nearly abeam—clearly a bit closer—but you really want to get over to the left side of the next beat. This means rounding the other side of the gate. For now, as stated above, your main goal should be to sail the shorter distance. If that won't work,

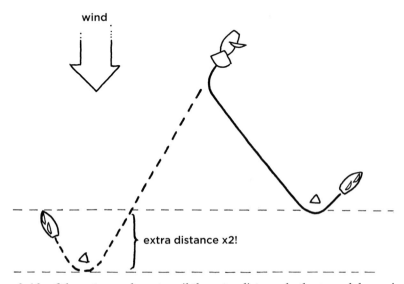

wind

extra distance x2!

At the unfavored side of the gate, you have to sail the extra distance both up- and downwind!

your next goal should be to follow the path of least resistance: go for the side with the fewest boats and the cleanest air. As is the case with slowing down when faced with a crowd at a single leeward mark, losing a couple of boatlengths by sailing to a mark that is a bit farther away is nothing compared to wallowing in a pocket of dead air while a half-dozen competitors go walking by.

Beyond that, if you know you're going toward one side of the next beat, ease your way over to that side of the gate well ahead of time, so you will be in a position to round with a minimum of trouble.

Whichever side you choose to round, bear in mind when approaching a gate that boats may be coming in from all sorts of unexpected directions. So keep a sharp eye out, both when steering for the mark and formulating your strategies. Come to think

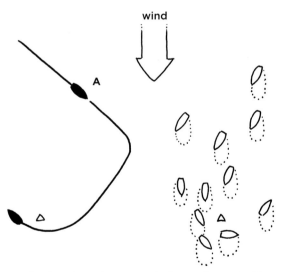

wind

*All other things being equal, choose the path of least resistance at a gate. Here, by rounding the right side of the gate, boat **A** avoids a tangle with the rest of the fleet at the left side.*

of it, that's not a bad thing to remember at any kind of mark rounding. Sailboats may not be the speediest contraptions in the world, but things have a way of happening with amazing rapidity on a racecourse, and this goes double for the crowded water around marks!

FINISHING

At long last the finish is in sight. You've managed to pull off a decent start, figure out the windshifts, and even survived one hell of a hairy rounding at the first leeward mark. Now it's time to sail fast and bring it on home. For the most part this is a fairly straightforward process. But of course, this is sailboat racing; even something as seemingly simple as crossing the finish line can be a little complicated on occasion. Among other things, there are two very different ways of finishing a sailboat race: on either an upwind or downwind leg. Then there are those pesky competitors again, all out there trying to go through the same small piece of water at the same time. Not surprisingly, when two or more sailboats are converging on one spot at this point in the race, neither is usually in a hurry to give way.

RULES AT THE FINISH LINE

Basically, the rules are the same as anyplace else on the course: the mark-rounding rules hold sway near the ends of the finish line and the other standard rules apply along the rest of it. When finishing on a beat, for example, a windward boat that is closer in toward the buoy or the committee boat has the right to slip inside, so long as it has an overlap at the moment either it or its competitor to leeward reaches a point two boatlengths away from the obstruction. The same goes when finishing to leeward, whether on the same or opposite tack. Note, however, that as was the case with mark roundings, we are talking about buoy room here, not freedom to go anywhere you want. Furthermore, if two boats are converging on a point that is greater than two boatlengths from either end, the upwind boat must keep clear, just as on any other part of the course.

Let's say, for example, that Rich and Adam are converging at the starboard end of the line on a downwind finish. Rich is on starboard tack on a course that will take him just to leeward of the buoy. Adam is on port, trying to slip around the buoy to finish ahead. Because he has an overlap when Rich crosses the two-boatlength circle, Adam is entitled to room to round. He does not, however, have the right to continue on a straight-line course. Instead, he must make a seamanlike rounding of the mark, even if that means letting Rich surge ahead.

Also, as was the case at the windward mark, when finishing upwind a boat on port tack cannot demand buoy room just because it has an inside overlap with a starboard-tack competitor. Neither can it flop over onto starboard tack within two boatlengths of the pin and expect a competitor coming in on starboard to have to stay clear. If you want to tack over onto starboard at any other point on the line, fine. As long as your sails are drawing, you're on starboard and the overtaking boat astern has to keep from hitting you from behind. But, within two boatlengths of the buoy at the port side of the line, this is strictly forbidden if it causes a boat on starboard tack to sail above close-hauled. Of course, if you are far enough ahead of your competitor to throw in this kind of a tack, you shouldn't really need to do so anyway. Simply cross your competitor's bow and finish on port, shooting for the finish line by rounding into the wind at the last moment, if necessary, to make sure you get across first.

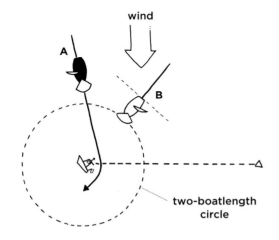

*The port-tack boat **A** has an overlap as the starboard tacker **B** crosses the two-boatlength circle, so port gets room at the mark.*

CLEAR AIR

When it comes to finishing, the two main considerations—as is the case with the rest of the course—are clear air and sailing the shortest course possible.

Clear air is obvious. Whether you're going upwind or down, sailing in somebody else's bad air is a bad idea. Remember, the speediest of sailboats can grind to a halt in the blink of an eye if you take away their wind. With this in mind try to anticipate clear-air problems in advance, so you won't be left gasping for breath at the last minute. When going upwind, don't tack into somebody else's wind shadow or into a position where your archrival can tack on top of you. When going downwind, don't hesitate to jibe away from a boat or a group of boats, if continuing on a converging course will put you at their mercy. The last thing you want is to be rolled just a few boatlengths from the finish.

As an example, let's say Adam is making his way downwind on starboard tack, and there are three boats threatening to cross his track on port tack just a few boatlengths away. Even if he could manage to sneak across with minimal loss of speed, there's the forbidding prospect of one or more of them jibing over to keep him in their wind shadow and driving a stake into his heart on their way to finishing a mere boatlength or two ahead. This is ugly even to contemplate. Don't allow yourself to fall under their power, even if there's only a hundred yards to go to the finish. Hopefully you've been practicing your jibes on your days off and can maneuver about the course at will. Remember, always finish fast. And whatever you do, keep sailing those jibe angles just as you did when approaching the leeward mark. Don't deadhead to the line.

FAVORED END

Sailing the shortest course means finding the favored end of the line—the part that is closest to where you are. As is the case with starting lines, finish lines are rarely perfectly even, which means one end can be a couple of boatlengths closer—a sizable difference in the event of a close finish, whether upwind or down. With this in mind always try to figure out which is closer as far in advance as possible. That way you can factor in the condition of the line when calling for those last couple of tacks or jibes.

One way to do this is to watch the competition. If the boats in the other sections up ahead all seem to be converging on one side or the other, that's a pretty good indication it's the favored end. If you have to figure things out for yourself, designate a crewmember who is not busy trimming sails to try to determine which end you should steer for. Have him or her use a pair of bi-

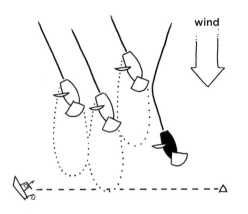

Don't sail into bad air, even if the finish line is just a few boatlengths away.

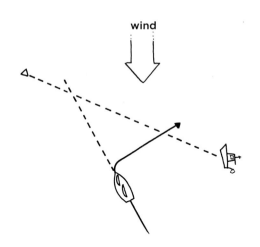

If you are sailing more along *the line than* at *it when finishing to windward, by all means tack!*

noculars if you have them on board. Picking the favored end is especially important when finishing upwind, because even a slightly skewed line will mean sailing a much greater distance on the unfavored tack. If you feel you are sailing more along the line than at it, by all means, flop over onto the other tack and bring the race to an end!

SHOOTING FOR THE LINE

In the event of a photo finish you can sometimes put yourself ahead by shooting for the line, especially when finishing to windward, in much the same way runners thrust out their chests or bicycle racers push their bikes forward to break the tape at the end of a sprint. Basically, shooting for the line entails rounding up into the wind at the last moment, say a boatlength or two from the line, and driving directly over, as opposed to sailing the longer course with your sails

full. The exact point at which you should round up depends on the type of boat you're sailing and the conditions. If you're aboard a light dinghy in choppy seas, your momentum isn't going to carry you very far. On the other hand, if you're powering along in a 50-foot keelboat in 15 knots of wind and flat seas, you should be able to travel a fair distance with your sails luffing. There's nothing wrong with taking up a boat to leeward and astern. However, remember that you lose your rights once your sails start flogging, because you are no longer on a tack. You also have to allow your competitor room and an opportunity to stay clear.

Another trick when sailing downwind is to ease off both the sheet and the guy, so your spinnaker will float out a little farther forward. According to the rules, you officially finish when the leading part of your boat crosses the line, whether it be a bow pulpit, bowsprit, or a magnificently full spinnaker. This maneuver might only give you an extra foot or two, but then again that might be all you need.

CLOSER IS BETTER

When finishing a sailboat race there is one final consideration to keep in mind that has nothing to do with seamanship and everything to do with human psychology. Specifically, if a number of competitors are all finishing within a boatlength of one other, a boat that is finishing closer to the committee boat will often get the horn before another boat farther down the line. The

Finishing Tips

- Maintain clear air right up until you cross the line.
- Try to determine the favored end of the line, and then arrange the last couple of tacks or jibes so that you finish there.
- Don't deadhead to the line on a downwind finish: keep sailing fast jibing angles right up to the very end.
- All other things being equal, in a close finish cross the line closer to the committee boat rather than far away; race committees tend to "see" a closer competitor finish first.

reasons for this are obvious. It's much easier to determine when a closer boat has crossed the line than one farther away. Remember, race committees are only human, and they've been out there rolling on the waves in the hot sun for just as long as you have. If the line looks pretty even, why not set yourself up to finish closer to the committee boat as opposed to farther away? Every little bit helps.

Q & A

Q. Adam is to windward and has just the slightest overlap from astern at the moment Rich's bow crosses the two-boatlength circle at the leeward mark. Both boats are sailing on a broad reach on port tack. Moments later Rich surges ahead on a wave, breaking the overlap. Rich steers high to make a close rounding and force Adam to go to the outside. Adam says he is still entitled to room to round inside. Who is in the right?
A. Adam is correct. Rights at the mark are

determined at the moment the lead boat pierces the two-boatlength circle. It does not change if the overlap is broken moments later.

Q. What is the best course to steer when rounding a jibe mark or leeward mark?
A. Wide-in, tight-out. This allows you to steer a nice gentle turn, conserving boat speed and making it easy for the crew to handle the sails, while losing as little as possible to windward when coming out on the next leg. The latter is especially important if the next leg is a beat.

Q. Adam and Rich are both heading for the right-side buoy of a gate rounding. Both are sailing on a broad reach, but Rich is coming in on port tack and Adam is on starboard. Rich reaches the two-boatlength point first and on the inside. Adam says he has right-of-way because he is on starboard. Rich says he's entitled to make a seamanlike rounding. Who is correct?
A. The rules for buoy room trump the starboard-port rule when the first of the two boats in question pierces the two-boatlength circle.

Q. On a downwind finish, two boats on opposite tacks are approaching the same point near the center of the line. The port-tack boat is slightly ahead and calls for room when it reaches a point two boatlengths from the line, so it can finish. Is he entitled to room?
A. Dream on, sailor! Unless you are within two boatlengths of the committee boat or

buoy, the rules regarding right-of-way are the same at the finish line as they are on the rest of the racecourse.

Q. Adam and Rich are both close-hauled and driving for the right side of the finish line on starboard tack. Rich is slightly ahead and to windward as they reach a point two boatlengths away from the committee boat. Adam sails as high as possible to pinch him off. Rich demands room at the mark. Does Adam have to give it to him?

A. Yes; because Rich has an inside overlap when one of the two boats crosses a point two boatlengths away from the mark, Adam has to allow him room to finish.

BASIC TACTICS AND A FEW TIPS

So you're out on the racecourse having the time of your life. The sun is shining and you're moving well in a good, steady 15-knot breeze. Then all of a sudden you run into traffic. Maybe you're reaching along with the chute up, and a boat appears behind you and takes away your air. Maybe you're close-hauled on port tack and you see a boat coming your way on starboard that puts you in a crossing situation. Suddenly what seemed like a promising leg is starting to get damn complicated.

In this chapter we will look at some basic techniques and rules of thumb for managing your boat on the course. We'll talk about both tactics—the techniques and tricks you can use for dealing with the here and now—and strategy, or the big picture. This is one area in which many books on sailboat racing get really complicated really fast, when in fact a few simple techniques

should serve you just fine 90 percent of the time and will be more than enough to get you around the racecourse. Get to know these techniques until they become second nature. Then you can start worrying about the esoteric stuff.

SMART PORT-STARBOARD CROSSING

All too often, especially for beginners, the success of a beat can boil down to a single port-starboard crossing. One moment you're tearing along on port tack, executing your race strategy; the next, another boat on starboard tack appears as if out of nowhere, apparently on a collision course, and your en-

106

tire crew is thrown into a panic. Everybody shouts out their opinion, but no one knows what to do. Maybe you throw in a crash tack at the last moment to avoid disaster. Maybe you bear off in a flurry of white water in order to pass astern. In either case you suddenly find yourself almost dead in the water. Everybody is flustered, frowning, no longer thinking ahead. The recriminations fly. Nobody is bothering to keep track of windshifts or boat speed anymore. Sailboat racing has suddenly become a whole lot less fun.

The real pity is all of this was unnecessary. There's no reason why any single crossing situation should be a disaster. In fact, if you put the following principles into practice, the situation should not be a setback at all.

Be Aware. As noted in chapter 3, The Windward Leg, *always* keep an eye out for other boats. With forewarning there is seldom, if ever, a reason to panic. If you are sailing on a keelboat with a larger crew, make sure those sailors on the windward rail know they're more than just ballast: they're also your eyes and ears. In heavy air they should be looking ahead and to leeward, especially when you're on port tack. Don't hesitate to send somebody to the low side every now and then to peek around the leech of the genoa and make sure there isn't anybody hiding on the other side of all that sailcloth. If someone is on the low side trimming the headsail, he or she should take a quick look around as a matter of course. It's also not a bad idea to have that crew take

out the winch handle again after trimming, just in case. That way, if you do ever find yourself having to do a crash tack, at least you'll be able to get the jib sheet off.

In order to determine well ahead of time whether you're going to pass ahead or behind a competitor in a crossing situation, check to see whether you are making land. In other words, try to determine who will pass ahead, based on how the other boat appears to be moving relative to the land or other objects in the area. For example, if the other boat appears to be moving forward relative to a stationary object behind it, it will pass ahead of you; if it appears to be slipping backward relative to its background, you will pass in front; and if it is stationary relative to the background, you are on a collision course. Another way of judging this is with a handheld compass. If your bearing on the other boat (or any other object, for that matter) is constant, you are on a collision course. If the angle relative to your heading is decreasing, the other boat will cross ahead. If the angle is increasing, you are the one who will be in front. A compass can be especially helpful at night or if there is nothing but water behind the boat in question. Otherwise, it is generally easier to simply watch how the other guy is doing relative to the shore.

In the event you see a boat approaching on the opposite tack and it looks like it's going to be close, don't fret. Make a mental note of the bearing and distance, but *keep sailing your own race*. Don't let the presence of the competition put you off your game. Warn your crew to be on the alert, but focus on speed. With a little luck, and if you sail fast enough, that other boat will be sailing safely through your wake and all that worry will have been for nothing.

Dipping. In the event a starboard tacker has you beat, the best thing to do in most cases is fall off and sail behind and around him, trimming your sails as you do to ensure you are sailing as fast as possible throughout the maneuver. Warn your crew of your plan and make sure somebody is ready to ease the jib and main. Then when you are a good five or six boatlengths away from the starboard tacker, begin to fall off smoothly and easily, while your trimmers crack off the sails to keep them working efficiently. You should only have to change course a little to slip behind the other guy's transom. In fact, if you find yourself falling off dramatically to avoid a collision, you probably had the other boat beat and didn't need to dip in the first place. Ideally, when you are a boatlength away from the starboard tacker, you should be headed right for his mast; in the time it takes you to sail that last boatlength, he should have plenty of time to sail the necessary half-boatlength to get out of the way. Of course, if you're sailing a much faster boat, you should aim closer to his transom. Whatever the case, do your best to keep it tight.

Once you have passed behind the other boat, steer smoothly and evenly back up to your original heading, with your trimmers bringing the jib and main in to match your heading. If the helm and sails are working together, you should actually have been

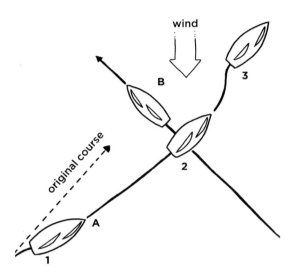

*A well-executed dip will cost you very little. Here, a starboard tacker (boat **B**) is about to cross boat **A**'s course. Boat **A** falls off smoothly, easing the sheets for speed and to avoid developing excessive windward helm (**1**). As he passes behind boat **B**, he trims the sails again while hardening up (**2**). Then he uses his extra boat speed to pinch up a little and gain back a few feet to windward (**3**).*

able to gain speed as you were footing off to make your pass. If so, try using that speed to pinch up a little and gain back a few feet to windward. In the end, if you do it correctly, a dip can result in little if any real loss of distance on your competitor. You certainly lose less than if you had thrown in an unnecessary tack. Best of all you're sticking with your original game plan, instead of flopping over before you want to.

Of course, in heavy air you'll want to be especially careful. Maybe even give yourself a bit of cushion when you make your dip, in case something unexpected happens. Always try to anticipate how your boat is going to respond when you crack off sheets.

Look ahead to see how the competition is faring. Make sure there are no puffs in the offing and that things won't suddenly get hairy as you foot off for speed. One time while racing in Japan, the International 50 *Insatiable* had to dip a competitor named *Diane* about ten minutes into a heavy-air race. Despite the fact that the crew was easing the sheets as the boat bore away for the dip, the boat accelerated to the point where the surge in power caused the helm to load up, becoming overwhelmed as it fought the boat's urge to turn into the wind. *Insatiable* crashed through *Diane*'s cockpit, creating a hole big enough for two men to walk through. (Of course, because the race was in Japan, there was no lack of photo boats to document the event!) *Insatiable*'s crew had actually eased the genoa and main so they were luffing. But the boat still heeled so much the rudder began to cavitate, causing turbulence and catching air instead of water as it was lifted out of the water. There was nothing the helmsman could do to keep her from rounding up and causing a hell of a collision. A bit more communication and anticipation could have prevented a pair of $2 million campaigns from running into one another. The one bright spot was that *Diane* was up and sailing again the next day.

Tacking Smart. Of course, there are times when it may be best to tack instead of dip. For instance, if you're well into the second half of the beat and are planning to tack soon anyway to avoid hitting the layline, by all means put the helm down so you don't end up in a corner. Another situation in which it might be best to tack is when there are a number of boats coming toward you on starboard and dipping one might put you in a position where you would have to dip them all. Giving up a little to avoid a single starboard tacker is one thing. Giving up a half dozen boatlengths to avoid a whole herd of starboard tackers is quite another!

When coming about in a crossing situation the main thing to remember is, unless you are roll-tacking a dinghy, it will take you a while to get back up to speed on the new tack. Therefore, be careful not to flop over in such a way that you end up in his wind shadow. If you can lee-bow your opponent, great. (Although in most cases, if you were in a position to lee-bow, you probably could have passed him anyway.) Otherwise, tack at least two or three boatlengths early, preferably more, to ensure that you and the other fellow won't tangle. Make a good tack and get up to speed, so you don't fall back into his wind shadow. Then sail like hell, using your competitor as a gauge of your own speed. Note that, in addition to the possibility of being blanketed, a real danger of tacking in response to a crossing situation is you may find yourself with the other boat so close to windward that you are pinned, or unable to tack. If after a couple of minutes the tactical situation changes and you want to go back on port, a few boatlengths between you and the guy to windward will mean you can do so at will. If, on the other hand, the other guy is camped on your hip, you're stuck sailing on starboard until he decides to go around first (see illustration next page).

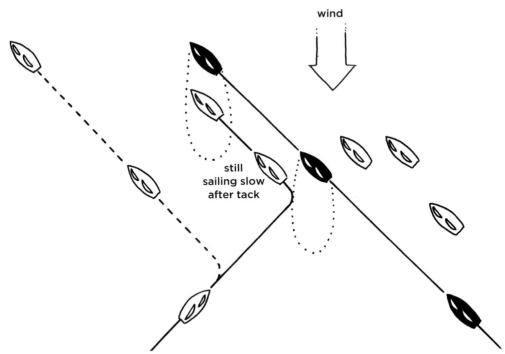

In a crossing situation, tack early to ensure you don't end up in the starboard-tacker's bad air. Remember, it will be a few seconds before you get back up to speed after the tack.

CLEARING YOUR AIR

Almost as upsetting as a bad port-starboard crossing is having a competitor tack on top of you so you're being gassed by his bad air. Moments earlier you may have been charging ahead like a house afire. Now someone has literally taken the wind out of your sails. Bummer. This, however, is not the time to feel sorry for yourself. It's time to act. As was the case when you realized you couldn't make the windward mark, the main thing here is not so much *what* you do, but that you do *something*. Don't just sit there and take it. That's a sure way to the back of the fleet.

As is the case with crossing situations, if you're aware of the boats around you, you'll be able to anticipate problems; you can have a plan of action in mind before you find yourself gasping for breath. This also will prevent you from doing something that could leave you in even worse shape than when you first got in trouble—such as tacking around, only to see another guy you hadn't noticed before coming straight at you with some choice words on his lips and eyes the size of saucers. If you see one of your competitors approaching from an angle that will afford him the opportunity to gas you, warn your crew to be ready, make a mental note of any other boats in the area, and look for signs that the other guy is planning a change of course. Be especially attentive to what the other crew is up to. If they all start tumbling off the rail to their stations, you can be pretty sure the other guy is looking to make things bad. Again, as a general rule of thumb, the wind shadow to leeward extends about ten mast lengths from the boat, sweeping aft with the general flow of the wind. This is true on either a beat or a beam reach. You can actually be a couple of boatlengths to leeward and directly abeam of a competitor and still have clear air. But beware. A whole lot of turbulence is right behind you, nipping at your heels!

In the event that you do find yourself gasping for breath, there are really only three options you can try in response. Again, the important thing is to suck it up and do *something*, as opposed to just sitting there wallowing in self-pity.

Footing Off. Let's say you're on port tack, the mark isn't that far off, and you're heading for the layline when some other guy camps on top of you. He's not doing it to get your goat necessarily, but that doesn't mean his presence is any less devastating in terms of your boat speed. Or maybe you're still in the first half of the beat and doing a great job staying in phase; you're getting

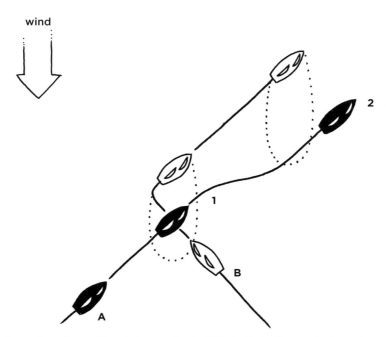

*If a competitor tacks on top of you, dive to leeward out of his bad air. Say you're boat **A** and a competitor, boat **B**, tacks on top of you, putting you in his wind shadow. To get out of it, ease out your jib and main for speed as you foot off (**1**). Then trim in again as you steer back up on course (**2**). If you can't get clear of his bad air this way, you must tack.*

gassed, but you really don't want to change your overall plan.

The thing to do in either case is foot off to leeward and drive through his shadow, working with your trimmers and bearing away a boatlength or two, much like you would if you were dipping a starboard-tack boat in a crossing situation. As always, warn your trimmers ahead of time that there's a boat in a position to possibly blanket you—or cover you, as it's sometimes called—so they'll be ready. Then if that cover becomes a reality, foot off as soon as the other guy has you in his shadow—or better yet, while he's still coming around—because once you're being hurt by that bad air it may already be too late. Whenever you choose to make your move, do so aggressively, *diving* through the bad air to get to the good side. Otherwise you'll never escape that shadow. Unfortunately, some heavier boats just don't accelerate like others, which makes it that much harder to punch through a wind shadow. On these boats you may have no choice but to tack. However, if your boat is a nimble one, diving off for clear air can remedy an otherwise tough situation.

Pinching Up. If, on the other hand, your competition tacks so that he is either directly in front of you or in a lee-bow position, you'll have to escape by going high. As is the case when footing off, don't wait until your opponent's dastardly tactics are starting to hurt before you make good your escape. Even as the other guy is coming around and it's obvious what's happening,

More Advice for Pinching Up

When pinching up to escape from a lee-bow situation, the key is to be prepared before the lee-bow becomes a reality. If, for example, you are on starboard and a boat is trying to cross on port tack, make sure you are sailing fast—maybe even sailing a bit low to pick up a little more speed—so you will be able to respond if necessary. If and when the port-tacker comes about, trim in your sails just a touch and point up a few degrees to create some separation between you and your competitor to leeward. Depending on the boat, you should have plenty of time to create a boatlength or more of room to weather before you start slowing down. Watch the leeward boat. Don't slow down so much he starts going faster than you and is able to pull ahead while you are performing this maneuver. Be sure to practice this maneuver on a day off. That way you will know ahead of time how your boat responds to sailing higher than its optimal course.

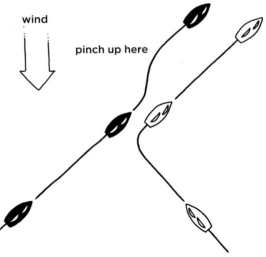

Pinch up to put some distance between you and a lee-bow. If you can't get out of the lee-bow you will have to tack.

begin hardening up while your mainsail trimmer takes in on the traveler and your jib trimmer cranks in on the sheet. You won't be able to hold this course for long without losing boat speed. But it will enable you to put some separation between you and your opponent.

Tacking. There's not much to say here other than just do it. If you've tried footing off with no success or are hopelessly buried in the middle of a bunch of muck, go around while you've still got the boat speed to do so. Here, as in other instances, it pays to be aware of the overall tactical situation vis-à-vis the competition; not only can you warn your crew to be ready for a tack, you can also avoid tacking into another bad spot or being suddenly surprised by another competitor appearing as if from nowhere.

COVERING THE OTHER GUY ON A BEAT

All this talk of escape is probably making you wonder when it will be your turn to make the other guy pay. However, before you get all fired up and bloodthirsty, you might want to ask yourself this one simple question: Why? Why camp on one of your competitors out of spite, or just because you can? Remember, this is supposed to be a friendly game. You better have a good reason for making the other guy's life more difficult, especially when sailing to windward. Otherwise, you will very likely leave him more than a little ticked off. More impor-

tantly, don't let the opportunity to pick up a couple of cheap boatlengths against a single competitor distract you from your overall game plan.

Still, there are times when blanketing a competitor is either unavoidable or perfectly justifiable. When approaching a mark, for example, it's every man for himself. The same is true of the finish. If there are two of you on opposite tacks near the end of a race, by all means do everything you can to ensure the other guy passes the committee boat behind you, not the other way around.

With this in mind, the key to covering an opponent when sailing to windward is knowing how long it takes for your boat to get back up to speed after coming through a tack. That way, you can make sure it is the other guy, not you, who's hurting at the end of the maneuver. For example, let's say Rich and Adam are both nearing the end of the race on an upwind finish. Rich is on port, while Adam is on starboard and slightly ahead as they approach a crossing situation. Adam is not entirely confident in his boat speed (racing against a veteran sailmaker can be *so* disheartening at times!), so even as Rich is falling off ever so slightly to pass astern, Adam throws in a tack to cover him on port. The only problem is Rich is plowing ahead at full speed and Adam has lost valuable knots while coming around. Next thing you know, it's Rich who's in the driver's seat from a lee-bow position and Adam who's feeling the pain.

A better plan would have been for Adam

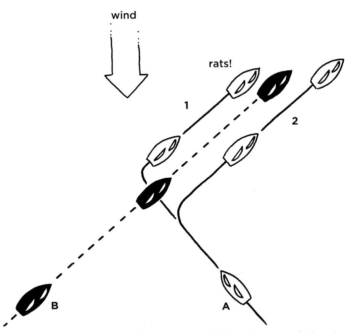

*As boats **A** and **B** approach a crossing situation, boat **A** must decide when to tack, bearing in mind how fast it will accelerate as it comes through the tack. By tacking later (**1**), boat **A** can't get up to speed fast enough to cover and ends up in boat **B**'s lee-bow. By tacking early (**2**), boat **A** is able to get back up to speed in time to lee-bow boat **B**.*

to tack a little earlier, moments before crossing Rich's bow, so he would be the one putting Rich in a lee-bow position instead of the other way around. In this case, Rich would have no choice but to tack around unless he wanted to follow his fellow author the rest of the way to the finish line. Note that this is a perfect example of a situation in which a quick response on Rich's part could make all the difference. If Rich were to throw in a tack or pinch up a boatlength right away—even while Adam is still in the act of coming around—he could head off into clear air with relatively little loss of speed, meaning the race would still be very much up for grabs.

Crossing Situations

- If you're on port tack and can't clear a starboard tack boat in a crossing situation, it is often better to dip below the other boat than simply tack over onto starboard. With a well-executed dip you lose very little.
- If a competitor tacks to cover, make your move to escape before the cover starts to slow you down.
- When tacking to cover another boat, make sure you can get up to speed after the tack so your competitor won't end up covering you.
- As a crossing situation develops, be sure to warn the crew in advance so the helmsman and trimmers can work together, whether the decision is to dip, tack, foot off, or pinch up to clear your air from a cover.

COVERING AND PASSING DOWNWIND

Sailing downwind offers the guys toward the back of the fleet plenty of opportunity to close in on the guys in front. When properly done, jibing—in contrast to tacking—results in very little loss of boat speed, so there's a lot more flexibility in where the fleet can go. A wind shadow downwind is also stretching in front of the boat, instead of below and behind, making it a much more effective part of your tactical arsenal when coming up from astern.

Having said this, there's all the difference in the world between walking up on a boat from behind and actually passing it. Remember, if you are overtaking from astern and to windward, your competitor has every right to luff you up as high as he wants to prevent you from getting by. If you're passing to leeward, even as you thunder ahead you will immediately find yourself getting gassed. Because of these two hazards, the key to passing on a run is to be patient and keep some distance between you and the other guy. Put yourself in a position where he is choking on your bad air, but don't go storming up on his transom or try to pass him from a boatlength to windward. Remember, your wind shadow will extend a good ten mast lengths away. If he jibes away, fine. You can jibe with him if you want, in order to cover him again when

he jibes back. Then again, you can stay where you are and play your shifts.

Ultimately, passing on a downwind leg is largely a matter of boat speed and being where the wind is—and positioning yourself for a good rounding at the leeward mark. As noted in chapter 6, Leeward Mark Roundings and Finishing, the leeward mark is an area in which boatlengths and places can be gained and lost in the blink of an eye. So instead of actually passing somebody on a run, the better goal is often to position yourself to pass him at the mark. Remember, you only have to overlap a bit to qualify for room at the mark. There is nothing that says you have to overlap by a certain amount. That one foot of overlap should be more than enough to get you around ahead of the boat in front of you. With this in mind, you can try to use your wind shadow to both close the gap and force the competition over to the right side of the course. Do this by allowing him to sail in clear air when he is going where you want, but covering him as he heads back to the middle. Ideally, at the very end of the leg, he will have no choice but to sail in your wind shadow as he approaches the mark, giving you your opportunity to establish an overlap. Execute a good spinnaker drop and mark rounding, and you will be the one in the lead at the start of the beat (see illustration next page).

Be aware that, although passing individual boats can be a real challenge, passing *groups* of boats can be a snap; they will often be so concerned with the immediate tactical situation they will let you sail along unmolested. In that case, the best thing to do is simply play the windshifts, concentrate on boat speed, and let the clump of boats in front of you battle it out as you work your boat.

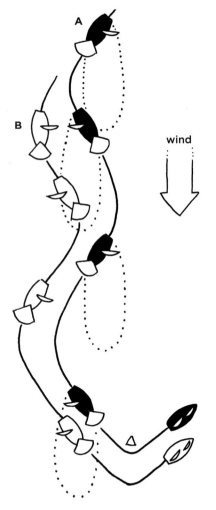

*More important than actually passing the competition on the downwind leg is positioning yourself to pass at the leeward mark. In this instance, boat **A** uses its wind shadow to force boat **B** to the outside. Then, as they approach the mark, boat **B** has no choice but to sail in boat **A**'s bad air, allowing boat **A** to establish an inside overlap.*

To avoid being passed or to maintain separation on the downwind leg, plan ahead for clear air. Watch where your competitors are steering behind you, and then go elsewhere. The downwind leg can be a heartbreaking place as the tail end of the fleet eats up all those gains you made earlier, while bringing in a new breeze. But that's no reason to throw in the towel. If a competitor starts closing in with thoughts of putting you in his shadow, anticipate this move by sailing a slightly higher and hotter heading early on. This will force him to make a dramatic change in course to put you in his bad air. Hopefully this will dissuade him from deciding to mix it up, and he will either fall back down onto a less aggressive angle or jibe away. As is the case on a reaching leg, you want to deal with the competition before it gets close enough to even begin thinking about a luffing match; you don't want that any more than he does. Be especially attentive near the end of the leg so you won't get caught up in traffic as you approach the leeward mark.

Of course all these strategic and tactical considerations will be irrelevant if you don't execute your jibes. For cruisers, spinnaker handling and jibes in particular are a source of more than a little trepidation. But for racing sailors they are just a fact of life. Practice your jibes over and over again until they become second nature, whether it's a drifter—when winds are light—or blowing stink. (For more information about sailing in light air, see chapter 10.) Remember, when jibing, the last thing you want is to stop the jibe while sailing dead downwind, especially in light air. Doing so will blanket the spinnaker with the main, causing the spinnaker to collapse and possibly wrap around the forestay. Jibe like you tack, with a nice, smooth, continuous change of course from one heading to another. If you are at the helm, make sure to keep the boat sailing under the spinnaker; i.e., not getting ahead of or behind the trimmers as they rotate it around. This will ensure the sail doesn't collapse.

While you're at it, practice jibing without the spinnaker pole. You will be surprised at how well it works. In tight races, places are often lost by crews that are more concerned about getting the pole jibed than keeping the sail full. Again, it's shocking how few racing sailors at the club-racing level spend time honing these skills. Doing so may yield even the beginner some surprising results. The key to sailing downwind is the ability to change course efficiently and with little or no loss of speed. If you can't do this, you're at a disadvantage before you even get around the windward mark.

KNOWING WHERE TO GO

Although it would hardly be classed as higher-order tactics, a real easy way to get a jump on a good part of the fleet is by simply knowing where to go; knowing not only the basic shape of the course, but also its length and the compass headings for each leg. Pay close attention to your sailing instructions and the signals from the committee boat. Then write this information down in pencil on the deck or on a plastic note board, so you can refresh your memory at a glance. Keep track of the true wind direction and your tacking angles so you'll know in an instant when you're sailing well or getting knocked.

This kind of planning ahead can be especially helpful when it comes time to figure out what course you want to steer on the next reaching or running leg. It's amazing how many boats just play follow the leader until they see the next mark, which can take a while on a larger PHRF or one-design course. You can make real gains on the competition if you can effect your strategy right off the bat or simply sail the shortest distance from one buoy to the next, instead of fumbling about.

Q & A

Q. What are the advantages of dipping behind a starboard-tack competitor in a port-starboard crossing situation?
A. You aren't changing your overall strategy and, if the dip is properly executed, you will lose little if any distance on the competition.

Q. At what point should a port-tack boat go around if it chooses to avoid a starboard-tack boat by tacking in a crossing situation?
A. As early as possible; that way it will have room to tack back onto port if and when it

wants, and there will be no chance of ending up in the other boat's wind shadow.

Q. You are sailing to windward on port tack, and there is a starboard-tack boat that is closing in on you in the distance. Studying it a little more closely, you see that it seems to be moving forward relative to the trees and hills in the background. What does this tell you?
A. The other boat is making land, which means it will pass safely ahead.

Q. You are bringing down a new breeze to the boats in the lead on a downwind leg. As you approach a boat directly ahead, should you: A) sail straight for his transom to maximize the effect of your wind shadow; B) set a course that will take you a few boatlengths to windward; or C) set a course that will take you to leeward?

A. Option B is the best. You will still be slowing the competition down because the other boat will be in your wind shadow. By maintaining some distance, you will discourage him from trying to engage you in a luffing match.

Q. You are in the middle of the beat on port tack sailing in a 10-degree lift in an oscillating breeze. A competitor crosses your bow on starboard tack, and then flops over so he is sailing parallel to you a boatlength ahead and to windward; you are in his turbulent air. What should you do?
A. Foot off a boatlength or two while easing the jib and main. The change in course and increase in speed should take you out of your competitor's wind shadow. Of course, you could also tack away to clear your air, but that would mean tacking into a knock.

Chapter 8

WEATHER

All too often the weather can be one of the most mysterious and frustrating parts of sailboat racing. The best sail trim and tactics in the world won't do you a lick of good if you sail into a dead spot or blunder your way into a windshift that makes the beat twice as long as it was just moments earlier. Obviously, predicting the weather is an uncertain business at best, but that doesn't mean it's completely impossible to anticipate what's coming. Some sailors have an uncanny ability to figure out what the wind will be doing in the next five, ten, or thirty minutes, or even in the next few hours. Possibly they have sold their souls to the devil or are making regular sacrifices to the sea god, Poseidon. Fortunately, you can often work out at least a close approximation of what the weather is going to do through a careful examination of wind, water, and the local weather report.

HOW WEATHER WORKS

At its most basic, weather results from the fact that the Earth's atmosphere is continually being subjected to uneven heating, both locally and globally. The areas of colder, high-pressure air that result displace areas of warmer, low-pressure air, creating winds. As air passes over the Earth's surface, and especially over water, it also picks up moisture. Warm air rises, cooling as it does so, and creates clouds and precipitation. Because it's dense, cold air falls and spreads as it displaces air from those warmer, low-pressure areas.

Of particular interest to sailors, cold air does not spread from a high-pressure area into a low-pressure area in a straight line.

Instead, because of the Coriolis Effect, it follows a circular pattern, rotating away from a center of high pressure in a clockwise direction in the Northern Hemisphere and in a counterclockwise direction in the Southern Hemisphere. Similarly, air flowing into a low-pressure area also moves in a circular pattern, flowing around the center of low pressure in a counterclockwise direction in the Northern Hemisphere and in a clockwise direction in the Southern Hemisphere. The Coriolis Effect also determines the directions of global winds such as the trade winds in the Atlantic and Pacific Oceans and such notorious wind belts as the Roaring Forties down in the Southern Ocean and off Cape Horn. It's also why the continental United States is in an area of prevailing westerlies,

which is why storms and other weather systems travel in that same direction.

When thinking about the weather, sailors need to be aware of how different areas of high- and low-pressure air are interacting at both the regional and local levels, since both dynamics play a role in generating the winds on the racecourse. Ultimately, the two main concerns are the strength of the wind and the direction from which it will blow; knowing these are necessary to formulate a race strategy. No problem, right? Hmmm . . .

REGIONAL WEATHER PATTERNS

When looking at the regional weather patterns and winds, you need to be on the

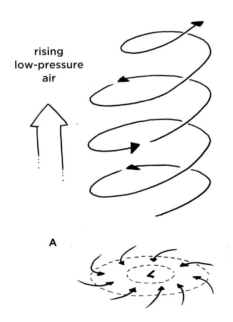

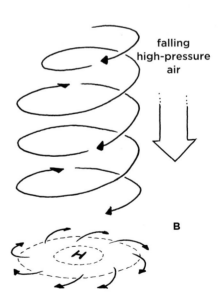

A   B

*In the Northern Hemisphere, air flows into a low-pressure system in a counterclockwise direction **A** and rises into the upper atmosphere. In a high-pressure system, air flows down from the upper atmosphere and away from the system's center in a clockwise direction **B**.*

lookout for three things: areas of high pressure, areas of low pressure, and fronts—situations in which an area of high or low pressure is pushing another air mass aside.

Highs and Lows. When observing high- or low-pressure areas, you need to keep in mind the direction in which the wind will circulate around the center of the region, the location of the area relative to your position, and the steepness of the pressure gradient, or the rate at which the air pressure changes within the air mass. This latter feature can most readily be seen by looking at the isobars—lines connecting areas of equal air pressure—on a weather map. When the isobars are close together, they indicate a steep pressure gradient with more wind. When the isobars are spread out, the pressure gradient is gradual and you can expect calmer conditions. This can be especially daunting in the middle of a large area of

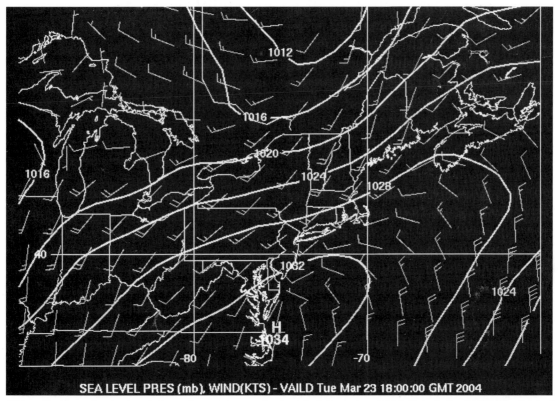

SEA LEVEL PRES (mb), WIND(KTS) - VAILD Tue Mar 23 18:00:00 GMT 2004

This map from the National Oceanic and Atmospheric Administration (NOAA) includes isobars and wind "arrows" that show wind strength and the direction in which it is blowing. Note how the wind is circulating in a clockwise direction around the region of high pressure centered near the mouth of the Chesapeake Bay. An arrow with one mark, or feather, indicates 8–12 knots of wind. An arrow with two feathers indicates 18–22 knots. An arrow with one feather that is smaller than the other represents 13–17 knots. And an arrow with three feathers represents 28–32 knots. (Courtesy the National Oceanic and Atmospheric Administration) high pressure. Given a situation in which there is heavier, high-pressure air near the ground with lighter, low-pressure air higher up, the weather situation is said to be "stable"; there is no reason for the air to rearrange itself. Add to this a shallow pressure gradient across the area and there is little reason for any air movement. This is why areas of high pressure and high, steady barometer readings are associated with clear, calm weather. The winds you experience on a racecourse that is in the middle of a high-pressure area will be largely local in origin.

Low-pressure areas, on the other hand, are often more unstable, with steeper pressure gradients as low-pressure air rises into the upper atmosphere, creating winds, lightning, and precipitation. Regions of low pressure, for example, are what bring about hurricanes and many other storms in the tropics. Because of the wind patterns around a low-pressure air mass, the winds in a particular area are determined by its position relative to the center of the weather system. In the Northern Hemisphere, if you are east of a low-pressure center, the winds will be from the south; if you are to the north, they will be easterly; if you are to the west, they will be from the north; and if you are due south, they will be from the west. These wind directions are reversed if you are in the Southern Hemisphere.

Of equal importance is the way the wind direction will shift as a low passes overhead. In the Northern Hemisphere, as a low passes from west to east, the wind direction will back, or shift counterclockwise, from east to north if you are north of the low-pressure center; and veer, or shift clockwise, from south to west if you are south of the low-pressure center.

If you are in the tropics of the Northern Hemisphere—in other words, south of the

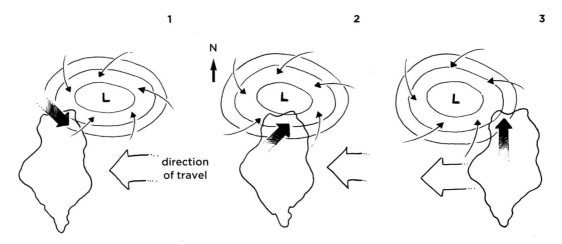

Wind directions will shift as a weather system passes. Here, the wind backs as a tropical depression passes to the north of an island in the Northern Hemisphere.

Tropic of Cancer—where weather systems can travel from east to west under the influence of the northeast trade winds, the situation will be reversed: the wind will veer as the low-pressure center passes westward and to the south, and will back if the low-pressure center passes to the north.

Frontal Systems. Frontal systems can be especially important to sailors, because the passage of a cold front in particular can result in dramatic changes in wind direction and strength. The mechanics of how frontal systems form and develop are beyond the scope of this book. But a basic knowledge of how they affect wind direction and strength can be very helpful if a front comes plowing through in the middle of a race or regatta.

In the continental United States, fronts often pass in succession—first a warm front followed by a cold front—after the formation of a low-pressure "kink" in the boundary between the cold air mass surrounding the North Pole and the warmer air to the south. When this happens, and if you are south of the low-pressure center, you will first experience southerly winds as the air in the region preceding the warm front circulates up toward the low-pressure kink. Then, with the arrival of the warm front, you will have thick cloud cover, rain, and a change in wind direction; the breeze will veer so that it's coming out of the west. The resulting weather will be warm—no great shock—and very likely quite clear. Eventually, however, a cold front will come barreling through, often heralded by a line of thunderstorms. These are sometimes dangerous

in their intensity and cause very confused wind conditions, with winds that oscillate back and forth as the two air masses vie for supremacy. Ultimately, the wind will veer yet again, until it is coming from the northwest. There may be some remaining showers to contend with after the front has passed. But eventually things will clear up and you will have blue skies, puffy "fair weather" cumulus clouds, and light, steady breezes.

Oftentimes when racing around the buoys, fronts are not a factor. Race committees will generally postpone a race if they think a dramatic shift is in the offing. They also prefer not to hold races when

Race Committees and Weather

In addition to its many other duties, the race committee has to ensure that weather conditions are suitable for racing. If there is severe weather in the area, for example, the race committee may cancel or abandon racing for the day, either while still on shore before the fleet has set out for the racing area or midway through a day's racing. In the event of calms or rough conditions, the race committee may also decide to postpone racing, again either before or after the committee boat and fleet have left the dock. Whether it postpones or abandons racing, the committee will use the same signals on land that it would use on the water, as outlined in chapter 1. Some race committees, especially those administering bigger regattas, will notify the fleet via VHF radio when the committee boat is underway and headed toward the racing area. The sailing instructions for the regatta will detail how and when this will take place.

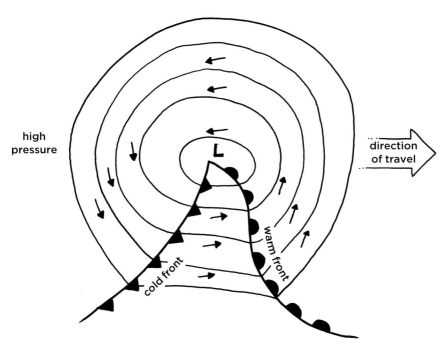

The passage of a frontal system will bring a series of changes in wind direction. As the warm front passes, the wind will veer from the south to the southwest. The cold front will then often bring a line of storms, after which the wind will veer into the northwest.

there have been reports of extreme weather in the area. Still, there are times when fronts will pass through during the course of a regatta, or when a windshift makes its presence known midway through a race that has been started in the wake of a thunderstorm.

Surprisingly, given all the excitement to the south, things are relatively calm north of the low-pressure center as you experience a more gradual transition from high to low pressure, with the wind slowly backing into the north. Depending on the pressure gradients in your area, you might experience a good breeze at times. But you won't get the storms associated with a front.

LOCAL WEATHER

Of course, as you've probably noticed, many times there will be a great difference between what has been predicted by your local weather forecaster and what you actually experience when sailing. This is because the weather at any given point on the Earth's surface can be as heavily influenced by local factors as by the great air masses that go careening across continents and oceans. In fact, unless you are a couple of miles or more offshore, away from the influence of the land, it is these local factors that can make the real difference during a sailboat race.

Sea Breezes. The most common and best known of the local breezes is the sea breeze, an almost daily occurrence over all larger bodies of water, including large lakes and harbors. Sea breezes result when the sun warms the land faster than the water, creating a difference in temperature and air pressure. Think of the air as moving in a circle. Specifically, as the air over the land warms and begins to rise, the colder, heavier air over the water moves in to take its place, creating a breeze. This new air over the land then warms up, rises, and is replaced by yet more cold air coming in from over the water. As the air over the land rises, it cools and forms the small cumulus clouds that you often see along the shore on a sunny day. Eventually it falls back down toward the water.

Typically, a sea breeze won't get going until late morning or early afternoon, but the exact strength and timing of the breeze can vary appreciably depending on weather conditions. For example, on a cloudy day you will have less breeze than when the sun is out. In fact, you might not have any breeze at all. A strong wind also can delay or even obviate a sea breeze, for example, if a strong weather system is passing overhead.

In some places the strength of a sea breeze, the time it comes in, and the direction in which it blows are very predictable. The Fremantle Doctor off Fremantle, Australia, for example, is a very powerful and reliable sea breeze caused by the intense warming of the desert outback a few miles inland. In San Francisco some people describe the sea breeze as "the Napa Valley

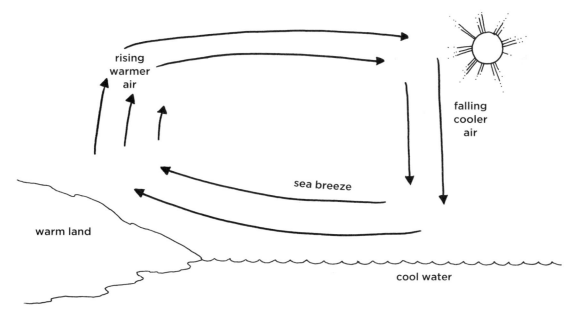

As warming air rises over land it is replaced by the cooler, higher pressure air over the water. The movement of this cooler air creates the sea breeze.

sucking," because the warm air over that region powers the Bay's notorious winds. Unfortunately, over most of the world the sea breeze is far less reliable; on light days in particular, anticipating the "if" and "when" of the sea breeze can mean the difference between finishing a race at the top or the very bottom of the fleet.

If, for example, there is a light wind out of the north and you are sailing a beat a mile or two east of a north-south shoreline, you should stay on the right side of the course; once the wind veers it will lift the starboard tack and knock the port tack. (Remember, sail to the shifts!) If you are on the right side of the course you may actually end up on or close to the layline, whereas if you go over to the left side you will have to slog your way almost directly to windward all over again.

By the same token, if the sea breeze comes in at some point during the run, the boats on the right side of the course will have the advantage, because they will be headed on port tack as they come in to the mark and have a hotter angle of sail. Meanwhile, the boats on the left side will have the mark nearly dead downwind once again.

As described above, sea breezes can be fickle creatures, so getting a good slant doesn't necessarily mean you're home free. Sometimes the wind will shift around slowly; sometimes it will oscillate back and forth before settling in; and sometimes it will switch around all at once. Even if it does come around all at once, it will often continue to waver back and forth so that, whether sailing upwind or down, you will still want to play the shifts.

It can also be tough to tell where exactly the sea breeze will fill in. Usually, it first appears a mile or so offshore and then spreads both toward and away from the land as it grows in strength. It might also lift a little as it first comes over the land, leaving a dead zone immediately along the shore. If you're not careful, on fluky summer mornings in particular you can find yourself sitting motionless in the water while one of your competitors goes gliding, or ghosting,

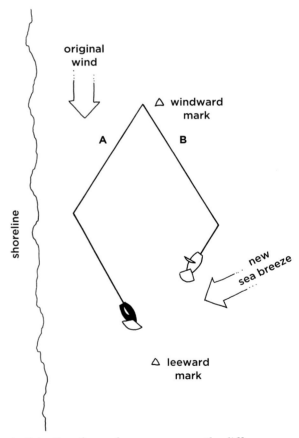

*Anticipating the sea breeze can mean the difference between sailing low and slow or on a hot angle. On this run, going to the right (**A**) means sailing a hotter angle when the sea breeze comes in, whereas going to the left (**B**) means sailing nearly dead downwind.*

by a quarter mile or less to windward. In many cases the only way to know where the wind will be is through experience. So keep track of how the wind behaves when you are out sailing and chat it up with your fellow sailors back at the dock. You can also look for signs such as dark patches of rippled water and the flutter of flags or drift of smoke from smokestacks on shore. And of course, keep an eye on the other sailboats in the area—whether they be racing or cruising. If the boats toward one side of the racecourse are carrying their spinnakers nice and full while the chutes on the other side are hanging limp, there should be little question where you want to be.

Shorelines and Geography. In addition to creating a sea breeze, a shoreline or island can also affect the direction and strength of a wind, depending on its direction and the geography of the land. Gaps between islands and breaks in the shore, for example, can funnel and intensify the breeze, making it much stronger at certain points than in the general area. The wind can also wrap around hills or points of land and create small lifts or headers, depending on the direction in which you're sailing. For example, if a westerly breeze is blowing around the northern tip of a headland, it will tend to back first, and then veer a little so that, directly to leeward of the point, it will be from the northwest. Finally, winds blowing nearly parallel to a shoreline will often blow even more parallel right where the shore meets the water.

Because the land can have such a dramatic influence on wind, many race committees try to set their courses as far offshore as conveniently possible, especially when staging major regattas such as class championships. But if you're sailing on an inland lake or confined harbor, the land and its effect on sailing conditions is a fact of life. Upstate New York and the upper Midwest are both hotbeds of small-boat sailing, much of which takes place within spittin' distance of

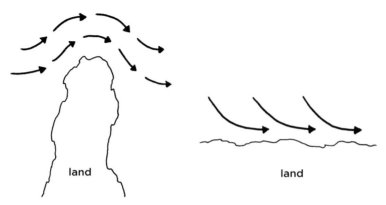

There are a number of ways the land can influence wind direction: For example, a breeze will bend around a headland (left); and a wind nearly parallel to the land will become more parallel (right). But beware: you can never be entirely sure how land will affect the wind.

shore. Out West there are all kinds of sailing taking place on inland lakes, including small alpine lakes in the Sierra Nevada range in California.

As is the case with the sea breeze, the only true way to know the winds in the area is through observation, personal experience, and asking around. And, no, this latter option is most definitely *not* cheating. Many Olympic hopefuls, for example, will hire a coach before competing in a qualifying regatta at a location such as San Francisco Bay, and part of that coach's job is pointing out how the wind behaves in the area. The fabled schooner *America*, which brought the Hundred Guinea Cup over from England in 1851, had a British pilot on board. You can bet the crew was asking him for some pointers on where he thought the breeze would be coming from!

Finally, if you want to gain a little insight into how the wind behaves in your area, make a habit of taking a walk along the waterside every now and then to see what's doin'. This can be especially helpful if you can gain a little height by climbing a bluff or hill overlooking the area where you race. Note how the various boats are performing, based on their location relative to the land. Look for those dark patches that indicate wind on the water. Where are they forming and how do they behave? Do they tend to develop in one particular area? Are they forming in a particular direction? Bring a pair of binoculars. Maybe even bring a handheld compass to help you determine the direction of the winds you are observing. The next time you are out racing in

similar conditions, you might be able to use this knowledge to get a puff or favorable windshift ahead of the competition. But beware. Studying other boats and the water can become addicting. Wisconsin's Pewaukee Lake, for example, is at first glance a fairly benign body of water, oftentimes crowded with fishing boats and personal watercraft. However, it is also the home of the Harken sailing company and a hotbed of scow racing. Before important regattas in particular, it's not at all unusual to see a sailor or two haunting the hills, their eyes on the water below, looking for tips that might help them out on race day.

Clouds. Clouds are formed by moving air and can therefore be an indication of wind. Be careful, though: different clouds can mean different kinds of breezes. The clouds accompanying a front, for example, will almost always have wind in advance of them, so be sure to get to that side of the course. In this case, it can be especially helpful to check the weather radio beforehand, because it will give you some indication of what the wind will be like after the front passes.

On partly cloudy days, on the other hand, you need to use a different strategy. Specifically, when there are medium-size cumulus clouds overhead, the rule of thumb is to sail toward them, but not directly under them; there is wind on the edges of the clouds, but less underneath. It can be difficult to tell what windshifts might come with these puffs so try to see what happens to the boats that get to them first. Luckily, once you have determined how the wind is behaving

Weather Tips

- In the Northern Hemisphere, air circulates in a clockwise direction around a high-pressure area and counterclockwise around a low-pressure area.
- A sea breeze will often first appear about a mile offshore and spread both toward and away from the land.
- Because of the land's influence, winds blowing almost parallel to a shoreline will sometimes bend so that, at the water's edge, they are blowing parallel to the land.
- On a partly cloudy day, there will often be wind around the edges of medium-size cumulus clouds.

in the vicinity of one cloud, it will generally be the same with the other clouds in the area.

WEATHER SOURCES AND RACE DAY

One of the best things to do when figuring out the weather outlook for race day is start looking at the weather picture the night before. Before you turn in (nice and early, of course, so you'll be at your very best when it comes time to bend on sails), check the local weather forecast, either by going online or listening to your weather radio. Weather broadcasts on television or in the newspaper can also give you some insight, although they tend to be too superficial for sailing purposes. The idea behind checking the weather the night before is to get a feel for how things change over time. Weather is very much a continuing process. It's a lot easier to keep track of developments over

the course of a few hours than to absorb the whole picture at a glance.

On race day, check the weather when you wake up and again before you head out the door. Also consider buying a portable weather radio for monitoring reports broadcast by the National Oceanic and Atmospheric Administration (NOAA), especially for day-long regattas. Jot down information such as predicted wind speeds and directions, and even such specifics as barometric pressures if you think it might help. Getting into the habit of noting these kinds of data will make you that much more comfortable with the general weather picture in your area.

We are truly living in a Golden Age of easy-access weather information, thanks to sources such as the Internet, and NOAA and the National Weather Service, which broadcast detailed and continually updated weather reports 24 hours a day from some eight hundred different weather stations nationwide. Detailed satellite images, radar maps, and Web cam images, showing a particular stretch of lake or harbor as it appears at that very moment are only a mouse click away. In some localities, NOAA weather radio can be accessed via telephone (look for an NOAA information number in the yellow pages; as long as it's a local call it shouldn't cost you a thing). If not, you can listen to the forecast either on your boat's VHF radio or with a NOAA weather radio receiver, which can be purchased at just about any chandlery or electronics store.

Finding a good Internet site can be as simple as going to the weather page of your local newspaper or logging on to the NOAA weather Web site. You can also visit the Web sites of yacht clubs or even marine suppliers in your area. Nearly all will have at least some kind of basic weather information available; many will have links to the appropriate NOAA Web pages for their immediate area; and some will have data from their own personal weather stations online, so you can know exactly what is happening down at the waterside. Other valuable resources include the Intellicast Web site and cable television's The Weather Channel Web site. These last two sites in particular give all kinds of background information if you want to study meteorology in greater depth. (See the Appendix for more information on weather resources.)

When looking at weather maps, try to correlate what you see on the screen or in the paper with what you read or hear on the forecast. Note the location of fronts and air masses and look at the pressure gradients indicated by the isobars. Try to understand how the information you see in the maps is causing the weather in your particular area. Again, write things down if you think it will help. Get in the habit of studying the weather all the time, whether or not you are racing, and it will become less and less mysterious.

For those who want to learn more about meteorology, there are literally stacks of books on the subject (see Recommended Reading in the Resources section of the Appendix for starters). By learning about the nu-

ances of meteorology, observing the weather in your area, and talking about wind patterns with your fellow sailors, you too may become one of those lucky sailors who always seems to find a puff or windshift.

Q & A

Q. How do winds circulate around a center of low pressure in the Northern Hemisphere?
A. Counterclockwise.

Q. How will a shoreline influence a general wind blowing roughly parallel to it?
A. It will bend the wind so it is flowing parallel to the shore.

Q. Do closely packed isobars on a weather map indicate more or less wind?
A. Closely packed isobars represent a steep pressure gradient, so they indicate more wind.

Q. Under what conditions will the sea breeze play an especially important role?
A. When you are sailing within a mile or two of shore on a sunny day in relatively calm conditions.

Q. How will a headland affect the wind blowing past it?
A. The wind will bend around the headland, causing it to back or veer depending on which side of the headland the wind passes.

Chapter 9

BOAT SPEED
Part 1: Sail Controls and Concepts

If there is one aspect of sailboat racing that is more frustrating and mysterious for beginners than weather, it's boat speed. Getting from point A to point B under sail is one thing. Getting there ahead of the competition is quite another. In the next three chapters we will try to keep things as simple as possible, since the end result of too much sail trim talk is usually confusion. The idea here is to sail intelligently and efficiently as you first set out on the adventure that is sailboat racing. Unless you decide to start out your racing career sailing in, say, the red-hot Farr 40 class, these recommendations alone may yield surprising results. Later on, as you begin to feel more comfortable on the racecourse, you can plunge into the more esoteric aspects of sail trim in an effort to wring out that last fraction of a knot of speed.

BALANCE

It is at this point that most discussions of sail trim start talking about the aerodynamic shapes of sails, things such as sail controls and the curvature of your foils. The reasons for this are obvious. The sails are what make you go, right? What better place to start?

As any seasoned racer will tell you, however, you need more than just sails to go sailing, especially when trying to get to windward. Your hull and underwater appendages—the keel and rudder—are just as important. In fact, these underwater foils and those pretty white foils up in the air need to work in concert if your boat is to go anywhere at all, let alone go well.

The operative term here is balance, the net result of the various forces at work on your boat's hull, rudder, keel, and sails. Below the waterline, your boat's hull, rudder, and keel together create a center of lateral resistance, a kind of pivot point around which the boat will spin as it resists the temptation to drift to leeward in reaction to the wind. Overhead, your sails create an analogous center of effort, representing the cumulative effect of the wind on your rig as it tries to push your boat both sideways and through the water. If the sideways component of the center of effort is forward of the center of resistance when sailing close-hauled or on a reach, it will push the bow to leeward. This condition is called leeward helm. If it is aft of the center of lateral resistance, it will try to push the boat up into the wind. This is called, not surprisingly, windward helm. If the centers of lateral resistance and effort are in line, the boat will be balanced, a point at which it is said to have neutral helm.

While centers of resistance and effort can be calculated theoretically (in fact, this is a big part of what a naval architect does when creating a new design), in practice the best way to judge whether a boat is in balance is through the helm. If you have to use a lot of rudder to keep your boat on course, that should tell you something. If the helm feels light, so that all you need is fingertip pressure to keep your boat on course—even if it's blowing 20 knots—you're doing the right thing. Balance is crucial to boat speed because the more rudder you use—in other words the more you have to angle the rudder off centerline—the more resistance it creates to forward motion. In the chapters

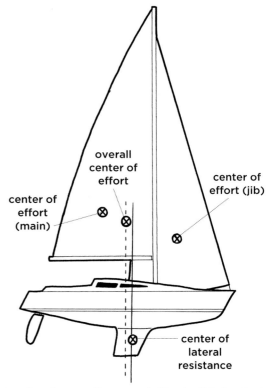

Note that the overall center of effort is slightly aft of the center of lateral resistance when the sails are sheeted in, so that this performance cruiser will have a tendency to want to turn up into the wind. A little of this phenomenon, known as weather helm, is good because it gives the helmsman a feel for the water passing over the rudder.

about mark roundings (see chapters 4 and 6), we talk about using as little rudder as possible to maintain boat speed while making your turn. The same goes for straight-line sailing. The helmsman should think more of "guiding" the boat upwind, rather than just steering it; a well-trimmed boat will pretty much sail itself.

Of course, it is this interaction between the sails and underwater appendages that makes it possible to actually steer a boat with just the sails. By manipulating the trim of the jib and mainsail you can move the center of effort fore and aft. In chapter 3, The Windward Leg, for example, we emphasize that it's important to ease the main when rounding the windward mark, but that it's fine to leave the jib strapped in. This is because by easing the main you are reducing the amount of lateral force it's generating, which causes the overall center of effort to move forward and create leeward helm. This is precisely what you want when falling off from a beat to a reach at the end of that first leg.

The same thing goes when rounding the leeward mark, only in reverse. In this case, trim in the main first. This will move the center of effort aft, especially if you let the jib lag behind a bit to reduce the amount of lateral force it contributes to the overall lateral force being generated by the rig. The resulting windward helm will bring the boat around and up to a beat, with very little need for the rudder.

As a practical matter, most sailboats go fastest to windward or on a reach with just a touch of windward helm. There are two reasons for this. First, it gives the helmsman a good feel for the water passing over his foils. Second, it means the keel is providing lift, actually pulling the hull to windward to help counteract the downwind pressure being exerted on the boat by the sails. On modern racing boats, the rudder also provides some lift when sailing to windward—yet another good reason to use as little helm as possible; moving it about disrupts the flow of water over the rudder's surface. Remember, don't just wiggle that rudder up and down in the waves: control it.

When thinking about balance and helm, it's also important to keep in mind the amount of heel the boat is experiencing, since a boat on its ear exhibits far more weather helm than when it's sailing upright. The reason is, as the hull heels over, it no longer presents a symmetrical hydrodynamic shape as it works its way through the water. Specifically, as one side of the hull is forced deeper into the water, the forward portion of the hull—where it tapers in from the point of maximum beam to the leading edge at the bow—acts like a rudder pushing the bow to windward. The rudder itself must compensate for this force.

In fact, this source of helm can be even more crippling than any disparity between the centers of resistance and effort, which is why the helmsmen and main trimmers on well-sailed boats inevitably work in tandem to keep the boat under control in heavy-air conditions. When a puff hits, the main trimmer will ease off his sail, using the sheet or traveler to dump off the extra wind, minimizing the degree of heel so the boat won't want to round up into the wind. By doing this, he also reduces the mainsail's contribution to the total lateral force exhibited by the sails, causing the center of effort to move forward. This further decreases the forces creating windward helm. When the puff passes, the main trimmer will bring the sail back in, once again harnessing the power of the wind as completely as possible. Ideally, throughout this process, the helmsman will barely have had to adjust the helm at all. On powerfully rigged racing boats, the sail trimmers are often said to be the ones truly steering the boat. This is not an exaggeration.

SAIL SHAPE: THE JARGON

But enough of all this balance stuff! When most sailors think boat speed, they're thinking sails. And if the sail development budgets for the average America's Cup campaign are any indication, they aren't half wrong. Before getting into the nuts and bolts of sail trim, however, we need to nail down some terms. Good sail trim isn't just about deciding how far in or out you should place your sails; it's about the curvature, or "shape," of your sails, ensuring that they are performing as efficient aerodynamic foils. We need some jargon in order to discuss both that shape and sail aerodynamics in general with some degree of precision. We also need to look at the sail controls and theory that are used when manipulating shape. Those sails overhead are anything but big flat pieces of sailcloth.

Draft—The term draft is used to describe the curvature, or camber, of the sail as determined by the way the sail was originally built by the sailmaker, the way it is flying on the rig, and the way it is being trimmed. More importantly, it is often used as shorthand for the point of maximum draft of the sail, the point of its deepest curvature. This draft depth, or chord depth, is measured from the point of deepest curvature to the chord, a theoretical straight line drawn from the luff of the sail to the leech. The distance between the luff and leech, or the length of this line, is referred to as the chord length. A "full" sail is one with a deep draft for its chord length. A "flat" sail is one with a shallow draft. Draft depth is often represented as a percentage of chord length. To calculate this figure, divide the draft depth by the chord length and multiply the result by 100. A 15 percent draft depth is fairly full for a main, while a 10 percent draft is pretty shallow. A 12 percent draft is pretty flat for a jib while 20 percent is quite full. In practice you need to be able to estimate the amount of draft in the sail by looking up at the sail from below.

Of equal importance when looking at sail shape is the fore-and-aft location of the point of maximum draft as a percentage of the total chord length aft of the luff. For example, on most sloops, the point of maximum draft will be 45 to 50 percent, or about halfway aft on the main, and 35 to 40 percent aft on the jib—a little bit forward of halfway. On boats that carry just a mainsail, such as MC-scows, Beetle Cats, Lasers, or

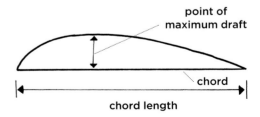

Draft describes the amount of curvature in the sail. Draft depth is measured from the point of deepest curvature to the chord.

Wyliecats, the draft is carried a bit farther forward, around 35 to 40 percent aft of the sail's leading edge, since without a headsail the main is essentially acting like a genoa. Again, you can generate these numbers mathematically, in this case by dividing the distance from the luff to the point of maximum draft by the total chord length and then multiplying the result by 100. But in practice you need to be able to make an educated guess by looking up at the curvature of the sail as the boat is underway.

Twist—This term refers to the degree to which the leech of the sail falls off to leeward. If you look up along the trailing edge of either your jib or main, you will see that the angle the sailcloth forms relative to the boom or chord changes the higher you go. On the lower part of the sail, the leech will usually be curved slightly to windward; midway up, it will be approximately parallel to the boom; and near the top of the sail, it will angle away slightly to leeward. Each sail is designed with a certain amount of twist, but this twist can also be adjusted using your sail controls.

Attached flow—When sails are working efficiently, especially when sailing to windward, they do not *push* a boat through the water so much as they *pull* the boat through the water, due to differences in air pressure on either side of the sail. For this to happen efficiently, the wind passing over both sides of the sail must be "attached." In other words, there can't be a large area of turbulence or disturbed air between the general airflow and the sail. When this happens the air is said to "separate" or "detach," and the sail itself is "stalled" like the wing of an airplane. Note that, while in a perfect world there would be a smooth, or laminar, flow of perfectly attached air over both the main and the genoa, in reality the air passing over the main can be fairly turbulent because of the mast at the leading edge. This turbulence isn't enough to cause the airflow to detach

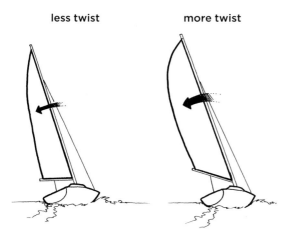

less twist   more twist

Twist refers to the degree to which the leech falls off to leeward. When the angle of the sail's trailing edge is cupped to windward, there is less twist. When the leech is allowed to curve off to leeward, there is more twist.

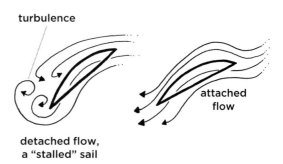

turbulence

attached flow

detached flow, a "stalled" sail

The airflow must remain attached if it is to efficiently interact with the sail.

completely. But it still results in a reduction of power and lift and an increase in drag.

Lift—We've already been throwing this term around a bit, but it's time for a more exact definition. Basically, it refers to the net forward force that results from the air passing over a sail when sailing into the wind. Somewhat like the centers of lateral resistance and effort, the overall force generated can be summed up as a single line, or vector, showing direction and amount. This vector can then be broken down into a forward and lateral component. The forward component is the good one, the one that causes your boat to go forward. The lateral component is the one that your keel and rudder must compensate for if you want to avoid drifting off into oblivion.

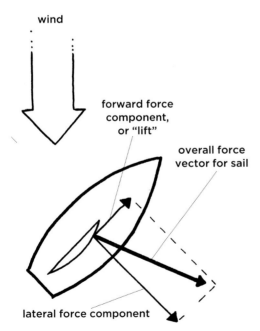

Lift is the result of the forward component of the overall force generated by the sail.

Angle of attack—This term refers to the angle between the chord of the sail and the apparent wind direction as it strikes the leading edge of the sail. Note that this is different from the attitude of the actual leading edge of the sail—the material immediately behind the mast—because that material is inevitably angled to leeward relative to the boom.

Apparent wind—As discussed in chapter 5, Downwind Legs/Reaches, there are actually two kinds of wind to be aware of aboard a well-run sailboat. The first is the true wind: the wind you experience when standing still at a given point. The second is apparent wind: the wind you experience while you're moving. Apparent wind can be either greater than or less than the true wind, depending on your angle of sail. When sailing on a beat or close reach, for example, the apparent wind will be greater and from an angle that is farther forward than the true wind. When sailing on a run, the apparent wind will be substantially less than the true wind.

Velocity made good—Velocity made good, or VMG, refers to the speed with which you are making progress toward your goal—in other words, the mark—as opposed to simply your speed through the water. This concept is of particular interest when on a beat or jibing downwind, because you often need to strike a balance between the angle of sail that carries you through the water fastest and that which will get you to your destination most efficiently. On a beat, for example, steering a lower course and cracking off the sheets will increase your boat speed. But because you are no longer sailing as directly toward the mark, your VMG will actually fall.

SAIL CONTROLS

Fortunately, despite the apparent complexity of many rigs, the controls used to regulate sail shape are fairly few in number and easy to use. The tough part is knowing how to use them. First we'll look at sail controls for the mainsail. Then we'll look at the jib. In many ways the two sails are controlled in much the same way. But there are a few differences.

MAINSAIL CONTROLS

Halyard tension/cunningham—Both the halyard and cunningham are used to control luff tension, which in turn controls the location of the draft. In a sail made of a woven fabric such as Dacron, they do this by first taking out any extra sailcloth or wrinkles coming off the mast and then stretching the material so it realigns the weave. This pulls forward on the fabric making up the middle and front of the sail. With higher-tech sails, such as those made of Mylar or Kevlar, the cunningham or halyard controls the excess cloth in the leading edge of the sail, but does not stretch it. Doing so would ruin the sail by permanently distorting the material.

For those who don't have one, the cunningham is a piece of line that is led through a block near the base of the mast to an eyelet in the sail a foot or so above the tack, where it is generally attached with a small hook. When you take in on the cunningham it pulls down on the luff, increasing the tension on that part of the sail.

Outhaul—Increasing or decreasing the amount of tension along the foot has a

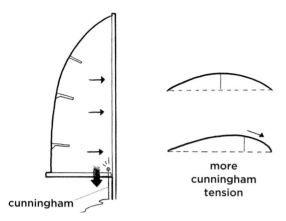

cunningham

Luff tension, which is controlled by the halyard or cunningham, pulls the draft forward by stretching or taking out any of the extra material in the leading edge of the sail.

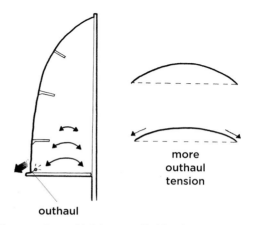

outhaul

Foot tension, which is controlled by the outhaul, flattens the lower part of the sail by increasing the tension along the foot of the sail.

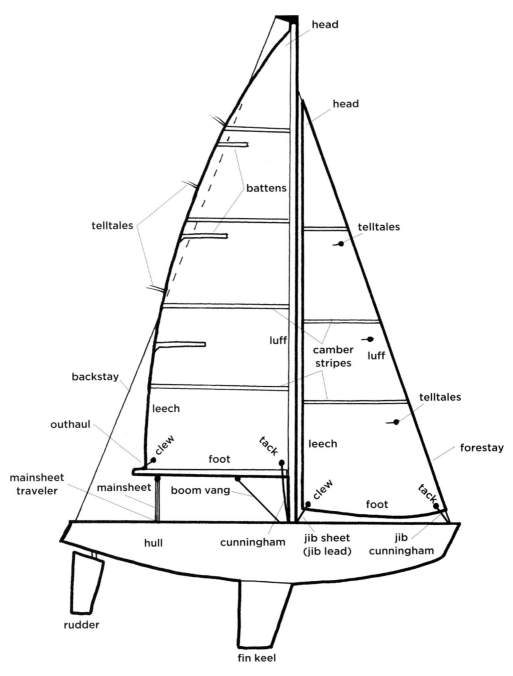

There are many controls available to help with sail trim.

direct effect on the amount of draft in the lower part of the sail. Specifically, easing out on the outhaul results in more draft, while trimming in flattens the sail. Some sails are built with flattening reefs that accomplish much the same thing by increasing tension along the foot and cinching down a panel of sailcloth that otherwise adds curvature to the lower part of the sail.

Mainsheet—In the past you may have thought the mainsheet's only job was to let the main in and out. But not anymore! When trimming sails for windward performance, the mainsheet is your means of controlling leech tension, or twist. Take in on the mainsheet and you pull down on the boom, removing twist from the sail, cupping in the leech. Ease it out and the leech falls off, giving you more twist. In general, unless you are dumping air in heavy conditions, a good rule of thumb is keep the top batten parallel to the boom, something you can easily judge by sighting up from the center of the boom. On a boat with a masthead rig you can sheet in a little tighter, because the wind in front of the main is deflected toward the boat's centerline by the genoa all the way to the top of the mast. Therefore, the top of the mainsail is sailing in a bit of a header like the rest of the sail. On a reach or run, you will still use the sheet to control the main's angle of attack, while the boom vang controls twist by holding the boom down. But that is not its job on a beat.

Main traveler—So if we can't use our mainsheets to control angle of attack on the beat, what *can* we use? The answer is the main traveler, the track to which your main-sheet is attached, running athwartships either near the back of the cockpit or up on the cabintop. The advantage to changing the angle of attack by this means is that, with the mainsheet and other sail controls set, the aerodynamic shape of the sail remains unaltered.

Backstay/mast bend—While the outhaul works great for flattening the lower part of the mainsail, the best way to flatten the sail farther up is by taking in on the backstay to bend the mast. By doing this you pull the central panels of the sail forward, which reduces the amount of material that is used to give the sail its curved shape. Note that because you are reducing the amount from the leading half of the sail, mast bend also causes the draft to drift aft. Therefore, it's important to add some luff tension to keep the draft forward where it belongs. Also note that the mast can bend when the mainsheet pulls down on the leech, especially on boats with flexible

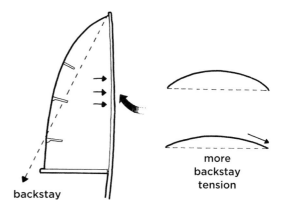

Taking in on the backstay creates mast bend, which flattens the upper part of the sail by pulling the material from the center of the sail forward.

masts. Finns and Lasers, for example, both rely heavily on mainsheet tension because they are built without backstays. Finally, be aware that as you crank in on the backstay, you will also be putting some twist in the leech as the top of the mast moves aft toward the clew of the mainsail.

Running backstays—These adjustable stays serve the opposite purpose of standard backstays. Because they pull aft on the upper-middle part of the mast, as opposed to the very top, they straighten out the spar, putting camber back in the sail even as the backstay is trying to take it out. Note that fewer and fewer boats are equipped with runners these days; only the largest boats have them anymore.

Boom vang—Although the primary job of the vang is to control twist when sailing off the wind, on occasion it can be used to control twist to windward as well, as has become the practice aboard some top-end racing boats. Also, by using a technique known as vang sheeting, it can provide a very fast way of controlling angle of attack. However, in this capacity it can also break your boom and gooseneck, so for starters don't use it.

Having said that, the basic idea behind vang sheeting is to trim in on the vang to set your twist, which in turn relieves the tension on the mainsheet and allows you to play it as if it was the traveler (in total contradiction of our admonition above!). As an additional benefit, because the vang also pushes the boom forward, it bends the mast down low, reducing draft in the bottom portion of the main and opening the slot

between the main and the jib. In most cases when a vang breaks a boom, it happens because no one bothered to ease it off again at the weather mark. Falling off onto a reach, the main trimmer eases the mainsheet, which transfers all the upward pressure to the vang. Then when someone eases off the backstay, the mast straightens, the leech transfers the entire load to the vang, the tremendous pressure moves from the end of the boom forward to the vang and—snap!

JIB CONTROLS

Halyard tension/cunningham—These work the same on the jib as they do on the main, although few boats have cunninghams on their jibs. Instead they rely on halyard tension.

Forestay sag—Although the two might not seem similar at first, forestay sag influences headsail shape in much the same way that mast bend affects the main. Even on the most sophisticated race boats, it's impossible to completely eliminate forestay sag because of the tremendous forces involved. So when sailmakers build their sails they design them to fly on a forestay with a moderate amount of sag. This way the draft and the leading-edge angle will be correct, even with the luff curving off to leeward a little. Straightening the forestay pulls material from the middle of the sail forward a few inches, flattening the sail. As was the case with the main, a little extra luff tension is needed to keep the draft forward. Note that the best way to straighten the forestay on most boats is by taking in on the back-

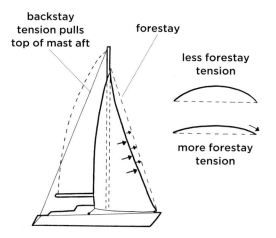

Taking in on the backstay straightens the forestay, removing draft from the headsail by pulling forward on the material from the center of the sail.

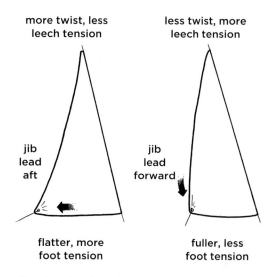

Adjusting the sheet lead fore and aft changes the overall shape of a headsail. With the jib lead forward there is more downward force on the leech and less tension along the foot of the sail. Therefore the sail will have less twist along the trailing edge and more curvature, or draft, in the foot. With the jib lead aft there is less downward force along the leech and more tension along the foot. Therefore you have more twist and less draft in the lower part of the sail.

stay, which means that the same sail control that flattens the main also flattens the jib. Isn't that nice? If, on the other hand, you want to keep some camber in the main while you're taking in on your backstay, put on some running backstay (assuming you've got them) to keep the mast straight. Be aware that sometimes all that backstay and mainsheet tension can be a bit much when the winds fall light, so in a drifter consider taking a spare jib or spinnaker halyard to the bow and tightening it to induce sag. Otherwise, your mainsheet and backstay tension may straighten the forestay more than you want.

Jib lead—In contrast to the main, which has an outhaul, mainsheet, and main traveler for controlling things such as angle of attack and leech tension, the jib has just its sheet. This single line, however, can wield a tremendous influence on sail shape depending on how it is set. The two main

variables are the amount of sheet tension—the amount you pull in on the line—and the position of the sheet lead fore and aft. The latter is determined by where you place the jib-lead block on its slide or track.

At its most basic, adjusting the sheet controls both the angle of attack and the amount of draft in the sail. Trimming in, for example, brings the leading edge toward centerline and pulls the sailcloth aft, flattening the draft. Easing out does just the opposite. Many cruisers, however, largely ignore the effect that jib-lead angle has on twist; i.e., that it exerts a substantial downward force along the leech of the sail as well as a horizontal force aft along the foot.

When you move the jib lead forward, for example, you exert that much more downward force on the sail's trailing edge, cupping in the leech. When you move the lead aft, less of the sheet tension transfers to the trailing edge, thereby allowing the leech to twist off to leeward.

Because they determine how much of the line's tension will be directed horizontally, jib-lead adjustments also affect angle of attack and the amount of draft in the sail. If the lead is well forward, for example, the sail will be fuller and the angle of attack less dramatic, because much of the sheet's force is taking in on the leech. If the lead is aft, the sheet's force will be directed along the foot of the sail, pulling the leading edge in toward the centerline and flattening the sail.

Obviously, the key to headsail trim is finding the right balance between these two competing forces. As a general rule, the sheet angle should bisect the angle made by the foot and leech. A good way to determine this is by measuring to the center of the luff and then drawing a line from the clew to this point. The sheet lead should be along this line. This angle, however, sometimes needs to be modified depending on the conditions and angle of sail.

MAST TUNING

In addition to these sail controls there are a couple of other things to keep in mind when thinking about boat speed. The first concerns that big aluminum (or possibly carbon or wood) thing sticking up out of the middle of your boat. If you're just cruising around on a sunny day, all that really matters is that it stays upright. But if you want to be competitive on the racecourse, you need the thing to be straight athwartships and have the right amount of rake (the angle at which the mast is inclined aft of vertical), and prebend fore and aft. (Prebend refers to the amount of bend in the mast without the backstay on. Bend is the amount the mast bends under tension from the sails and other adjustments.) Even a couple of inches of curvature from one side to the other can mean a big difference in performance. Sight up along the luff groove of your mast and you might be surprised at what you see. Does your boat always seem to be a bit livelier on one tack than the other when sailing close to the wind? Now you may discover why.

To tune your mast, first make sure the entire thing isn't leaning to one side or the other. While you're at it, take a close look at where it's stepped to make sure it's in the center of the boat. Believe it or not, due to builder error, many boats' masts are not actually set at the exact centerline.

The first step to making sure the spar is upright is measure from the bow back to the chainplates and mark a common spot on the rail on each side. Then loosen the entire rig (make sure to back off on the backstay and topping lift as well), attach a metal tape measure (or any other kind of tape that won't stretch) to the main halyard, and haul it to the top of the mast. Pull the tape down to those common points on each rail. Do you get the same measurement on each side? If so, great. If not, position the tip of the mast so it is in the center of the boat by tightening or backing off on the upper shrouds; i.e., the ones that go straight up to the top of the rig. At this point keep things loose. You're not tensioning the rig yet, just getting it centered and creating a starting point for the rest of the process.

Once this is done, straighten the rig using those shrouds running on a diagonal. Whether you have one set of spreaders or four, the process basically involves starting from the top and working your way down the rig, tightening and backing off on either side, and sighting up the length of the spar until everything is in column. This will take some time, so be patient. Don't worry about tension yet. Again, you're just establishing a kind of a baseline. For now you merely want to get the mast straight.

Once you have this basic tune set, you can begin tightening things down, once again working your way down from the top. If there are tuning guides for your boat, use a tension gauge and tighten the stays to the proper settings. The proper tension not only has to do with the boat, but also how the sails are cut. In fact, setting the tension is in many ways as much an art as it is a science. Ask around and see what the rest of the guys in the fleet are doing. If your boat is a popular one-design, you should have no trouble at all finding a tuning guide by calling your class association or a major sailmaker that caters to the class. If your boat is of a less common design, you can contact the manufacturer or your local rigger. Unfortunately, there are so many different rig

styles it would take an entire book to cover them all, so you need to do a little independent research of your own.

During your research make sure that, before you go out and copy the tension settings or prebend on some other guy's boat, you understand why it was set up that way. What works for one boat may not work for another. Not only that, asking around may reveal that nobody really knows *why* a rig has been set up the way it has. Prebend in particular sets the mainsail on the rig, so if your sail is built to fly on a straight mast, even a little prebend can impact its performance. Also, remember that a straight mast is a stiff mast, and that tighter rigs are better in heavy air, while looser rigs are best when things fall light. As a general rule of thumb, rake makes a boat faster to windward, but slows it on a reach or run. There are different theories about why this happens. One is that the angle of exit of the foils (sails) is better when the trailing edge is more perpendicular, because that is more consistent with the way the main and genoa interact with one another. Iceboats, for example, sail with incredible rake.

With your tension set, it's time to go sailing and see how the rig performs when it's put under load. Trim the main and backstay so the sails look good. Then sail from one tack to the other, looking up the length of the mast and tightening or loosening the stays if any portion of the spar is sagging to leeward or curving to windward. Use the same number of turns on each side so the mast will still be in column when it isn't under load. If you are like most people, chances are you tightened the lowers too much and the uppers not enough when you set the tension back at the dock. Take your time, and after each adjustment, take another sight up the groove of the mast. When you are satisfied, secure the turnbuckles with cotter pins and tape or put a line through them so they can't spin off. On boats with swept-back spreaders, be sure to check the straightness of the mast in all conditions, because the stays on these rigs tighten unevenly as the mast bends. Before each race readjust both sides to get the mast good and straight. On a fractional rig boat don't worry if the tip of the mast sags to leeward. Everyone else's is doing the same thing. In light air you can try letting the middle of the mast sag to leeward slightly for more power, but in general a straight mast is best.

NEW SAILS: HOW DO YOU KNOW YOUR SAILS ARE GOOD ENOUGH?

Unfortunately, all the rig tuning and sail trim in the world can't compensate for bad sails: bad, in this case, meaning sails that are not necessarily falling apart, but are distorted to the point of having lost their efficient aerodynamic shape. At one end of the spectrum are cruisers using ten-year-old mains that have all the aerodynamic sophistication of an old bed sheet; at the other end are grand prix racing programs that can count the total number of hours of sail usage on one hand. Obviously, the vast majority of sailors fall somewhere in between these two extremes. The question is, how do you know when to replace your sails to avoid total frustration on the racecourse?

The answer—not surprisingly—is it depends on the kind of racing you want to do. If you hope to do well in a highly competitive fleet, you will probably have to invest in new canvas at least every year or two. If you plan on racing in a more casual venue, say a relaxed one-design or PHRF fleet, you will get a lot more mileage out of your canvas. In either case take your sails to

Finding a Good Sailmaker

The best sailmaker for one sailor might not be the same for another. Especially if you are a beginner, look for a sailmaker who is local and willing to spend some time with you. An internationally renowned company with fancy, space-age, molded sails might be perfect for some guy with a 40-foot carbon fiber racing machine. But if you are still as much a cruiser as a racer, a local outfit will often be more willing to accommodate your individual needs, thereby giving you the better sails. Ask around and see what the other sailors in the fleet have to say. Similarly, while a number of sailmakers have stock sails for the more popular one-design classes, it pays to ask around and see how one brand stacks up against another in the local conditions, as opposed to just looking at the race results in the flashy magazine ads. While you're at it, take a look at the tuning guides put out by the different manufacturers. Are they understandable? The best sails in the world aren't going to do you a lick of good if you can't make them work.

a sailmaker, so he can look at them in the loft and give you a rundown on their shape and condition. To make his job a little easier, take a picture of your main and jib under sail.

The first sign of a main going bad is a wrinkle from the clew to the lower batten. This indicates that the lower leech of the sail has stretched, which reduces power, pointing ability, and feel in the helm. After that the luff will get too full as it stretches under the force of all those puffs. This will make it difficult, if not impossible, to flatten the sail to decrease its power in a blow. Congratulations, you now have a great sail in your inventory for the next drifter! You'll see the first sign of a bad genoa when the upper part of the sail loses its smooth foil shape and goes tubular. This is clear evidence that

the middle of the sail has stretched, compromising the sail's ability to perform to windward. All of these conditions can be fixed with a recut. But keep in mind there is only so much you can do. Think of that sail as your engine: you wouldn't want to enter a car race with four cylinders under your hood when everyone else has eight. Same goes with your sails. Sometimes you just have to get new ones to be competitive.

If your entire inventory is shot and your credit limit won't let you replace the whole thing in one fell swoop, a new headsail should be your first purchase. The reason for this is the main can be recut more easily and also is easier to modify under sail. In fact, if you are a one-design sailor, always keep your headsails up to date and never use the new one during practice. If you sail

The first sign of a main going bad is a wrinkle from the clew to the lower batten. This indicates that the lower leech of the sail has stretched, which reduces power, pointing ability, and feel in the helm.

Repairing Old Sails

Your sailmaker can give new life to an old sail by having it re-cut, taking out a strip of sailcloth to tighten up a part of the sail that has stretched under the force of the wind, returning the sail to its original, aerodynamic shape. To do this, a sail-maker takes apart a seam or slits the sail to make a new one. He or she then puts a new piece of material, or a "bandage," over the cut to make a new seam. Recutting as little as one-eighth inch can make a big difference in speed. Bear in mind that a stretched-out sail is not only less efficient, but will also age more quickly because the strain from the wind is diverted to areas of the sail that are not designed to take that kind of force.

While conventional Dacron sails are the easiest to work on, Kevlar sails can also be tweaked to improve their performance as they age. If you are having doubts about the condition of your sails, take a picture of them next time you are out on the water, so you can show it to a sailmaker and get his or her advice. You may be surprised at the kind of performance your sails are capable of after a little TLC!

PHRF or under some other handicap rating and have a more extensive sail inventory, fill it in as follows. First, get the sails you need for your boat to sail best in its optimum conditions. For example, if your boat sails great in heavy air, get new heavy-air sails to ensure you win in those conditions. Then fill in where your boat is weakest. After all, no one likes to finish dead last.

In terms of spinnaker wear, these sails tend to get "slow" as the material they are made of breaks down. Put the cloth from the middle of the sail in your hand and try to blow through it. If you can, you have a leaker. If the shape of this sail hasn't changed too dramatically, it could still be good on reaches or in heavy air. But a sail that lets air through will be slow in the light stuff. Other signs that a sail is getting older are a wrinkle coming in from the clew and a collapse in the center of the head, referred to as an "EA," or elephant ass. Both are symptoms of stretch around the leeches and can often be fixed with a recut. If the tapes on your spinnaker flap, have them tightened as well.

Whether your sails are new or old there are a number of things you can do to preserve your canvas and cut down on those trips to the sailmaker. Most important, avoid flogging your sails: there are few things that break down sailcloth fibers faster than letting your sails flap in the wind. For example, if you are in the habit of raising your sails while motoring into the wind, back off on the throttle a bit so you aren't creating your own personal gale while the main is going up. Also, as outlined in chapter 2, Starting, don't round up into the wind to find its true direction, since that is another great way to shake the life out of your sails. After you've finished a day on the water, be sure to dry your sails. If you sail on salt water, rinse the sails regularly, because salt crystals can work their way into the weave, where their sharp little corners will wreak havoc on the delicate fibers that make up the fabric. Finally, at the beginning or end of the season, give the entire inventory a close inspection to look for cuts, worn spots, or rotten thread.

Q & A

Q. A few minutes before the start, Rich is fine-tuning his sail shape and wants to figure out whether or not he has the right amount of leech tension in the mainsail. What is the easiest way to do this?

A. He can sight up from the center of the boom and make sure the top batten is parallel to the boom.

Q. The main and jib on Adam's one-design centerboarder are both looking pretty tired, but he's only got enough in the bank account for one new sail. What should he do?

A. He should replace the headsail and recut the main. Mains respond better to this kind of overhaul and can also be more effectively controlled under sail.

Q. Rich is trimming the mainsail in heavy air. A puff hits and as the boat heels the helmsman says he's having trouble controlling the boat. What should Rich do?

A. Rich needs to ease the main traveler to dump off some wind and reduce the amount of heel. That will reduce the amount of weather helm making it easier for the helmsman to steer.

Q. What is the primary function of the mainsheet when sailing to windward?

A. The mainsheet controls leech tension/twist. It can also be used to induce mast bend, especially on smaller boats without backstays, such as Finns and Lasers.

Q. What is the first step in mast tuning?

A. After backing off on all the shrouds, use the main halyard to haul a tape measure to the top of the mast and check to see if it is straight up and down in the boat.

Chapter 10

BOAT SPEED
Part 2: Sailing to Windward

N ow that we've got sail controls and the language of sail trim straightened away, it's time to put those tools and ideas to work. First we're going to talk about theory and how it is that sail shape affects performance. After that we'll look at sail trim settings for different conditions. Every boat is different, so you'll have to experiment on the water to see what works best for you. But these settings will serve as a good baseline and general guide.

THE WAY SAILS WORK TO WINDWARD

As most sailors know, modern sails work much like airplane wings when sailing to windward. Because of the way they are curved, and because of the angle of attack when trimmed properly, the air passing over the leeward side speeds up relative to the air passing over the windward side, since it has a longer distance to travel. As discovered by the eighteenth-century Swiss scientist Daniel Bernoulli, (a fellow whose name has been evoked in pretty much every discussion on sail theory since the dawn of time—or at least the mid-1700s), air pressure falls as air speed increases, which means the sail creates a region of low pressure on the leeward side relative to the air pressure on the windward side. It is this difference in pressure that creates the force on the sail that allows a sailboat to move in the very direction from which the wind is blowing—albeit at a fairly oblique angle. In fact, most modern sailboats sail to windward most efficiently at approximately a 45-

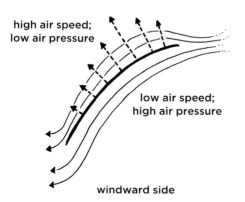

leeward side

high air speed;
low air pressure

low air speed;
high air pressure

windward side

Differences in air speed and air pressure allow a boat to sail to windward. Here, the parallel lines running along the sail represent the wind. As the air traveling along the leeward side of the sail speeds up to keep pace with the airflow on the windward side, it creates an area of low pressure relative to the windward side. This difference in air pressures creates the force illustrated by the arrows emanating from the sail. This force carries the boat to windward.

degree angle to the true wind. In ideal conditions, top-level racing boats can sail within 40 degrees of the true wind direction, and any boat can pinch up a few degrees high of 45 degrees of the wind for a few seconds if necessary. After that, however, they soon begin to lose boat speed and the VMG falls precipitously.

MORE ABOUT DRAFT

So much for the basics. In order to get any kind of real performance out of your sails—as opposed to just being blown around on a reach and firing up the iron genny when you want to go to windward—you need to

know how altering the different parameters of this basic aerodynamic shape will affect its performance. Of central importance, for example, is the amount of draft in your sails. Basically, draft provides power, since the more draft a sail has, the more the air on the leeward side has to speed up to keep pace with its windward-side counterpart. Therefore, all other things being equal, the more draft the better. Of course, this being sailboat racing, all other things are *not* equal. For example, when the breeze is very light, the air has trouble making sharp turns. This means too much draft will cause the airflow to separate from the sail, both in the deep belly of the sail on the windward side and in the area of the leech to leeward. Not only that, when the wind pipes up, that power can result in excess heel, which is not good either; it can cause a crippling amount of weather helm. Therefore, when sailing in light- or heavy-air conditions you will want to keep your sails flat, while in moderate conditions you will want to give your sails plenty of draft. Full sails also work well in chop, especially in lighter conditions, because they can give you some extra "oomph" for punching through waves.

The location of that draft is equally important when sailing to windward, for two reasons:

1. because it determines how the sail will translate the force of the wind into forward motion, and
2. because it determines the leading-edge angle of the sail relative to the chord.

The first consideration is fairly straightforward. Basically, you want the point of maximum curvature to be forward, since that is the area where the air must speed up most dramatically if it is to reconnect with the windward-side airflow as it passes the leech. Because the area of maximum speed has the lowest air pressure, it is also the area in which you will get the most lift. Bringing the draft forward, then, will angle the force generated by the sail closer to the direction in which you want to go.

To understand the second aspect of draft location, imagine two sails, each with the same amount of draft depth, but with the point of maximum draft in different parts of the sail. Note how the sail with the draft farther aft offers a leading edge angle that is much closer to the angle of attack. In general, the leading edge of a sail needs to be in line with the apparent wind. Therefore, a draft-aft sail will have better pointing ability, because its leading edge is closer to the boat's centerline. Of course on the downside, the sail's ability to create lift will decrease, because the air will be speeding up farther aft. It also means that, because the air has to make a tighter turn at the leech, there will be a greater tendency for the airflow to become detached in this area. As a result the helmsman has to be especially careful not to stall the sail by steering off his ideal course. In the end, you should always try to keep the draft in its designed location; i.e., around 35 to 40 percent aft in the jib and 45 to 50 percent aft in the main (35 to 40 percent aft for mains on boats without jibs). By doing so you are effecting the carefully considered compromise position cre-

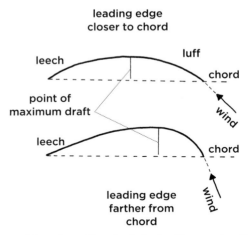

Draft location affects both the leading- and trailing-edge shape. Note the different angles of attack for the chord and leading edge of the sail.

ated by the sailmaker. One notable exception to this rule of thumb comes into play when you're in heavy seas or an ugly chop: in these conditions, it often makes sense to pull the draft a little farther forward than you normally would, since it will then be that much easier to keep the leech from stalling. This is referred to as giving the helmsman a wider "groove" in which to steer the boat.

MORE ABOUT TWIST AND ANGLE OF ATTACK

Finally, there are twist and angle of attack, both of which relate to power. Regarding angle of attack, the greater the angle relative to the wind direction, the more bend there will be in the flow of air and the more the air on the leeward side will have to speed up to keep pace with the air to windward. This means force on sails. As is the case with draft, however, too much of a good thing can result in excess heel, which is why it is often necessary to ease the sail out in heavy air, even allowing it to backwind if the boat becomes overpowered. No matter what the conditions, creating too great an angle of attack will cause the airflow to detach on the leeward side of the sail, resulting in speed-robbing turbulence.

Twist is much the same, although it concerns the upper part of the sail primarily. Specifically, when the leech is tight—i.e., when there is very little twist—the angle of attack of the upper part of the sail is nearly that of the lower part; when there is a lot of twist the angle of attack falls off appreciably. The same considerations are at work here as in angle of attack; all the more so in terms of heel, because of the tremendous leverage afforded the forces at work near the top of the mast. Note that, no matter what the conditions, you should always have at least a bit of twist in the sail. This is because air speeds are always a little greater as you get higher above the water (because friction between the air and water near the water's surface slows the air down). As outlined in chapter 5, Downwind Legs/ Reaches, an increase in wind speed causes the apparent wind to shift aft. As a result, the upper part of the sail is always working in a bit of a lift. In addition, because of its triangular shape, there is less genoa in front of the main up high; therefore it has less effect on the wind direction than down low. Again, as a general rule, if the upper batten is parallel to the boom when you sight up

from its center, you have the right amount of twist. In the genoa, the sailcloth in the leech near the top of the sail should be parallel to the chord at the bottom of the sail. This can be hard to see, however, so it's generally best to simply make sure the curve of the leech on the genoa is parallel to the curve of the mainsail.

Another important point is that twisting the sail affects the groove in which the sail works best by allowing it to work efficiently over a broader range of headings. For example, imagine you have a sail shaped from top to bottom like an airplane wing. Nice shape, you say, and you would be right as long as you are sailing upwind in 6 knots of wind apparent and in perfectly flat water. Put that boat in waves, however, and things will begin to change immediately. At one point the sail will travel through the air at 6 knots. But a moment later, as the boat rears up to go over a steep wave, the top of the sail will experience 2 knots apparent. Then as the boat lunges over the top of the wave and crashes down into the trough, the top of the sail will travel through the air at 10 knots or more. At those moments when the wind speed is at its highest, the hard wing shape will create an overpowering force that may actually stall the trailing edge. Then, when the boat is traveling up the face of another wave, the sail may stall yet again, this time because it doesn't have enough wind. Add to this dilemma the helmsman's need to steer both high and low of his optimum course to get around the worst of the chop and you have a situation in which the upper portion of the sail is hard pressed to make any kind of significant contribution to the overall race effort.

In these kinds of conditions, putting a little extra twist in the sail in order to allow the leech to fall off a bit provides a much more forgiving trailing edge. Specifically, whether the apparent wind at the masthead is high or low, the air will remain attached. Same goes for when the helmsman has to shinny around an especially steep wave. Think of it this way: trim the sail at the bottom for pointing high and at the top for reaching. The combination will allow the sail to perform well, even if it is not trimmed to perfection. In short, twist allows the sail to work well, even if you are not the best helmsman in the world.

Sail Shape Tips

- Camber, or draft, provides power but can also result in excess heel. A 15 percent draft depth is fairly full for a main, while a 10 percent draft depth is pretty shallow.
- In extremely light conditions the air has trouble making sharp bends. Keep your sails a bit flatter so the air doesn't detach in the belly or along the trailing edge.
- Pulling the draft forward with luff tension can provide extra power in chop; otherwise it should be kept in its designed locations—35 to 40 percent aft in a jib and 45 to 50 percent aft in the main.
- A little twist is necessary because the upper part of the mainsail is always sailing in a bit of a lift. More twist also can help keep the sail working efficiently in choppy conditions by giving you a wider "groove." In general you have the right amount of twist if the upper batten in the mainsail is parallel to the boom, and the leech of the genoa is parallel to the curve of the belly of the main.

A FEW WORDS ABOUT THE JIB AND MAIN TOGETHER

As most sailors know, sailboats go faster and point higher on a beat when they use two sails—a jib and a main—as opposed to one. This is due in part to a phenomenon called upwash, in which the low-pressure region on the leeward side of a sail draws in the surrounding air, deflecting the wind ahead of the sail's leading edge so it is angled toward the leeward side of the boat. As a result, because of the upwash in front of the main, the jib or genoa is continually operating in lift. In addition, because the main is accelerating the air on its leeward side, the air on the leeward side of the jib has to work that much harder to catch up. In other words, it accelerates more than it otherwise would if the sail was on its own, creating more lift. (In less refined circles, this process is described by saying the main "sucks.") On the downside, because the airflow is deflected slightly to windward as it exits the trailing edge of genoa, the main is forever operating in a slight header. But the positive effects on the headsail outweigh these negative effects, so there is a net gain. In terms of trim, it's this interaction between the two sails that allows the main to be trimmed in closer to centerline than the headsail. It's also why in heavy air you always want to ease the main first; easing the jib first will hurt your pointing ability.

The area between the jib and the main is called the slot. It's important because it accelerates the air flowing along the side of the main, enabling both it and the headsail

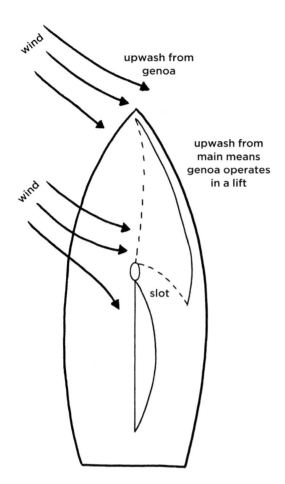

wind

upwash from
genoa

wind

upwash from
main means
genoa operates
in a lift

slot

The jib or genoa and main work together when sailing to windward. Specifically, the upwash, or deflected air drawn around the mast by the low-pressure air on the leeward side of the main, allows the jib to operate in a lift. Furthermore, because the air accelerates as it goes through the slot and along the leeward side of the main, the air on the leeward side of the jib has to accelerate that much more, creating additional lift.

to develop that additional lift. Ideally, the leech curve on the headsail should parallel the curve of the belly of the main so there will be a smooth, even flow through this area. If you've got decent sails the slot will

pretty much take care of itself on the beat. But if you are flying a jib or genoa on a close reach, you should try to get those curves to match up by adjusting the lead. In heavy air, opening up the slot allows more air through, sloughing off power and reducing the heeling force on the rig.

A FEW WORDS ABOUT TELLTALES

We are just about ready to start talking about specific trim settings. But before we do, a bit of advice: if you don't already have telltales on your sails, you should put them on—immediately. Racing without telltales is like playing hockey wearing dull ice skates: you can do it, but not half as well. The telltales on the jib should be set along the leading edge a few inches back from the luff. An additional pair can be installed on the leech, about two-thirds of the way up from the foot. The telltales on the main should be installed along the leech. Some people also put telltales in the body of the mainsail, but they don't do much good there.

Telltales basically show whether the airflow over the sail is smooth or turbulent. When the leeward-side telltales are fluttering on the jib, for example, they tell you the sail is sheeted in too tight or you are sailing too low for your jib trim. As a result the angle of attack is so great the airflow is separating from the leeward side. If the inside telltales are lifting, the airflow is separating on the windward side and you need to either sheet in the sail or steer a lower course. Similarly, if the telltales are streaming aft from the main leech or the leech on the jib,

Telltales on the genoa or jib (left) let the helmsman and trimmers know if their sails are working efficiently. When telltales stream aft there is smooth airflow on both sides of the sail. If the leeward telltales flutter, you are pointing too low or the sail is overtrimmed. If the windward telltales flutter, you are sailing too high or the sail is undertrimmed. A telltale on the shroud gives you an easy reference for apparent wind direction. The mainsail telltales (right) are placed on the end of the battens. The top telltale is the most important. When trimmed properly it will stream out and tuck behind the sail every so often. (RICHARD STEARNS)

you know the air is flowing smoothly off the sail. If, on the other hand, the telltales are getting sucked over to the leeward side, you need to ease the sail out or put some more twist in the leech because the angle of attack is so great the airflow on the leeward side is no longer remaining attached along the entire length of the foil.

Note that in addition to putting telltales on your sails, you might want to tie a piece of yarn on each of your side stays. This little wind direction finder is often the most accurate device on the boat, especially in light conditions. By sailing with the genoa telltales and the side-stay telltales in your line of sight, you have two excellent wind indicators on hand to help you sail your very best.

Also consider having horizontal stripes called camber stripes installed on your sails. With these it's much easier to see both the depth and location of the draft. They should

This offshore racer is carrying camber stripes on both its jib and main to help the crew visualize sail shape.

be evenly spaced along both the jib and the main. The traditionalists in the crowd might not like the look. But then again, the view from the front of the fleet is a hell of a lot better than the one from the back, aesthetics notwithstanding!

Bear in mind when sailing to windward that telltales are a guide, *not* the boss, and that feel and speed take precedence over the telltales if the three seem to be contradictory. Remember, the trimmer is concerned with shape, not just those fluttering pieces of red nylon. If for some reason the telltales are not all working, there may be a whole host of things going on—bad air, tactical maneuvering, or the simple fact that the telltales might be in the wrong position—so make sure you are paying attention to the boat as a whole. Then again, if a trimmer accidentally has the sail in too tight or too loose, blindly keeping the telltales streaming will mean sailing too high or low. Both the trimmer and driver need to concentrate on speed. Who cares what is flying if you are going fast?

PUTTING SAIL CONTROLS INTO ACTION

Finally, it's time to start trimming sails, adding a few comments about boat handling along the way. After that we will finish the chapter by paying a second visit to your keel and rudder.

LIGHT AIR (2–6 knots)

Most sailors hate drifters. But especially as a beginner, it is this kind of sailing that can yield the best results. The old salts in the fleet may feel this kind of racing is below them and may only be half trying.

As noted a little earlier, in drifting conditions, the air tends to be sluggish and reluctant to make sharp turns. Therefore, you'll want to make things as easy as possible for the little breeze you have by keeping your sails flat and the leech open. You also should resist the temptation to pinch, since sailing too high a course will immediately slow you down. This is especially dangerous in light air because the apparent wind you generate once you get moving becomes a crucial part of overall boat speed. Allow yourself to come to a complete stop and you could be a long time in getting that speed back. One time at the Milwaukee Grand Prix regatta the smaller one-design divisions were just ghosting around the leeward mark and getting set up for the next beat when a couple of the leaders from the PHRF 1 division came sliding down, including *SAILING* magazine publisher Bill Schanen's bright red J/145 *Main Street*. With its towering rig and gigantic asymmetrical spinnaker, *Main Street* quickly overran the rest of the boats trying to drift their way around, so they came to a grinding halt. Bill wasn't being a bad guy. In fact, he is one of the true gentlemen of the sport. But given the conditions, *Main Street* definitely put the smaller boats in the area in a pickle, and it took what seemed like the better part of the next leg for some of them to get back up to speed.

In terms of specific settings, in very light air you should use a moderate amount of outhaul and set your jib leads back a notch or two to keep the sails flat. Setting the jib lead aft also will allow the leech to twist open—which is a good thing—and help compensate for the jib's natural tendency to develop a deeper draft whenever it is eased. Take in on the mainsheet until the top batten is parallel to the boom, then use the traveler to position the boom at the centerline, or even a bit higher if you want to induce a little windward helm to give the helmsman some more feel. Note that the traveler may need to be positioned all the way to weather to keep the boom at centerline while easing out the mainsheet to induce the necessary twist.

Draft should be about 45 to 50 percent aft for the main (around 40 percent aft for main-only rigs) and 38 to 45 percent aft in the jib, with a 10 percent depth to the main and a 12 percent depth to the jib. If the upper portions of the main are a bit full, try putting in a bit of mast bend to flatten it. However, remember that doing this will also tighten the forestay, flattening the jib. Use your halyard or cunningham (preferably the latter) to place the draft where it belongs fore and aft. If you have a new sail with some horizontal wrinkles in the luff don't worry. They won't have any negative impact on performance.

Note that crew weight can have a dramatic effect on boat speed in light air, even aboard larger boats. Have some of the crew

A few horizontal wrinkles in the main won't adversely affect performance.

sit to leeward, for example, to induce a bit of heel so gravity will help the sails belly out. This can also give the boat a bit of weather helm, allowing the helmsman a better feel. Avoid movements that rock the boat, since that will cause the air to detach from the sailcloth. As a new wind comes in, have the crew come back in slowly and smoothly, avoiding any sudden movements and making sure the boat is retaining a fast heel angle. You can also try moving the crew forward in light air to help lift the stern out of the water, thereby reducing wetted surface area and the drag associated with it.

This is definitely a time when less is more in terms of the amount of rudder you use: every time you put the wheel or tiller down, you put on the brakes. With this in mind, make sure the entire crew works together on the tacks so you lose as little speed as possible. In these conditions, dipping a

The crew here is sitting to leeward to help induce some heel during a light-air day.

competitor in a crossing situation, as opposed to throwing in an unnecessary tack, makes all the sense in the world.

Finally, when it comes to sails, ugly and old are often fast in light air. New sails will

Light-Air Sailing

- Make it as easy as possible for the air to flow over your sails by keeping them flat and the leech open. Use a moderate amount of outhaul on the main and set your jib leads back a notch or two. Maybe use a little mast bend as well, if the upper sections of the sails are a bit full.
- Resist the temptation to pinch, because you will both slow down and kill whatever apparent wind you have generated.
- Also fight the urge to strap your sails in tight, which will create the illusion of power; keep things loose: "when in doubt, let it out."
- Keep crew movements to a minimum so the boat won't knock about and detach the air from the sails.
- In a drifter, use crew weight to leeward to induce a little heel and help the sails belly out.

often have the draft built too far forward for light air because they are intended to work in heavier conditions. As a sail gets old, however, the draft naturally moves aft, making it perfect for drifters.

MODERATE AIR (8–15 knots)

As the wind comes in, the first things you have to look out for are your leech and draft location. Under the influence of the increased air pressure, the leech will begin to sag to leeward, so you need to take in on the mainsheet and move the jib lead forward a bit. (On many boats you may find yourself moving the jib lead forward in as little as 4 to 5 knots of wind.) Adding some luff tension to both sails will bring the draft back where it belongs, as it will inevitably have blown a little aft. Since bringing the mainsheet in will also bring the boom a little more to windward, you might need to drop the traveler a bit to keep it on centerline. Conversely, you might need to sheet the jib in a little tighter, since moving the lead forward will open up the angle of attack at the luff.

This is the time when you want the sails nice and full so they will provide maximum power. The wind now has enough energy in it to make relatively sharp turns, and you don't have to worry about excessive heel. You especially want your sails to be full if there is any chop; there's nothing like short, sharp waves for slowing you down. In moderate conditions you should make the effort to keep your sail controls nice and loose, always fighting the temptation to strap things in tight, creating the illusion of power: ease the outhaul to power up the main; ease the backstay to keep both sails nice and full up high. Make sure your telltales are streaming, especially off the leech. The idea here is to keep your sails working as efficiently as possible, especially in the lighter part of this range.

As puffs come and go, the trimmers should be watching their sails, making small adjustments to keep the draft and leech where they want them. "Moderate conditions" actually encompass a fairly wide range of wind speeds and pressures on sailcloth. Note we're talking about moving your control lines by inches here, not feet. Does the draft in the main seem to be shifting aft? Then take in the cunningham just a touch. After that wait a few seconds to see what it does to boat speed. Are the mainsail telltales beginning to disappear behind the leech? Crack off the traveler just a hair to get them streaming again.

Crew weight, especially at the top end of this range, is very important: being able to hike out in order to control heel instead of depowering your sails will make you that much faster. If, however, you start developing too much heel in spite of your crew's best efforts, try putting on some backstay in the puffs to twist the leech open. Then if the wind continues to build and becomes steadier, use even more backstay to flatten the sail, trimming in on the mainsheet to keep the top batten parallel to the boom. If your sail has one, you might want to start thinking about taking in on the flattening reef. At this point the top telltale should be al-

ternately flowing and tucking behind the leech.

As always the helmsman should be using as little rudder as possible, letting his trimmers—his main trimmer in particular—know if he has to make any extra effort to stay on course. If the water is fairly calm, this might be the time to try sailing just a hair higher. Ease the genoa halyard or cunningham as you do in order to move the draft back, giving the sail a fine entry and rounding up the leech to pinch more air through the slot. If, on the other hand, there is some chop, it might be best to foot off a few degrees for speed; pull the draft forward with a little luff tension to cup the leading edge and make it a little easier to steer. Cupping the leading edge also helps when driving over the top of another boat to leeward: it will give you the power you need as you foot off a little to put your competitor back in your wind shadow. Of course, no matter what course you choose, always be sure your trimmers know what

Moderate-Air Sailing

- Keep sails full and drawing with plenty of draft; this is when you want maximum power, especially in choppy conditions.
- Keep the boom at centerline and the top batten of the mainsail parallel to the boom; add some luff tension to the jib and main to keep the draft from blowing aft.
- Hike hard to prevent excessive heel at the top end of the range.
- Once again, fight the urge to strap your sails in tight, creating the illusion of power. Keep things loose.

your intentions are so you are all working together.

HEAVY AIR (18–27 knots)

The idea of "heavy air" can be very subjective. What constitutes a lot of air for, say, a performance racer-cruiser such as a Farr 395 may feel like a fresh breeze to the crew of a solid, full-keel boat such as an Alberg 30. In the end, however, no matter what kind of boat you're on, heavy air means a change of priorities from more moderate conditions. Although you want to continue deriving as much power as possible out of the rig, you *don't* want to induce a crippling amount of heel. Hike hard! (While you're at it, encourage your crew to eat plenty of cheeseburgers and fries.) In heavy air the boats in the lead have very little helm and just sail themselves. The back of the fleet has helm and is constantly overpowered.

When heel starts to become a problem, the first thing you should do is begin flattening the sails: trim in on the outhaul, move the jib lead back a couple of notches, and put on some more backstay tension; definitely take in on that flattening reef if you've got one. While you are doing this, use your halyards and/or cunningham to put more luff tension in both the main and jib; the increased wind pressure will have blown the draft aft again. You will also want to trim the mainsheet to keep that top batten parallel to the boom. Check to see if you need to lower the traveler to keep the boom on centerline. Trimming in the mainsheet may have brought the boom too far

to windward. On a boat with a large, overlapping headsail think about changing to a smaller sail. On a jib boat, a boat with small, non-overlapping headsails and a main that provides a hefty share of the driving and heeling power, you may want to change to a flatter headsail made from a heavier material.

As the wind continues to build, start dumping that excess air in earnest, especially on more modern rigs with larger mains. Again, the best way to do this is to drop the main traveler. Don't worry if the main is backwinded by the jib or begins bellying up near the luff. As long as it isn't actually flogging, the air is still attached across the sailplan—all the sails that are flying on a boat's rig—and you aren't losing as much aerodynamic efficiency as you might think. In fact, that bubble in the main is a great way to allow more wind through the slot (see photo next page).

If things have yet to get too hairy, try playing the backstay, quickly hauling it in during the puffs and letting it back off during the lulls. This works especially well on small or midsize boats with large mains, such as Lightnings, Melges 24s, or the ubiquitous J/24. Think of your backstay as your fine tune in heavy air, your traveler as your medium tune, and the mainsheet as the control of last resort. Be aware, however, that although easing the main works to depower the rig on some boats, there are times it can slow you down. This is especially the case with boats with fractional rigs, because the mainsheet plays an important role in keeping the forestay tight (in much the

A Tartan Ten carrying a substantial bubble in its main in heavy conditions. Note how the rudder is still being lifted out of the water because of excessive heel, indicating the crew needs to depower the rig even more.

same way that it influences mast bend). Therefore, when you ease the mainsheet the forestay will sag as well, causing the jib to develop deeper draft. This, of course, is exactly what you don't want to happen in heavy air, so be prepared to compensate with more backstay or a new jib-lead setting.

As things get heavier still, dump yet more power by moving the jib lead even farther aft and/or outboard to put more twist in the leech and open up the slot. If necessary, ease the sheet in the puffs, so the helmsman isn't fighting too hard to keep the boat on course. Then take it back in for the lulls. In these conditions the helmsman and main trimmer in particular should be in constant communication in order to keep the boat under control while maintaining

maximum power. Be careful, however, not to over-flatten your sails, since that can make things hard on the helmsman as well. Imagine a situation in which you have two flat triangles on your mast. If you point even the least bit too high the sail will luff. If you head even a little bit too low, you will stall the sail and heel over. Therefore the sail needs at least a little shape and twist to widen the steering groove. If the main starts to develop a truly serious backwind bubble—with the sail bulging dramatically to windward as a result of the air coming off the jib—consider moving the genoa or jib lead outboard, which will open the slot to relieve the pressure, instead of just flattening sail.

Finally, crew weight in heavy air is absolutely critical, especially if there are waves.

Heavy-Air Sailing

- As heel starts to become a problem, flatten the sails by using the outhaul and backstay, and by moving the jib lead aft. Try playing the backstay in puffy conditions: put it on to depower the rig and let it off in the lulls.
- Drop the traveler to dump power from the main; only let out the mainsheet as a last resort.
- Trimmers and helmsman should be in constant communication in an effort to keep the boat under control while maintaining maximum power in the sails.
- Don't worry if there's a bubble in the main; as long as the sail isn't flogging, the air is still attached.
- Hike hard!

In smooth water you can pinch up, feathering into the wind in the puffs, shedding some of that extra power, and cheating your way to windward in the process. But in a chop, feathering up can result in bashing headlong into a wall of water, stopping your boat in its tracks. For this reason you need all the crew weight you can get on the windward rail so you can keep heel to a minimum while you're keeping as much power as possible in the sails.

BEYOND HEAVY AIR—REEFING

Especially in one-design fleets, whether to reef or not has to be one of the most agonizing decisions in sailboat racing. The wind is whistling in the rigging, waves are breaking over the bow, you're flogging the livin' bejesus out of the main . . . but hey, none of the other guys has reefed yet. Still, putting in a reef—reducing the total sail area by cinching down some of the lower part of the mainsail against the boom—not only means sparing your sailcloth an unnecessary thrashing, it can also mean greater relative speed. A good set of reef points will allow you to reduce sail area and flatten the sail, giving you just the shape you want for heavy conditions. Unfortunately, the exact point at which a reef becomes necessary varies dramatically from boat to boat, although in the beginning especially, discretion is probably the better part of valor. You'll have enough to keep track of with the growing seas and general chaos. Why not make it easy on yourself and take in a tuck? You can always shake the thing out again.

Having said that, be sure to talk to your sailmaker about reefing beforehand if you have a main made out of Kevlar or some other exotic fiber. Because Kevlar sails have threads aligned directly to the clew, taking in a reef also takes the load line off the threads and can ruin the sails. Newer sails are getting better, but be careful.

A QUICK LOOK AT KEELS

At this point we're just about ready to crack off, easing sheets as we round the mark into the next chapter and start talking about sail trim on the downwind legs. But before we do, let's take a final look at your keel. Hidden as it is beneath the water, it's easy to forget that poor fin down there, what with all the tweaking of sails going on topsides.

Still, even the most basic understanding of the way your keel works will make you a better sailor, because you will be able to work your helm and sails with it in mind.

In fact, your keel works very much like a sail: it is built with a similar curved cross section and depends on an angle of attack to provide lift in the direction opposite those forces trying to push your boat downwind. This angle of attack is created because when a sailboat is sailing into the wind or on a reach, it is not actually sailing in a straight line, but slipping sideways a bit. As is the case with your sails, the water on the leeward side of the keel has to travel farther than the water on the other side, so it has to speed up, creating a low-pressure area and lift. Note that in terms of water flow the *leeward* side of the keel is actually the *windward* side of the boat, because the water's angle of attack when striking the keel is a consequence of the boat slipping away from the wind. As a result the lift forces generated by the keel are trying to carry the hull to windward, which—wonder of wonders!—is precisely where you want to go.

It's important to keep this dynamic in mind when you are sailing, especially when going to windward. When you are pinching, for example, you aren't just making life difficult for your sails. By allowing your boat speed to drop away you are also making it impossible for your keel to provide lift, thereby making your bid to defy the laws of physics that much more futile. As stated in the previous chapter, many modern race boats (and performance cruisers as well) are

built with large, deep rudders designed around a highly efficient foil cross section, so they can provide lift as well. Again, if you are sailing this kind of boat, you have all the more reason to keep your helm fairly neutral, since putting the helm down abruptly also means compromising the amount of lift this underwater appendage is able to generate.

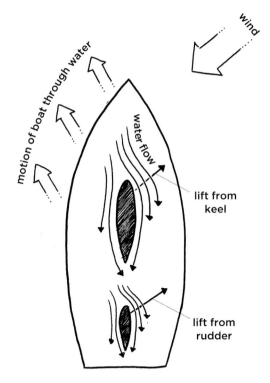

This is a fish's-eye view of how the keel and rudder produce lift. Because a sailboat travels through the water at a slight angle when sailing to windward, the water hits the keel and rudder at an angle. This causes the water on the windward side of the two appendages to travel farther and faster than water on the leeward side, which results in a force to windward: lift.

Q & A

Q. What are the optimum fore and aft draft locations in most sails?
A. The draft should be 35 to 40 percent of the way aft in headsails, and 45 to 50 percent aft in the main. If a boat carries a main with no jib the draft should be 35 to 40 percent aft.

Q. Adam is sailing to windward in 10 knots of wind and a moderate chop. How should he trim his sails?
A. He needs to use some halyard or cunningham tension to pull the draft forward in both the jib and main. He should also ease the mainsheet to increase twist in the main. These two settings will give him a wider groove in which to sail, making it easier to steer without stalling the sails. It's important in these conditions that both sails have plenty of draft to provide power. If the waves are slowing him down appreciably he might also want to consider steering a slightly lower course, footing off for speed.

Q. The wind is building to the point where crew weight alone can no longer keep the boat on its feet. What's the first thing you should do?

A. The first step is to depower the sails by flattening them: with the main this means taking in on the outhaul and backstay; for the jib this means moving the jib lead aft. If the mainsail has a flattening reef this is the time to use it. If the wind continues to build the main trimmer can dump some more power by easing the traveler to leeward. Only ease the mainsheet as a last resort.

Q. Rich is out in a wind so light that the boats in the fleet are barely moving. What kind of draft should he use to make the best of these very light conditions?
A. A shallow draft will work best because light air has trouble making sharp changes in direction. A deep draft can cause the airflow to detach from the sail.

Q. Adam is sailing to windward in moderate to heavy conditions and wants to flatten the upper portion of the main and jib in an effort to reduce heel. How can he most easily do this?
A. He can flatten both sails at the same time by using more backstay tension. This will both bend the mast and straighten the forestay, pulling sail material forward and leaving less material in the middle of the sail for curvature.

BOAT SPEED

Chapter 11

Part 3: Sailing Off the Wind

First, a confession: Originally, this book was supposed to have just one chapter on boat speed, but the more we thought about it, the more it made sense to spend a bit more time than we'd originally planned on this aspect of sailboat racing. If there's one thing more hackneyed than evoking Daniel Bernoulli's name in the context of a sail theory discussion, it's repeating the old adage that "nothing makes you look more like a tactical genius than boat speed." Or something like that . . .

In this chapter we will be looking at sail trim on a reach or run, and spinnaker trim in particular. After that we'll reveal a cruel fact of sailboat racing that may come as a great disappointment to some and an inspiration to others.

SAIL TRIM TO LEEWARD

As is the case with tactics and strategy, boat speed on the downwind legs often doesn't get the respect it deserves. As is the case with racing in light air, however, the rest of the fleet's nonchalance presents the beginner with an opportunity. If the rest of the fleet is relaxing in the sun and drinking beer, that affords you the perfect place to put some boats behind you. Not only that, paying attention to downwind sail trim can also yield big gains when the wind picks up. Good sail trim makes it easier to carry sail in heavier conditions. Therefore, while the rest of the fleet is hanging on for dear life you'll be making knots.

TRIMMING THE MAIN

Because you are no longer trying to sail in the same general direction from which the wind is blowing, trimming the main on a broad reach or run is much less complicated than on a beat. That does not, however, mean you just ease the thing out and forget about it. It's still a foil, as opposed to a bedsheet flapping in the wind.

The first thing to do as you fall off around the windward mark is ease off your various sail controls. Because the boom is no longer trimmed in near centerline and more of the overall force of the sail is being directed forward, heel is no longer as big a problem; you are therefore free to create a much more powerful sail. Ease off your backstay and your outhaul to increase the draft of the sail. While you're at it, ease the cunningham or lower the halyard, since the draft is no longer being blown aft as it was on the beat. This adjustment is also necessary because, with the backstay eased and the mast straighter, the distance between the head of the sail and the tack just got a little longer. Not only that, if your halyard is at all stretchy it will now tend to pull up on the head of the sail because the mainsheet is no longer exerting the same downward force that it was when the boom was near centerline.

As the main is eased out beyond the range of the traveler, take in on the vang to control twist. The mainsheet can now be used as an extension of the traveler to control the angle of attack. If you start to heel too much, ease the mainsheet to dump that excess air loading up the helm. When trimming the main on a close or beam reach, the top telltale on the leech is the one to watch. It should alternately stream then tuck behind the main. While this is going on the other telltales should be flying as well. Also look for a bubble in the front of the main and regulate it in heavy air by trimming the main or easing the genoa.

As you fall off farther to a broad reach or a run, the sail is less able to act like a foil, and the name of the game is to project as much surface area as possible. If necessary, push the boom out so it is perpendicular to the apparent wind direction. You can even have someone lean against the boom to keep it there if the wind won't do this on its own. On many boats you can try shifting crew weight to induce some windward heel, getting the sail to project a little higher off the water, where it will catch a little more air.

In heavy air downwind, the vang plays an important role in controlling heel and stability. If you have the vang on hard, the sail will pull the boat to leeward. If you ease the vang, the boom will lift and the boat will want to roll to weather (see illustration next page). Letting the boat roll to weather is very fast in medium to heavy air, but it can also be dangerous because it can easily lead to a windward broach. If the boat heels too far to weather you can pitchpole, digging the spinnaker pole in the water, which either spins the boat into a wild jibe or breaks the mast.

In the end, sailing on a run ain't the

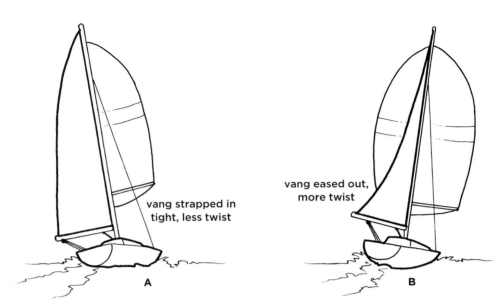

*Twist in the main when sailing downwind controls heel and stability. With the vang on hard, the boat heels to leeward (**A**). With the vang eased, the boom lifts, the main is twisted, and the boat wants to roll to weather (**B**).*

most sophisticated thing in the world. But then again, unless it's blowing stink, you shouldn't be sailing dead downwind anyway, remember? And if it is blowing stink, you'll have a hell of a lot more to keep you busy than fiddling with the cunningham!

TRIMMING JIBS

In many ways, trimming a jib on a beam reach or off the wind is a lot like trimming the main. Everything needs to be loosened up so you get a nice full draft around 35 to 40 percent aft of the headstay. Of paramount importance is controlling the amount of twist in the leech. This means moving the jib lead forward, where it will exert a downward force on the trailing edge of the sail, instead of just letting it twist away at will. In terms

of adjusting the angle of attack for a genoa or jib on a broad reach, the best thing to do is work it as you would a spinnaker. Ease the sail until it shows a bit of a bubble in the luff, and then trim that bubble out. Don't ease and trim as much as you do when playing a spinnaker, but don't just leave it cleated either. Luff telltales can be problematic on a broad reach, because they are usually too far forward for all the camber you get on this angle of sail. You could try sticking on a few "reaching" telltales. But depending on your exact angle of sail only a few of them will ever really work at any given time anyway. So it's best to play the bubble.

Unfortunately, a good upwind genoa generally does not make a very good reaching sail because the upper leech is too open, falling off to leeward as you ease the sail. In

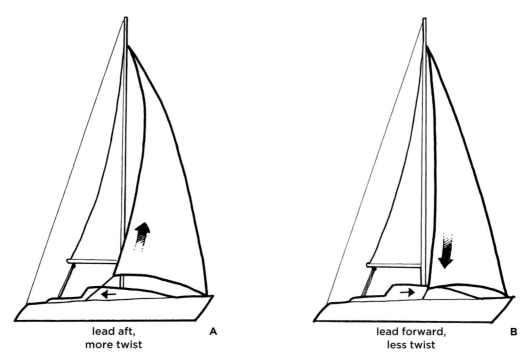

*Control twist in the jib by moving the jib lead forward. Having the lead aft allows the clew to rise (**A**). Having the lead forward (**B**) exerts downward force on the clew and leech, reducing the amount of twist.*

fact, an old blown-out headsail is sometimes faster on a reach than a new one, since it has more belly in the middle. Whether your genoa is new or old, adjust the lead so the center of the sail looks good. This will probably give you a sail that is a bit too full, with the leech cupped in at the bottom and too open at the head. But unless you have a specialty reacher, you will have to live with a compromise.

Beyond that, try to get the slot between the main and the genoa as even as you can so the leeches are roughly parallel. Reaching headsails are built with high clews that naturally blow away from the boat and therefore keep the slot open, but with a con-

ventional all-purpose sail you'll have to do the best you can. On a close reach or a beam reach you can try rigging up a type of jib-lead fine tune called a barberhauler to help open up the slot at the bottom of the sail. To do this, bend a third sheet to the clew of the headsail and then run it through a snatch block shackled to the toerail. Take up on this new sheet and ease out on the original one. The new outboard sheet will take up the strain, effectively giving you a whole new lead. You can then use these two leads in concert to fine-tune the jib lead even farther, moving it inboard and outboard at will. Sometimes a slight pull outboard of just a half inch can make a big difference.

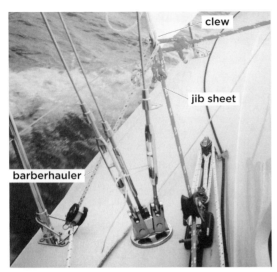

Looking forward, the dark line is the jib sheet and the white line is the barberhauler. The clew of the jib can just be seen at the top of the photo. Easing out the sheet and taking in on the barberhauler will move the jib lead outboard, opening up the slot. (RICHARD STEARNS)

Off-Wind Jib Trim

- Since telltales are not very effective off the wind, trim the genoa much like you would a spinnaker, easing the sheet until the sail shows a bit of a bubble in the luff, and then bringing the sail back in.
- Move the genoa lead forward to keep the leech from twisting off to leeward; try to get the slot as even as you can so the leech on the genoa is parallel to the belly of the main.
- Trim the genoa so the center of the sail looks good, even if that means the upper leech is too open and the lower leech is curled in.
- On a close reach try rigging up a barberhauler to get the jib lead outboard, opening up the slot.
- Be careful not to overtrim the main in the event it is back-winded by the lower part of the genoa—it's better to ease the headsail.

Unfortunately, even with a barberhauler there's no way—on a monohull at least—that you can get the lead far enough outboard to trim the sail properly on a broad reach, so you will constantly be trimming to compromise. In fact, you would have to have a lead well outboard of the deck if you were to position the lead correctly. Because a general-purpose headsail will usually be overtrimmed along the bottom, it will often backwind the main. So you need to be careful not to overtrim the main in an effort to open up the slot: overtrimming will result in *neither* sail being trimmed correctly. Remember, the main is a great reaching sail, but overtrimming it can result in excess heel. In the end, sailing off the wind with an upwind jib or genoa will always mean having to compromise. However, knowing the nature of the problem will help you experiment with trim and find out which compromise is the best.

SPINNAKERS

When most beginning racers think of spinnakers, they think about all the things that can go wrong instead of how to make things go right. This much-maligned headsail, however, is just as sensitive to shape controls as the other sails in your inventory. Treat it right, and it will be more than happy to give you a bit of a boost in boat speed. This goes for both symmetrical spinnakers and asymmetrical spinnakers.

SYMMETRICAL SPINNAKERS

Ultimately, symmetrical spinnaker trim is all about balancing the sail—in other words, carrying the sail so it is flying symmetrically, as designed. As the first step in this process, hoist your spinnaker as high as it will go. That's right, as *high* as it will go, despite what all those other guys in the fleet might say. The only time you might not want it at full hoist is on a fractional boat on a tight reach, in which case allowing the head to float a foot or so away from the mast will also get it away from the main. Otherwise, hoist it all the way. Once the sail is up, square the pole to the wind; i.e., set the pole so it's perpendicular to the apparent wind, and trim the sheet until the sail begins to fill. Then, once the sail is flying, come aft with the pole just a touch to direct the force of the sail as far forward as possible, continually playing the sheet as you do so by trimming it in and out to keep the luff just curling. Many sailors leave the pole square to the wind, but that is not far enough aft. If it were then on a tight reach with the wind forward of abeam, the proper place for the pole would be to leeward of the forestay, which is obviously not the case. You can tell if the pole is too far aft because the sail will be hard to trim and will break or curl low on the luff. It will also cause the sail to fly at a crooked angle off to leeward. As a final step, adjust the pole so the tack is level with the clew of the sail. When you do this, remember to adjust the inboard end of the pole as well, so it will be perpendicular to the mast. You want to keep the tack of the spinnaker as far out as possible so it will get plenty of clear air.

At this point your spinnaker will be trimmed to about 85 percent efficiency. In fact, by using just these simple rules of thumb you will already have a sail that is pulling well and allowing you to keep pace with the better part of most fleets. As is the case with your working sails, however, there are a number of sail controls at your disposal with which to fine-tune that basic shape for even better speed. The goal here, in addition to maintaining that balance, is to shape the sail so the wind moves across its surface smoothly and evenly. To accomplish this you can adjust both the pole position and sheet lead. These adjustments will yield the following results (see illustration next page):

1. Pole up—Makes the head of the sail flatter
2. Pole down—Gives the head more camber
3. Pole aft—Flattens the bottom of the sail
4. Pole forward—Gives the bottom of the sail more camber
5. Sheet lead forward—Curls in or rounds the trailing edge of the sail; also makes the head fuller
6. Sheet lead aft—Flattens the trailing edge of the sail and flattens the head

When playing the sheet, the curl should start just below the seam where the head joins the rest of the sail. From there it should reach up about two-thirds of the way to the head. In other words, it should stretch from

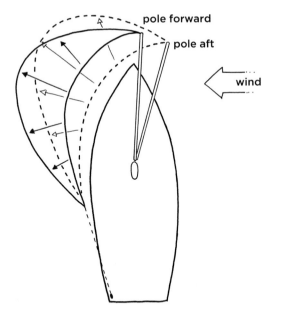

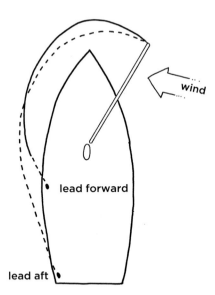

Moving the pole aft flattens the sail and directs the force more forward. (Change in sail shape indicated with dashed lines.)

Moving the sheet lead aft flattens both the trailing edge and the head of the sail. (Change in sail shape indicated with dashed lines.)

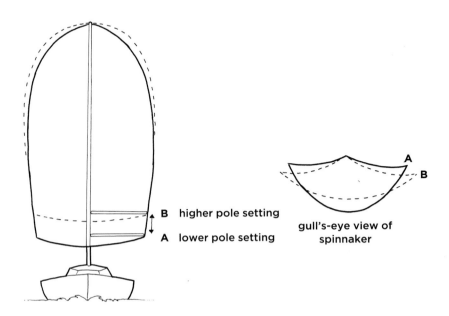

B higher pole setting

A lower pole setting

gull's-eye view of spinnaker

*The height of the pole affects the amount of draft up near the head. With the pole down, the leeches are tight and the head full (**A**). With the pole up, the leeches are eased and the head is flatter (**B**).*

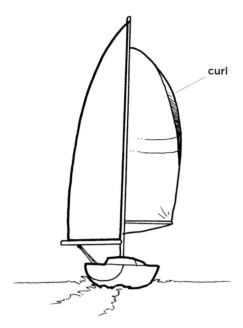

curl

When trimming the spinnaker, the curl should be between 45 and 80 percent of the way up the sail. If it's higher, raise the pole to flatten the head.

about 45 percent of the way up the sail to about 80 percent of the way up. If the sail curls higher than this, the head is too full and you should raise the pole to flatten it. As noted earlier, if the sail is curling low and down near the clew, you can ease the pole forward.

When sailing on a beam reach or a close reach, make sure to keep the sheet lead well aft; this allows the wind to flow off the trailing edge, much as it does off the leech of the main or jib. The reason for this is that when carrying the spinnaker at a higher angle of sail, it has an attached flow much like that on your working sails. Cupping in the trailing edge of the sail will produce turbulence and drag.

Along these same lines, always be sure

to keep the pole off the headstay. In addition to moving the center of effort forward, this flattens out the foot of the sail by stretching it out. In terms of pole height, you have the choice of carrying it high or low, depending on the conditions and the exact angle of sail. When carrying the spinnaker at higher angles of sail with the apparent wind forward of abeam, a high pole flattens the head of the sail and, combined with the pole off the forestay, results in the entire sail being as flat as you can get it. This is good for pointing. Be aware, however, that setting the pole too high lets the center of effort fall aft in the head, which can make the sail prone to stalling (much as it did with the draft well aft in the main). It can also cause excessive heel. To remedy this problem, drop the pole to a low position. This will tighten the luff and pull the draft forward. The boat won't point quite as high, but it will cut down on the amount of heel because the forces generated are directed in a more forward direction. In fact, in this position the sail acts more like an asymmetrical spinnaker or even a genoa. Note that in those heavy-air situations in which you are concerned about being overpowered (excessive heel is just as bad on a reach as a beat), always be sure to keep someone close to the vang and the mainsheet. That way if the helm starts to load up in a puff you can ease them both off, the helmsman can steer a slightly lower course, and the spinnaker trimmer can ease his sheet until the puff goes away.

When sailing on a broad reach or a run in heavy air, the sheet lead should be well forward, so use a twing to bring the line down to deck level up near amidships. (A twing is either a hook installed on deck or a piece of line with a block on the end through which you run the sheet to pull it down near the toerail.) There are two reasons for this. First, making the head fuller by using a forward sheet lead helps support the sail; i.e., keeps it from collapsing. Second, by firming up the leech, you help prevent the sail from rolling back and forth if there is any kind of a sea. Also, the pole should be kept low to further help create a full sail and keep it from rolling. As the wind gets even heavier on a run, ease the pole forward. This will give the sail even more fullness (stability) and hide more of it behind the main.

When steering in heavy air, always try to anticipate what will happen; once you feel the helm beginning to load up, the crew must be ready to act quickly if you are to avoid a broach. The danger of having to use excess helm to keep the boat on course is that, at some point, the rudder will start to cavitate, or stall, catching more and more air on its leeward side until you have lost all steering. When that happens there is nothing you can do to stop the boat from rounding up. To avoid this situation, always have a crewmember keep an eye out for puffs in heavy air. And when a puff hits, immediately steer a lower course while the crew

Looking aft, the twing has been eased so that the spinnaker sheet lead is as far aft as possible. (The spinnaker is not visible.) Trimming in the twing would bring the spinnaker sheet forward to a point near the snatch block attached to the stanchion base at the very bottom of the photo. (RICHARD STEARNS)

Spinnaker Trim

- Hoist the sail all the way; the only time you might want to let the spinnaker float out a foot or so from the mast is when you're aboard a fractionally rigged boat on a tight reach.

- Set the pole so it is slightly aft of perpendicular to the apparent wind; on a close reach keep the pole off the forestay whenever possible.

- On a close or beam reach keep the sheet lead aft in order to flatten the trailing edge of the sail; on a broad reach or run move the sheet lead forward to help support the sail and prevent it from rolling back and forth.

- Raise the pole a bit on a close reach to flatten the head and help with pointing; if heel becomes a problem, lower the pole to move the draft forward.

- Off the wind, lower the pole to help support the sail with plenty of camber in the head; a low pole setting also helps keep the sail from rolling; in heavy air, if the spinnaker is becoming difficult to control, ease the pole forward a bit so it will be partially blanketed by the main.

On the edge: The sails are beginning to overwhelm the helm on this performance keelboat. Note how the helmsman is trying to steer down to a lower course, but the rudder is already beginning to lift out of the water, rendering it useless.

eases off the spinnaker sheet and main. Again, you can ease the pole forward just a touch to blanket it behind the main. But whatever you do, don't ease the guy out dramatically or let it run. That will just cause the sail to fly out away from the mast. If you feel the cavitation getting out of control, try giving the helm a few fairly violent tugs. By steering down hard, then relaxing the pressure, you can reattach the flow. Jerk it again and again, each time easing off to let the flow reattach for just a second. Alas, if this fails and you still wipe out, you have no choice but to ease the sheets and let the sails luff until the boat gets back on its feet. Once it does, steer low, but *don't* immediately trim in. Remember, you are starting again from a complete stop, so the apparent wind is now much higher than when you were underway. This in turn means the loads on the rig will be that much more extreme. If you trim sails and try to sail back up to your original course before gaining speed, chances are all you will do is wipe out again.

ASYMMETRICAL SPINNAKERS

Because they use a fixed bowsprit as opposed to a spinnaker pole off the mast, asymmetrical spinnakers are generally much simpler to fly. In fact, all you are really left with is the lead position and luff tension, much as was the case with the genoa.

As a first rule of thumb, be aware that an asymmetrical can sail with a much larger luff curl and still not collapse, so be careful not to overtrim the sail. In terms of luff tension, the luff length of the sail is quite a bit longer than the straight line between the hoist and the end of the bowsprit, so in general, and especially on a close reach, you will want to sail with the spinnaker fully hoisted and the tack all the way to the pole. As you sail more downwind, the sail will want to pull itself out in front of the boat. At this point you can ease the tack line so the sail will come around the bow that much more. Downwind, the tack line should extend either straight up and down or slightly to weather. If it falls off a little, but the sail is still pulling forward, you should be okay. Otherwise, if it sags off dramatically to leeward, the forces in the sail have shifted too far aft and you need to pull the tack back out to the end of the bowsprit. Very seldom do you have to actually move the sheet lead, since the boom automatically does that for you by pushing down on the line as it is eased out. Note that rolling is generally not a problem with asymmetrical spinnakers. With symmetrical spinnakers rolling starts to become a problem as the pole is brought aft for a broad reach or run. But since an asymmetrical spinnaker's tack is always run to a fixed bowsprit in the bow, this is less of an issue.

A QUICK DOWNWIND TRIMMING GUIDE

Phew! This chapter has been packed with a lot of information in a fairly small space. Some readers might even be experiencing that very confusion we set out to avoid. The following is a quick survey of broad recommendations for boat trim off the wind. They are hardly all inclusive, but will serve as a good starting point for those new to the subject.

Tight Reach. Falling off 10 degrees or so from a beat, the first thing to do is ease the jib sheet and let the traveler down on the main. Don't ease the mainsheet; that will allow the leech to open up, spilling off air. Check the jib lead. It probably needs to move forward to tighten the leech. If it's not blowing too hard, ease off the backstay to power up the main by giving it a deeper draft. Easing the backstay will also put some sag in the forestay, making the genoa fuller and more powerful as well.

Close Reach. Falling off another 10 degrees, be sure to put the vang on; by this time you will have run out of traveler (unless you are on a multihull) and will have to ease the main with the sheet. As is the case when sailing upwind, keep the top batten parallel to the boom. Ease the outhaul and cunningham to keep the sail full and prevent the draft from going too far forward. Heeling is even less of a problem on this angle of sail, so you want lots of power. Maybe ease the backstay some more and/or begin to barberhaul the genoa outboard. Deflecting the lead as little as one inch can make a big difference in speed. At this point in heavy air, you may find that the genoa is blowing a bubble into the mainsail. Now it's decision time. Do you trim the main, let the genoa out, or barberhaul some more? Usually barberhauling will be your first choice, followed by some ease on the genoa. Letting it luff a bit—just a bubble—is faster than overtrimming the main while keeping the genoa full. Of course, if it is blowing hard don't forget to hike.

As you continue falling off, with the true wind around 70 degrees or more off the bow, your apparent wind will still be fairly far forward, but the forces on the rig will be starting to taper off. Keep using those same adjustments to maintain a nice full sail shape with the draft in the proper location. By this time the genoa telltales are no longer working correctly; they are too far forward, so ease the sail until you see a bubble and then trim it out. The lead will be forward and outboard as far as you can get it. In heavier air especially, keep the rig balanced so you won't have to use a lot of rudder to keep the boat on course, killing speed. Work the sails to make things easy on the helmsman. You may even have to

sail with bubbles in them. Remember, until the main actually shakes in a luff, you still have attached flow on the sails.

Beam Reach. Your heading now has you sailing with the true wind at 90 degrees. That will put the apparent wind anywhere from 85 to 70 degrees off the bow, depending on the wind velocity and the speed of your boat. Now is the time to put up that spinnaker, although in heavy air the apparent wind may still be too far forward. Keep the pole high to flatten the head of the sail and give you a good leading edge. Keep the sheet lead aft to flatten the leech.

Turning downwind another 10 degrees you definitely need the spinnaker, since the apparent wind is now shifting aft to where it is coming from abeam. To pull the center of effort forward and flatten the sail, keep the pole off the headstay. Don't neglect the main while you are doing this. Ease off the backstay, cunningham, and outhaul so it will be nice and full. If you are in heavy air, keep some outhaul on to slough off a little power and cut down on the amount of heel. Use the sheet to ease out the main, keeping the top telltale flying as much as possible. Control the leech with the vang, and hike if it is windy.

Falling off another 10 or 20 degrees puts the boat at the optimum angle for speed and comfort. Keep working the pole aft to expose more of the sail to the wind in front of the main. Lower the pole to put more draft in the head to support the sail. Put some twing on to take the sheet lead forward, cup the head of the sail further, and help prevent the sail from rolling. Have someone push the boom out if there isn't enough wind to do so.

Broad Reach/Run. With the apparent wind coming from 130 to 170 degrees off the bow, you have to just feel the boat and keep it going. The trimmer and the helmsman should be talking to each other about pressure, speed, and heading. If the clew of the spinnaker drops and the boat loses its edge, head up a little to get it going again. Don't deadhead, especially into the leeward mark. Always sail your angles unless there is an overwhelming tactical reason not to.

AND NOW . . . FOR THE "DISAPPOINTMENT"

Many readers look to sail-trim discussions like this one for some kind of "secret trick," a magic bullet that will solve all their boat speed problems once and for all and send them vaulting to the front of the fleet. Unfortunately, beyond nailing down a basic understanding of how sails work and how they can be manipulated, there's only one real way to sail fast—practice: take your boat out on the water and see how it performs in various conditions and after you make various adjustments. In some cases, you may be able to obtain impressive-looking polar diagrams for your boat, especially if it's a recent design. But don't forget: those

are just target speeds, a guide. You still have to get out on the water to figure out how to make your boat go, just like those poor America's Cup crews or Olympic hopefuls who are out on the water day in and day out, trying to pick up a fraction of a knot here and there.

As is the case when you're looking at the weather, a good way to hone your boat-speed skills is to get yourself a notebook to keep track of your boat's performance under various conditions and at different points of sail. Chances are you aren't half the masochist your average professional sailor is. But the good news is that boat speed, like sailboat racing in general, is a process and doesn't have to be done all at once. Figure out a little bit here and a little bit there. Every time on the water doesn't have to be a hard-core practice session. But, by the same token, what harm does it do to tweak your sails a little and jot down a few notes while you're out cruising? You can do the same after each race, scribbling down your thoughts along with the speeds you were able to achieve in different kinds of winds. Did the boat feel like it was moving well at a certain point in the second beat? Great! Write down what you were doing at the time, so it will be that much easier to repeat in the future.

As you get more comfortable with your boat's sails, try marking your halyards and sheets so you will be able to put them exactly where you want them for a given wind speed and angle of sail. (However, remember that sheets and especially halyards will stretch a little over time.) There's nothing

Finding More Speed Under Sail

Ultimately, finding more speed and getting to know your boat is largely a matter of trial and error. True, you can set your sails so that they look right. But to get that last fraction of a knot of boat speed, you need to experiment with different settings and shapes and see how they pan out in terms of performance. Even if you are just out on a daysail, try playing around with things like luff, outhaul, and leech tension, sighting up at the sail from the center of the boom to see what the sail looks like after each adjustment. Does one setting in particular seem to give you a boost in boat speed in certain conditions? Make a note of it so you will remember what you did the next time you're out in similar conditions. Does another setting slow you down or result in excessive weather helm? Make a note of that as well. As you become increasingly comfortable with your settings, try marking your control lines with a felt-tip pen so you can return to that setting with greater ease.

One thing to bear in mind whenever you are playing around with sail shape, whether out practicing or in the heat of competition: it takes even the nimblest of sailboats a few seconds to speed up or slow down, so the results of your new settings will take a few moments to show themselves. Don't just trim, say, the outhaul, and then expect your boat to surge ahead. Make a mental note of how fast you are going, trim in the line, and then watch your knotmeter (or pay attention to how the boat is moving through the water if you don't have one) to see what happens. Is there a slight increase after 10 or 15 seconds? Great! You're moving in the right direction. Take a look at the sail to see how deep the draft is and make a note where you've got the outhaul. Then see about adjusting something else.

Unfortunately, given the vagaries of wind and water, it can be tough figuring out when a change in speed is due to a change in the wind, your sail trim, your steering, or just a couple of sharp waves. But paying attention to your boat will give you a better and better feel for what's going on. Again, there's no substitute for time out on the water when it comes to boat handling. Books such as this can only go so far. You've got to go sailing to be a better sailor. And more often than not, in the heat of competition it's the better sailor who wins.

like being able to call for a specific setting, knowing it will get you the performance you want. Of course, you should also work on different sail trim configurations whenever you are out with the crew on a practice session. Try moving the draft back and forth to see how it affects boat speed and pointing ability. Do the same with the leech and chord depth. Let everybody take a turn at everybody else's job, especially the helm. If you're usually the driver, spend some time up on the foredeck and study your sails. What does it do to boat speed if you ease them out just a touch? How about moving the jib lead? If the main trimmer is at the tiller or wheel, try cranking in on the mainsheet to give him a taste of that weather helm you keep complaining about. There's nothing like standing in the other guy's shoes for a while to realize that maybe you aren't the only one working hard on board! One of the nice things about playing around with these settings on a day off is you can figure out what *not* to do without losing boatlengths to the competition. Take your time. Whenever you change one of your sail controls, give the boat a chance to settle in. Remember, even the speediest little racer takes a few seconds to speed up and slow down.

Finally, when you're out on the racecourse, never stop thinking about what you can do to make your sails perform at their very best. And always be alert to even the slightest changes in the conditions.

One time during the 285-mile Port Huron to Mackinac Island race, for example, the Santa Cruz 70 *Pied Piper* found itself rounding the northern turning mark with no air, with another Santa Cruz 70 named *Stripes* a mere fifty yards away. Contrary to conventional wisdom, the *Pied Piper* crew dropped its light No. 1 genoa and hoisted its "wind seeker," a much smaller sail with a wire in the luff that allows you to set it without bending it to the forestay. Next thing the crew knew, the boat started to move. Five minutes later *Pied Piper* was going 1.5 knots and the crew was sliding up the No. 1 and taking the drifter down. However, the boat stopped, so they hoisted the little drifter again and slowly took off. This time they kept it up until *Pied Piper* was going 2 knots. But once again, when they slid up the No. 1, the boat ground to a halt. Basically, the air was too light to attach around the larger sail; without attached flow there was no lift. The smaller sail, on the other hand, *could* keep the flow attached; *Pied Piper* was able to get moving and, because it's a light and narrow boat, she could develop some apparent wind. So off they went.

Seeing a small gray patch on the water to starboard, the crew worked its way through the early morning fishermen toward what it hoped was wind. Sure enough, that's what it was. *Pied Piper* started to slip away from *Stripes*, which was now five hundred yards away, looking for pressure in another small patch, or "cat's paw," of wind off in the distance. This time *Pied Pier* hit 3 knots, and when the crew hoisted the genoa it began to draw, due in part to the material from which it was made: a very lightweight Kevlar. In the beginning the crew sailed low for speed and kept the halyard loose so there were wrinkles in the luff; and as the wind began to pick up the crew, much to its delight, saw that *Stripes* was not in it. Now they could grind in on the halyard to get the wrinkles out and bring the draft forward for more drive. The sail was also starting to look a little full, so they moved the lead aft to flatten it. Soon the big boat was creating so much apparent wind it was time to change to the medium-weight No. 1, which the crew trimmed in so it was nice and flat for pointing ability in the gentle seas. If it had been light and choppy, they might have had to ease the backstay to induce a bit of sag in the forestay for more draft, but with the wind building they actually had to take in on the backstay to straighten it. This in turn started to bend the mast, flattening the main more than the crew wanted, so they cranked in on the running backstays to straighten it out. Eventually, with the wind continuing to build, they had to tighten the genoa halyard to pull the draft forward and move the lead aft again to flatten the sail some more. With so much activity going on no one had kept track of the competition. By the time someone thought to look, *Stripes* was nowhere to be seen.

Meanwhile, the wind kept building until it was time for another sail change. Instead of going with the heavy No. 1, however, the crew elected to go straight to the smaller No. 3. Again, the Santa Cruz 70 is a light and narrow boat, and by this time the rail was in the water. Not only that, the big genoa was forcing so much wind through the slot that the main was luffing wildly, even with the headsail eased. Once the No. 3 was up, however, the boat settled right down. The crew had a full main and the jib trimmed in hard as she powered directly toward Spectacle Reef. There was not one boat in sight anywhere on the horizon.

Eventually the crew had to go with a No. 4, and then a thin blade of a No. 5 headsail with the backstay on as hard as it would go and the running backstays straining to keep the mast from bending too much, putting overbend wrinkles in the main. Later, with the finish in sight, every boat the crew thought was in the race turned out to be a daysailer. Then, shortly after they crossed the finish line the wind shut down. When *Pied Piper* powered into the harbor there were no other boats. The crew went to the bar, and still no other boats. At 11:00 p.m. they braved the bats at the east end of Mackinac Island to look for boats, and still nothing. After that things got a bit foggy as a rum front came through, but still no boats. In fact, it was about twelve hours before the next boat crossed the finish line. None of the other boats in the fleet had experienced any wind that had required anything more than a light No. 1.

The lessons here are good ones: 1) Never stop thinking about your sail trim, and 2) it's the little things that can make big things happen in the end.

Q & A

Q. Why is a good upwind genoa less than ideal for sailing on a reach or run?
A. Because the leech is too open, which means it will just fall off to leeward as the sail is eased.

Q. How does the vang affect trim when sailing downwind in heavy air?
A. Using the vang to reduce the amount of twist in the main will cause the boat to heel to leeward. Easing the vang and putting twist in the sail will make the boat heel to windward.

Q. Rich is sailing on a beam reach with the spinnaker flying in heavy air when the boat starts to develop some strong weather helm as it heels with a puff. What should Rich do to avoid rounding up into a broach?
A. He should ease the mainsheet and vang, and ease the spinnaker sheet at the same time he steers about 10 degrees lower than normal. If he gets into real trouble and the rudder starts to cavitate, he can try jerking the helm a few times to reattach the flow.

Q. Adam is carrying a symmetrical spinnaker on as high an angle of sail as he can in light-to-moderate conditions. How should he trim the sail?
A. He needs to lead the sheet from as far aft as possible. This will give him a flat leech,

allowing the air to flow off the sail with very little turbulence. He can also carry the pole a bit higher. This will flatten the head of the sail, which is good for pointing. Finally, he should keep the pole off the headstay. This will flatten the foot of the sail.

Q. A little later Adam falls off onto a broad reach. What changes should he make in his spinnaker settings?

A. He could move the sheet lead forward by using a twing. This will put more draft in the head of the sail, helping to support it, and keep the sail from rolling if there are waves. He should also lower the pole, since that also puts more draft in the head.

Chapter 12

GETTING INVOLVED

Despite its reputation for exclusivity, getting involved in sailboat racing is one of the easiest things in the world. In contrast to the old days when your name had to be Vanderbilt or Lipton to be considered a "yachtsman," today there are hundreds of clubs, community sailing centers, sailing schools, and class associations that would like nothing more than to get you out there on the water with them. To tell the truth, it was never that hard to find some good sailboat racing if you wanted. It was just that, like today, it was the "big guys" who got all the press.

KINDS OF RACING

In some ways, the hardest part of sailboat racing is deciding which kind you want to do. All those boats sailing back and forth on the horizon may look the same to a landsman, but they are in fact radically different in terms of design and the way they figure out who is number one. Since the dawn of sailboat racing, yacht clubs and rule makers have struggled to ensure that different boats and different designs are as evenly matched as possible. The result has been a plethora of different design and rating techniques over the years, as the guys in the blue blazers struggle to keep up with the technological advances taking place both in boatyards and on the water.

One-Design Racing. Of course, the most obvious way to ensure that everyone is evenly matched is to require that everyone sail exactly the same boat, which is the basic premise of "one-design" racing. In fact, there are many who feel that this "pure" kind of racing is the only true way to determine the

POPULAR ONE-DESIGN BOATS

Name	Sailplan	No. of Crew	Comments	Similar Boats
Sunfish	single sail	1	good training boat, good racing	El Toro, Sailfish, Optimist
Laser	single sail	1	higher performance, worldwide racing	Megabyte, Force 5, Contender, Europe
Coronado 15	sloop, no spinnaker	2 trapeze	popular husband-wife boat	Sweet 16, Holder 14, Buccaneer,
JY 15	sloop, no spinnaker	2	no trapeze, tight one-design control	Vanguard 15, M 16, Lido 14, Snipe
505	sloop spinnaker	2 trapeze	high-performance dinghy	470, 420, M 20, Fireball
Flying Scot	sloop spinnaker	3	family oriented, large organization	Highlander, Ideal 18
Lightning	sloop spinnaker	3	planing hull, strong racing class	Y-Flyer, Thistle
Scows	varies	varies	16–38 feet, strong class organization	E-scows, A-scows, MC-scows,
Star	sloop, no spinnaker	2	complex, Olympic class	
Soling	sloop spinnaker	3	keelboat, former Olympic class	Etchells 22, Dragon, Yngling, Shields
J/24	sloop spinnaker	4 or 5	keelboat, with cabintrunk	Ensign, Sonar, S-2 7.9, Cal 25
J/105	sloop, asymmetrical spinnaker	4 to 6	high-performance keelboat	Melges 24
Tartan Ten	sloop spinnaker	5–7	larger keelboat	Mumm 30, One Design 35, Farr 40

best sailor on any given day. Today one-design boats come in all shapes and sizes, including everything from Optimist and El Toro dinghies to gaff-rigged Beetle Cat catboats to insanely fast catamarans and cutting-edge 49er sloops. Over the years, the world of one-design racing has resulted in the creation of such fine boats as the Lightning, the J/24, the Tartan Ten, the Santana 20, the Flying Scot, the C-scow, the Soling, the 470, the Ensign, and the Star—just to name a few. Many modern cruising designs, such as the legendary Catalina 30, the J/105, or the Farr 395, have also been designed with one-design racing in mind. Nearly every one of the world's top sailors cut their teeth on one-design sailing. And while you might not read about it in the sailing magazines, every one of those "rock star" racers continues to compete at the one-design level, both to keep themselves sharp and for the pure love of the sport. Dennis Conner, for example, isn't just Mr. America's Cup. He's also an Etchells champion. Paul Cayard, winner of the 1997–98 Whitbread Race aboard *EF Language,* is still active in the Star class.

Rating or Development Classes. Rating or development class racing is similar, but slightly different from one-design racing. These classes include those that have taken part in the America's Cup over the years, such as the 12-meter class, the International America's Cup Class, and the spectacular J class boats of the 1930s. As is the case with one-design racing, everybody starts at the same time and the first boat over the finish line wins. But in contrast to one-design racing, the boats are not identical. Instead, they are designed and built within the parameters of a design formula that is based on various measurements, including things such as waterline length, beam, displacement, and sail area to create boats that are similar, while still allowing room for innovation. A 12-meter sailboat, for instance, is not 12 meters long. In fact, over the years they have ranged in length from about 19 to 21 meters (about 60 to 70 feet) depending on the design. The number 12 simply refers to the required result when you plug a boat's various dimensions into the old International measurement rule, created in Europe around 1910. The same goes for 6-meters and 8-meters and the various "letter" boats of yesteryear, including the J boats, which were based on the parameters of the Universal Rule, devised by Nathanael Herreshoff around 1900.

A further variation of this idea can be found in various open classes, including the Moth class, Europe's extravagant Open 60 class, and the class of famous 18-foot skiffs of Sydney, Australia. The difference here is that the design rule is kept fairly wide open in a deliberate attempt to foster radical innovation. For years, for example, the main requirement of the Sydney 18 was that it be no more than 18 feet long. Everything from beam to sail area to the number of crew was up to the designer.

Of course, the problem with these various classes is they leave no room for anybody with a boat that is different from their own. Want to try your hand at racing your trusty old Tartan 30? Sorry, you've got to buy the same boat as everybody else in the fleet if you want to compete.

HANDICAPPING RULES

It is with this goal of making it possible for different kinds of boats to race against one another that various handicapping rules have been created over the years, including the venerable Cruising Club of America (CCA) rules, PHRF, MORC, the much-maligned IOR, the fast-fading IMS, and the new Americap II system in the United States. In every case, the rules adjust the finish time for each boat in a race based on a numerical rating and either the total time of the race (time-on-time correction) or the length of the race (time-on-distance correction). The actual rating can be based on the dimensions of the boat, as is the case with the IOR, IMS, and CCA rules; or on a subjective evaluation of a boat's speed by local race committees, as is the case with PHRF. The end goal, however, is the same: to ensure that the larger, faster boats in the fleet

POPULAR PHRF BOATS AND THEIR RATINGS

Boat Mfr. and Length (ft.)	PHRF Rating	Characteristics
Catalina 22	270	family cruising boat
Santana 23	172	smaller racing boat, light weight
Hunter 25	231	family cruising boat
Cal 25	223	family cruising boat
Colgate 26	168	daysailer/trainer
S2 9.1	135	performance cruiser/racer
Olson 30	105	narrow, light racing boat, fixed keel, also strong one-design
C&C 29	176	family cruising boat
Catalina 30	180	family cruising boat, occasional one-design racer
J/30	138	performance cruiser/one-design racer
C&C 99	102	performance cruiser/racer
Hobie 33	93	racer
Schock 35	72	racer
Beneteau First 36.7	75	performance cruiser/one-design racer
Farr 395	30	performance cruiser/one-design racer

don't have an unfair advantage over the smaller, slower ones.

The most popular handicapping system in use in America today is PHRF (Performance Handicap Racing Fleet). Based on an "administered handicapping system," as opposed to a strict measurement-based system, it is sometimes controversial because various rules committees subjectively decide on the rating. Still it works, and works well, in thousands of sailboat races across the country. Since ratings are determined locally, they vary for many boats depending on geographic location. If you ever decide the rating numbers are not correct, feel free to volunteer to be on the committee. The members will appreciate the help and you will meet some very knowledgeable, well-intentioned sailors.

Understanding how PHRF ratings work is relatively simple. Let's say, for example, that a C&C 29 with a PHRF rating of 176 is competing against a Pearson 26 with a rating of 210 over a race that is 6.5 miles long. The race is being scored using a time-on-distance correction system. To adjust the C&C 29's finish time you first derive its "time allowance," or TA, for the race: multiply the boat's rating by the distance of the race, and then divide by 60. This yields a TA of 19.07 minutes. This amount is then subtracted from the boat's finishing time. Plugging the Pearson 26's rating into the same formula results in a TA of 22.76. Therefore, since the Pearson gets to take off about three minutes more from its actual finish time, the C&C needs to beat its slower competitor by three minutes if it is to come out

ahead on corrected time. Clearly, big numbers are better when it comes to a PHRF rating because they mean you have that much more time to make your way around the course.

Another way to think about PHRF ratings when calculated as a factor of distance is to say that the boat with the lower rating has to "give" a slower boat the same number of seconds per mile that separates its rating from that of its slower competitors. In the above example, the C&C has to give the Pearson 34 seconds, or beat the Pearson by an additional 34 seconds, for every mile of distance. In some longer races this can yield some interesting results. In the 600-mile Millennium Mackinac race from Port Huron, Michigan, to Chicago, Illinois, the race was won by a 1965 Cal 40 with a brand-new 80-footer coming in second, even though the 80-footer beat the Cal to the finish line by 36 hours. Still, despite some occasional controversy, the PHRF system works and makes thousands of sailors happy all around the United States.

What follows is a sampling of the other different rating rules that have been used over the years. Some of them have been long since relegated to the dustbin of history. But it's still fun to know what people are talking about, either in esoteric sailing articles or when some crusty old sailor is discussing past glories at the yacht club bar.

Thames Measurement Rule—Based on the same principles that were used to measure the tonnage volume of large commercial sailing ships, this rule, which was established in England in the mid-1800s, resulted in the creation of some of the world's first "sailing freaks," or "rule beaters": boats designed to receive a favorable rating and seaworthiness be damned. Specifically, it was found that extremely deep, narrow boats with tremendous amounts of ballast in their keels and absurdly large rigs could receive "gift" ratings. Alas, some of these boats had a disturbing tendency to sink in heavy air.

Seawanhaka Rule—Developed in 1882 by America's Seawanhaka Yacht Club, this measurement-based rule incorporated both length and sail area in its ratings to discourage the construction of overcanvassed rule beaters on this side of the Atlantic. One of these boats, the top-heavy 150-foot centerboard schooner *Mohawk,* actually capsized while at anchor in New York harbor,

killing five people, including its owner. In recent years some traditional boat enthusiasts have decried the existence of modern racing boats, suggesting they are inherently dangerous and that such "unseaworthy" vessels would never have been built back in the "good old days." Alas, they have no idea what they are talking about.

CCA—Established by the Cruising Club of America in the 1930s, this system was displaced by the IOR system, but accommodated and resulted in the creation of some beautiful and seaworthy offshore boats in its day. These included the Cal 40 and many of the old Concordias. Like the Bermuda Rule from which it was derived, it gave a bonus to yawls, which is why many older offshore boats carry these rigs. Although traditional in appearance, many

Getting a PHRF Rating

To obtain a PHRF (Performance Handicap Rating Fleet) rating for your boat, first contact the fleet organization that assigns the handicaps for your area. Because the rule is locally administered, a rating from one area might not be the same as the rating for another. You can obtain the contact information for the dozens of PHRF fleets around the country from US Sailing (or the fleet captain at your yacht club). If yours is a standard production boat without any modifications, you may simply be assigned the standard handicap for that design after your boat has been duly measured and inspected to ensure that it is the same as the other boats of its type. Otherwise, if yours is a new design for a fleet or your standard production boat has been significantly changed over time—for example, with modifications to the keel or rudder—a new rating must be assigned by the committee or board of handicappers, often with input from the chief handi-

capper of the fleet. In order to assign a rating to a new or custom design, the chief handicapper and committee will compare the boat to similar boats already registered with the fleet. They may then add or subtract from the rating depending on differences in keel shape, rig, or displacement. They may also consider things such as materials used, the designer's reputation, and the age of the design.

Once a boat has been assigned a rating, that rating is subject to review in light of the boat's performance on the water. The goal is to make things as fair as possible. If one boat, for example, is suddenly running away with all the silver week after week, there must be something wrong. Keep in mind that the skill of the crew has no bearing on a boat's rating, the idea being that the boat needs to be sailed to its highest possible performance in order to succeed against the competition.

of these boats are actually rule beaters!

IOR—The International Offshore Rule, first implemented in the 1970s, was an admirable attempt at a truly "objective" numerical rating system. Unfortunately, it resulted in countless rule beaters with bumps and wrinkles in their hulls designed to "fool" the rule by creating artificially high or low measurements. It also favored boats with wide beams and pinched ends that were custom-designed to broach downwind. The failure of a number of IOR-based designs during the tragic 1979 Fastnet Race sounded the death knell for the rule.

IMS—The International Measurement System is the much vaunted replacement for the IOR. It has resulted in the creation of many beautiful and seaworthy racing boats. Unfortunately, because it's based on a sophisticated and expensive velocity prediction program and computerized handicapping system, it has fallen out of favor as being too darn much of a hassle for most sailors.

Americap II—A kinder and gentler (read less expensive and complicated) version of the IMS system. The jury is still out on the degree to which this will catch on.

MORC—The Midget Ocean Racing Club method is another measurement-based rating system for boats under thirty feet in length. Although very popular in the 1970s and early 1980s, it has been largely displaced by PHRF.

Note that these different kinds of racing are not mutually exclusive. For example, the Catalina 30 is successfully raced all around the United States under the PHRF rule, but there are also many regattas featuring one-design racing for the boat, including annual regional and national championships. Often the question of whether to race one-design or under some handicapping system is a matter of geography. On San Francisco Bay, for example, there is a thriving Folkboat fleet offering plenty of one-design opportunities. Elsewhere yours might be the only Folkboat for miles around, and you'll have little choice but to race against different kinds of designs.

If you already own a boat, it's only natural that you will want to see how it stacks up against the competition. And, thanks to handicapping systems, chances are there's some kind of venue whereby you can do that. Just about any boat that is twenty feet or more in length can get a piece of the action. If, on the other hand, you own an obscure little dinghy design, don't despair: there just might be a class association out there organizing some regional or national championship regattas in your area. The beamy little Beetle Cat, for example, would hardly be the first thing that comes to mind when you think of one-design racing. And yet there are active fleets on the East Coast mixing it up around the buoys throughout the summer.

Even if you own a big tubby cruiser or some obscure centerboard design that is unique to the world, do not be without hope; same goes if you live in an area where sailing is a bit scarce, say in Montana or Kentucky. If there's a decent-size body of water, you can bet there's a group of sailors trying to one-up each other at least a few times a year, and chances are you can get into the mix. Finally, if you are not yet an experienced sailor, there's always the possibility of crewing on somebody else's boat until you feel ready to campaign your own.

FINDING A FLEET

If you already have a boat and are a member of a yacht club, your problems may already be solved. It's a rare club that has a decent number of sailing members and doesn't have some kind of racing program. Find out who the fleet captain is, call him or her on the phone (or better still, buy him a drink the next time you see him at the bar), and you'll be on your way.

If, on the other hand, you keep your boat at a municipal marina or on a trailer in your driveway, you might have to do a bit more digging. Still, it shouldn't be too difficult. In fact, there are all kinds of people and organizations out there on both the local and national level who would like nothing more than to bring you into the sport.

National Level. On the national level, one of the best places to start is by calling US Sailing, the national governing body for the sport in the United States. In addition to helping set the rules for the sport and organizing the country's Olympic sailing team, its Council of Sailing Organizations helps coordinate sailing and racing programs na-

tionwide. By certifying different one-design classes it also serves as a clearinghouse for contact information on those organizations.

Let's say you own a Snipe dinghy. All you have to do is call US Sailing or go on its Web site and you'll be able to find not only the contact information for the fleet captain, but also the class Web site address. Or let's say you own a small Ericson racer-cruiser and are interested in finding a PHRF fleet in, say, Idaho. Giving US Sailing a call or visiting its Web site will provide you with the necessary information to contact organizations such as the Sailing Association of Intermountain Lakes, which covers Colorado, Montana, and—that's right—Idaho. Got the same problem in those hotbeds of sailboat racing known to the world in general as Kentucky and Tennessee? Never fear; there's always the Dixie Inland Yacht Racing Association to help you out.

Note that in addition to yacht clubs, one-design fleets, and regional sailing associations, US Sailing also provides information on sailing schools and community sailing programs. The latter can be an easy way to get into racing, especially if you don't have your own boat. Groups such as Boston's Community Boating Inc., Chicago's Lake Forest Sailing, the Milwaukee Community Sailing Center, or San Francisco's Treasure Island Sailing Center all have active racing programs in everything from El Toros to J/24s. In many cases, they will be more than happy to let sailors compete aboard their own boats to help build up the fleet.

Of course, in this age of the computer,

another quick way to find out what's happening in your area is to surf the Internet. Class associations exist even for boats that have been long out of production, and they are all looking to both grow their membership and bring in as many participants to their organized events as possible. Interested in possibly doing some one-design racing aboard your Hunter 28? The Hunter 28 Class Association will be happy to help. Many class associations also publish regular newsletters that not only list upcoming events, but also include articles on everything from boat maintenance to sail trim. You may find your sailing changing appreciably before you even cross the starting line.

Local Level. Locally, the best thing may be to let your fingers do the walking. Find the phone numbers for any local yacht clubs, marinas, sailing schools, community sailing programs, sail lofts, or marine supply stores in the area and tap them for information. Which of the area yacht clubs, sailing programs, or schools have active racing programs? What regattas in the area are open to all comers? Can you speak to the race director? Is there a bulletin board with posted race results to show you what kinds of boats are competing? Does that same bulletin board have "crew wanted" or "crew available" listings? Is one of the employees at your local West Marine or BoatUS a big racer? Can you chat with him or her for a few minutes? Take a while to stroll around your local marina or yacht club. Do you see a half dozen Rhodes 19s lined up on one of the piers or some Flying Scots on their trailers near the boat crane? That should tell you something. Go out to the waterfront after work on a Wednesday, and if there's any kind of racing action it should be immediately apparent.

True, you might have to be a bit of a detective. But then again, if you have your own boat and are familiar with sailing, you probably already have some idea as to what's out there. If you come across somebody who is less than receptive, don't take it personally. Remember, sailors have jobs and are busy just like everybody else. You may have caught him or her on a bad day. Rest assured, it's a rare sailor who doesn't want as many boats on the starting line as possible, since that makes the racing that much more interesting.

Joining a Crew. If you don't have your own boat, but are an experienced sailor, a quick and easy way onto the racecourse may be by crewing for somebody else. In fact, this might not be a bad idea even if you do have your own boat and want to get a taste of what it's like out there, without risking your own gelcoat. Go to one of those bulletin boards mentioned above and see what's listed, maybe put up a flier of your own describing your sailing experience and the fact that you're looking for a berth. Skippers are forever in search of good, reliable crew. Prove yourself on one boat, get to know some of the other sailors in the fleet, and you might find them calling you instead of the other way around.

YACHT CLUBS: SHOULD YOU JOIN?

You may already be a member of a yacht club with a racing program, in which case the question of joining a club is irrelevant. If, however, you aren't a member, don't worry. There are plenty of opportunities for sailors without insignias on their blazers. True, you may be barred from some opportunities, but you should still have ample opportunity to get out on the water.

For one thing, although the *owner* of the boat in a race might need to be a member, there are rarely such requirements for the crew. Even if you are a boatowner and want to race your own vessel, there are still opportunities out there. You probably won't be able to enter your boat into a club's regular Wednesday night summer series. But many regattas—both those organized for smaller one-designs and those that include larger handicap classes—are open to all comers. For example, in order to compete in any of the National Offshore One-Design (NOOD) regattas organized by *Sailing World* magazine and held around the country, all you have to do is be a member of US Sailing, which has a fairly reasonable fee given all the organization does. The same goes for most regional and national one-design regattas and for many local regattas. Throughout the Midwest, for example, there are dozens of small regattas held on lakes large and small for scows, Thistles, Lightnings, and Flying Scots, for which a class associa-

tion membership is required, but not a membership to a yacht club. Not only that, but in some cases you might be able to sneak your way into some club fleets if you play your cards right. If there are few small one-design boats at a club that hold informal practice races, for example, races that don't require the services of a formal race committee, they might be willing to let you join if you have the same kind of boat and you ask nicely. They're looking for practice, after all, so the more sparring partners the better.

Keep in mind that, if there is one membership that is pretty much universally required for racing your own boat, it's a US Sailing membership. But again, this only ap-

Joining US Sailing

Any skipper interested in racing his boat would be well advised to join US Sailing, the national governing body of the sport in the United States, as authorized by the U.S. Congress. Adult membership costs $50. A junior membership costs $20. The benefits of membership in US Sailing include eligibility for major regattas such as the National Offshore One-Design (NOOD) series, a subscription to the US Sailing newsletter, and discounts on everything from life rafts to US Sailing hats and shirts. More importantly, you are helping an organization that does a tremendous amount for the sport, including promoting the sport's various handicapping rules; certifying one-design classes; selecting and preparing the Olympic sailing team; training certified sailing instructors; developing curriculums for sailing schools around the country; researching various safety issues of concern to sailors; and helping with the Safety at Sea seminars that are held around the country to promote smart sailing on the water.

plies to boat owners. In fact, around the year 2000 US Sailing tried to require that all crew be members of the organization in order to compete. But there was such an outcry the proposal was quickly withdrawn.

Finally, if you've tried your hand at a few races and find you like it, why not look into joining a club? It's true that becoming a member of, say, the New York Yacht Club with its historic Manhattan clubhouse can be a pretty pricey, not to mention exclusive, proposition. But for every snooty blue-blood affair by the waterside there are dozens of down-to-earth organizations made up of ordinary people looking to have a good time, with reasonable fees and some damn good sailing. Not only that, membership can have some pretty neat privileges, such as being able to tie up your boat and use other clubs' facilities if you go cruising someplace else in the country. And while the food can be spotty on occasion, it's a rare club that doesn't have a heck of a good view of the water.

BUYING A BOAT

Let's say you've been crewing OPBs (other people's boats) for a while and are tired of that other guy getting to drive all the time. Then again, maybe you love your sturdy old Westsail 32 more than words can say, but there's just no denying that it's not exactly the best thing for racing in a light-air region such as San Diego, California. Maybe it's time to consider buying another boat for the sole purpose of racing.

Expense. As is the case with racing in general, buying a boat can be much less expensive than you might think. True, you can follow in the footsteps of Oracle founder Larry Ellison and have famed New Zealand designer Bruce Farr whip up a little 78-foot something for you. But there are also plenty of reasonably priced used boats out there, especially smaller one-designs and pocket cruiser-racers, that can get you on the racecourse without breaking the bank. Decent used Thistles, for example, can be had for as little as $1,000 if you look around a little, and it would be harder to find a nicer bunch of folks to race against. Same goes for Lightnings, although a decent one will set you back a little bit more, maybe $2,000. In both cases you will probably need to expend a little more cash and elbow grease in order to bring your new purchase up to racing trim. But hey, that's part of the fun, and there's no better way to really get to know your boat. Interested in something a little bigger, maybe a keelboat? How about looking into a used Santana 20, an Ensign, J/24, Soling, or Catalina 22? In fact, the list of great little boats out there goes on and on: MC-scows, 470s, Interlakes, Highlanders, X-boats, Fireballs, Flying Juniors, 110s. And let's not forget Lasers, Hobie Cats, or the ubiquitous Sunfish.

Class Association. When looking into buying a boat for racing—and this goes for whether you want to buy a used one-design or a brand-new carbon fiber grand prix racer—check out the class association and talk to a few of its members before writing any checks. How many races are held in your area each year? How far will you have to drive or sail in order to reach them? How big are the fleets? Are used boats available within your price range? Are used boats still reasonably competitive, or will you feel like you are trying to race with a bucket attached to your stern? And what about the boats themselves? Are you talking about an easy, comfortable boat to sail, such as a Harbor 20, or a touchy little planing dinghy, such as a 470, which is not only easy to capsize, but an incredibly cramped and athletic boat to manage, even in light air. Be honest with yourself. There's no denying that the 49er is a sexy racing machine. But is it *really* the boat for your middle-aged back?

Get to Know the Fleet. Finally, try to get to know some of the people. Are these the kinds of folks you want to spend time with back on shore? Half the fun of sailboat racing is hanging out with the other sailors before and after the actual racing, so it only makes sense to get to know them a bit before joining. Ask the local fleet captain if you can meet him after a day's racing at an upcoming regatta. Tell him you're thinking of buying a boat and joining the fleet. He'll most likely bend over backward to make you feel welcome, introducing you to some of the other sailors, and telling you all you need to know about the boat, maybe even giving you some insight into where you can find a good deal. If he or she isn't very friendly and nobody else seems particularly interested in talking to you either, that should tell you something.

Also, be sure to figure out what kind of expense you're thinking about getting yourself into and the nature of the fleet. Are there just a handful of regulars? Are they all buying new suits of sails with each new season? Are you ready to match these expenditures or possibly find yourself spending a lot of time at the back of the fleet? There's no shame in recognizing that you might be out of your league among a certain group, or that this particular approach to the game might be too rich for your blood. If a particular type of sailboat looks to be a little expensive for your tastes, don't hesitate to look around some more. One of the great things about sailboat racing is it's just as much fun racing in a closely matched bunch of cruisers as it is taming an overcanvassed sled in the company of millionaires. In fact, it can even be more fun. You think the Kiwis had an especially good time getting skunked in the 2003 America's Cup? Doubtful. In fact, it's often the old faithfuls, the classes that keep generation after generation of sailors happy, that elicit the most passionate loyalties. Try telling an Ensign sailor that his comfy 23-footer doesn't offer some of the best sailing around, and you'll get an earful to the contrary. In fact, you're liable to get an earful not only from him, but from every Ensign sailor within earshot. And you know what? They're right!

Q & A

Q. What is the difference between a one-design class and boats built to a design or rating rule?

A. In a one-design class the competing boats are identical. Boats built to a rating are similar because they must meet certain design parameters, but there is room for variation and innovation.

Q. A J/36 with a rating of 102 is competing against a Baltic 39 with a rating of 128. The race begins at noon, is 11 miles long, and will be scored using time-on-distance correction. The J/36 crosses the finish line at 2:58 p.m. and 55 seconds. The Baltic crosses at 3:03 p.m. and 30 seconds. Which boat is the winner?
A. To derive the time allowances for the two boats, multiply their ratings by the length of the race in miles, and then divide by 60. Using this formula, the TA for the J/36 is 18.7 minutes, or 18 minutes, 42 seconds. The TA for the Baltic is 23.5 minutes, or 23 minutes, 30 seconds. To obtain the two boats' corrected times simply subtract the TAs from their finish times. The corrected time for the J/36 is 2 hours, 40 minutes, and 13 seconds. The corrected time for the Baltic is 2 hours, 40 minutes, and zero seconds. The Baltic wins by the skin of its teeth.

Q. What is the major difference between PHRF and the Americap II handicapping system?
A. In PHRF, each boat's rating is determined subjectively by a rating committee. The Americap II system uses a boat's dimensions to determine its rating.

EPILOGUE
SOME FINAL WORDS FROM YOUR LONG-WINDED AUTHORS

Hopefully by this time you have a pretty good idea of what goes on during a sailboat race—at least in theory. Now it's time to get out on the water and see how things work for real. Before you do, however, here is one last piece of advice: have fun. Despite the fact that they are among the most beautiful things created by man, sailboats have an incredible ability to make some people absolutely miserable. Maybe it's because even the best of 'em still go pretty ridiculously slow if you stop and think about it. Then again it might be because even the most exotic, carbon-fiber racing machine depends on something as fickle as the breeze to actually get anywhere. (Then again it might just be that *damn* winch that keeps sticking you in the back!) Whatever it is, sailboats can turn the nicest people into incredible ogres, which is too bad.

Remember, even on those days when absolutely everyone except you seems to be getting the shifts, you are *lucky* to be out there sailing. You are truly *privileged* to be out beyond the dust and the clutter of the land, out where for some crazy, mysterious reason life seems to take on a whole new meaning, if you can just relax a little and let it happen. The vast majority of people in this world will never be able to share what you're experiencing at that very moment. To them sailboats and sailboat racing are as inaccessible as the moon, a collection of pretty white sails drifting by on the horizon, a whole different world. What you are doing is, for other people, literally a dream.

This is not to deny that sailboats and sailboat racing can be incredibly frustrating. There are few things in life as aggravating as watching one of your competitors slowly sailing away—and there seems to be nothing you can do to stop it. Still, don't let that cause you to lose perspective. Win or lose, always take a few moments to stop and look around, to appreciate how fantastic it is to be surrounded by a bunch of sailboats, to be out on the water, to be taking part in the great, centuries-old tradition that is sailboats and sailing. Try your hardest, give it your best shot, but remember: this is something that is *good* for you, good for the soul, no matter what place you finish at the end of the day. Did you screw up that beat? Did you go left when you just knew you should have gone right? Did you finish DFL (we'll let you figure that one out) just when you thought you were getting the hang of things? Fine. Regroup, figure out what went wrong, and fix it. It's all part of the process. It's all part of what makes the sport so rewarding.

Whatever you do, don't *ever* let sailing ruin your day. Life is too short. The simple fact that you're getting to play the game is pretty cool. Never lose sight of the fact that you're out on the water . . . that you're aboard a *sailboat* fer cryin' out loud, surrounded by the water and sky . . . that in that moment, no matter what else might be happening in the world, it's good to be alive.

Appendix

RESOURCES

Recommended Reading

Carr, Michael. *International Marine's Weather Predicting Simplified: How to Read Weather Charts and Satellite Images.* Camden, ME: International Marine, 1999.

Elvström, Paul. *Paul Elvström Explains the Racing Rules of Sailing, 2001–2004.* Camden, ME: International Marine, 2001.

Fox, Uffa. *According to Uffa: Handling Sailing Boats.* New York: St. Martin's, 1961.

Hancock, Brian. *Maximum Sail Power: The Complete Guide to Sails, Sail Technology and Performance.* Norwich, VT: Nomad Press, 2003.

Killing, Steve, and Douglas Hunter. *Yacht Design Explained: A Sailor's Guide to the Principles and Practice of Design.* New York: Norton, 1998.

Knox-Johnston, Robin. *Yachting: The History of a Passion.* New York: Hearst Marine Books, 1990.

Marchaj, C. A. *Sail Performance: Techniques to Maximize Sail Power.* Rev. ed. Camden, ME: International Marine, 2003.

Rousmaniere, John. *The Golden Pastime: A New History of Yachting.* New York: Norton, 1986.

Watts, Alan. *Instant Wind Forecasting.* Dobbs Ferry, NY: Sheridan House, 2002.

————. *The Weather Handbook.* 2nd ed. Dobbs Ferry, NY: Sheridan House, 1999.

Willis, Bryan. *2001–2004: The Rules in Practice.* East Sussex, UK: Fernhurst Books, 2001.

Weather Information Sources

Web Sites

Intellicast: www.intellicast.com. This site offers a number of sailing-specific pages, including wind forecast maps and planning pages for marine activities.

National Oceanic and Atmospheric Administration (NOAA) and the National Weather Service: www.nws.noaa.gov. This is an especially good site to go to for true weather maps showing wind directions and barometric pressures. Click on the buttons that will bring you information for your particular area.

The Weather Channel: www.weather.com. This site features marine-specific pages, local forecasts, and color weather maps.

Other Useful Web Sites

International Sailing Federation: The governing body for the sport of sailboat racing around the world, the ISAF is responsible for drafting the rules of the sport and organizing or sanctioning races and regattas around the world, including the Olympic Sailing Regatta.

Southampton, UK
44-23-80-635111
www.sailing.org

US Sailing: The national governing body
for the sport of sailboat racing in the
United States, US Sailing is involved in
certifying one-design classes, and organizing handicapping rules and sail
training.
401-683-0800
www.ussailing.org

GLOSSARY

Americap II—A recently developed handicapping system that uses a computer velocity prediction program to assign ratings to different racing boats; similar to IMS, but easier to use.

Apparent wind—The wind you experience aboard a moving boat, as opposed to the true wind you experience when sitting still.

Atomic clock—A precision clock whose operation depends on the natural vibration frequencies of an atomic system; used by some race committees to time the starts and finishes of races.

Attached flow—Air flowing with minimum turbulence across both sides of a sail so that, aerodynamically, the air and sail interact efficiently to create lift.

Back—Describes a counterclockwise shift in wind direction.

Backwind bubble—The effect created by easing a sail so the leading edge is blown slightly to windward without flogging. Can occur in heavy-air conditions on a beat or close reach.

Bad air—The turbulent or disturbed air that exists to leeward of a boat under sail; sometimes referred to as a wind shadow.

Barberhauler—A temporary jib sheet that moves the jib lead outboard when sailing on a reach; used to open up the slot.

Barging—An attempt by a boat to squeeze across the starting line immediately to leeward of the committee boat, while another boat to leeward is positioned to force it to sail high of the committee boat, thus forcing the first boat to circle around in order to start. A boat can also be caught barging in the middle of the starting line by reaching along the line when there are other boats in a position to take it up and over the line early.

Bear-away set—A spinnaker set executed at the windward mark whereby the crew hoists the sail as the boat simply falls off from a close-hauled heading to a reach or run.

Beat—To sail to windward on a close-hauled heading; the leg of a race that goes directly to windward.

Bend—Fore and aft curvature induced in the mast.

Blanket—To sail to windward of a competitor so he is adversely affected by your bad air.

Blow a halyard—To simply let a halyard run free when dousing a sail.

Boom vang—Primarily used to control leech tension on a reach or run; occasionally used when sailing to windward.

Broach—A situation in which the sails—often the spinnaker—overpower the boat, causing it to heel excessively so the helmsman can no longer control the boat's heading with the rudder.

Camber—The horizontal curvature of a sail as viewed between the luff and the leech.

Camber stripes—Horizontal bands of contrasting material attached to the sail to make it easier to see its camber.

Cavitate—When turbulence develops in the water flowing over the rudder, making the rudder less effective or useless; can result from moving the rudder far off centerline in an effort to correct course in rough conditions.

Center of effort—The point representing the combined effort of the sails to drive the hull of a sailboat through the water.

Center of lateral resistance—The point representing the combined effort of the hull, keel, and rudder to resist the sails' effort to drive the hull to leeward.

Chord—The imaginary line running directly from the luff to the leech of the sail.

Chord depth—The distance from the chord to the point of deepest draft in the sail.

Chord length—The length of the imaginary line running directly from the luff to the leech of the sail.

Class—A group of boats racing against one another in the same race; also called a section.

Class flag—A flag that designates when a particular class is due to race; usually indicates five minutes until the start; is taken down the moment the race starts.

Clew—The lower, aft corner of a sail.

Coming up from below—Establishing a position to leeward of another boat by sailing on a higher course from a point even farther to leeward (in contrast to establishing a position to leeward by sailing up on a parallel from directly astern).

Committee boat—Boat aboard which the race committee administers the race; also designates the starboard end of the start and finish lines.

Coriolis Effect/Force—The phenomenon whereby air movements follow a curved pattern as a result of the Earth's rotation.

Corner—The extreme right or left side of a beat or run; the point at which a boat would tack if it were to sail the entire beat in just two tacks.

Cover—*see* Blanket; also, to position your boat relative to a competitor so he cannot sail past you without being affected by your bad air.

Crack off—To ease sheets and sail a lower heading relative to wind direction.

Crash boat—Small motorboat used to arrange the drop-in buoys on the racecourse.

Crash tack—A sudden, unplanned, inefficient tack; often done to avoid a collision.

Cunningham—Used to control luff tension.

Deadhead run—Steering a direct course for the leeward mark or finish, as opposed to sailing a less direct (but generally faster) course using higher, hotter jibing angles.

Development class—A class made up of boats that are not identical, but similar since they adhere to a single rating formula or design rule.

Dip—To sail a course slightly below close-hauled to avoid a starboard-tack competitor in a crossing situation. Can occur when sailing to windward on port tack.

Dive—Making a dramatic course change to leeward, either to pass another boat on a reach or run or to escape from another boat's bad air on a beat.

Double rights—At the leeward mark or a jibe mark, an inside boat that is also on starboard and to leeward has double rights and is thus able to execute a tactical rounding.

Draft—The curvature of a sail as determined by a combination of the sail's original construction, the way it is flying on the rig, and the way it is trimmed.

Drifter—Especially light winds during which a sailboat cannot maintain steerage.

Drop-in buoy—A portable inflatable buoy used to designate a turn on a racecourse or the end of a start or finish line.

Ease—To let out a sail.

End run—During a leeward mark rounding, sailing a longer, wider course outside the other boats clustered around the mark.

Fall off—To steer down to a lower heading relative to the wind direction.

Favored end—The end of the starting line that is closest to the windward mark; the end of the finish line that is closest to you.

Feather—To temporarily sail a course higher than normal when close-hauled to gain distance to windward.

Flat sail—A sail with shallow draft.

Flattening reef—A device used to reduce the amount of draft in the lower part of the mainsail.

Fleet—A group of boats racing together, either in a single class or multiple classes.

Flier—A strategy whereby a boat follows a dramatically different course from the rest of the fleet in the hope of catching an advantageous shift or puff and thus making big gains; often considered a desperate strategy.

Flog—To ease a sail when close-hauled or on a close reach until the sail flaps in the wind.

Foot—Bottom edge of a sail.

Foot off—To sail a course a little farther off the wind than close-hauled in an effort to gain speed, avoid a competitor in a crossing situation, or escape an area of bad air on a beat.

Forestay sag—The curvature of the forestay to leeward under the pressure of the sail; can be controlled to influence sail shape.

Fractional rig—A rig in which the forestay does not run to the very top of the mast.

Front—The boundary between regions of high- and low-pressure air; often an area of dramatic weather.

Full sail—A sail with deep draft.

Gassing—When one boat causes another boat to sail in its bad air.

Gate—A configuration in which a pair of marks is used to designate the leeward end of the racecourse. Boats can round whichever mark they choose after sailing between the two marks.

Genoa—A jib that is large enough to overlap the mast.

Ghosting—Sailing very slowly in calm or near-calm conditions.

Ghosting conditions—Very light air, almost dead calm weather, in which sailboats can barely maintain steerage.

Hail—To signal another boat verbally, with or without a radio.

Harden up—To steer from a reach to a close reach or a beat, trimming in sails as you do so.

Head—Top corner of a sail.

Header—A windshift after which the wind comes from an angle closer to the bow.

Higher course—On a beat, the course that takes a boat more directly to the windward mark; on a run or reach, the course that causes a boat to sail at a closer angle to the wind.

Hot angle of sail—On a reach or run, a higher angle of sail that allows a boat to sail faster than on a lower course, due to the effects of apparent wind.

IMS (International Measurement System)—A handicapping system that uses a computer velocity prediction program to assign ratings to different racing boats.

Inside overlap—In a mark-rounding situation, this occurs when the boat closest to the mark has an overlap with a boat that is farther from the mark. This is particularly important when the first of the two boats—it doesn't matter which one—crosses the imaginary line two boatlengths from the mark. An inside overlap at this moment means the outside boat must give the inside boat room to sail around the mark, regardless of all other considerations.

IOR (International Offshore Rule)—A handicapping rule developed in the early 1970s that used a formula to assign ratings to different racing boats.

Isobars—On a weather map, lines connecting points of equal air pressure used to help meteorologists identify areas of high and low pressure.

Jibe—To alter course when sailing downwind so the stern passes through the eye of the wind; can also describe a boat's orientation to the wind on a reach or run; e.g., "The boat is sailing on a port jibe."

Jibe mark—The mark designating the turning point between the two downwind reaching legs on a triangle racecourse.

Jibe set—A spinnaker set executed at the windward mark whereby the boat jibes around the mark before the crew hoists the sail.

Jumping the halyard—A maneuver whereby one crewmember helps raise a sail more quickly by pulling on the halyard where it exits the mast a few feet above the deck, while another crewmember gathers up the resulting slack on a winch.

Knock—*see* Header.

Laminar flow—Smooth, nonturbulent airflow on the sail.

Layline—The imaginary line on a beat on which a boat can weather the windward mark.

Lee-bow—A situation in which a boat that is immediately ahead and to leeward of a competitor astern puts that competitor at a tactical disadvantage; the act of putting oneself in a lee-bow position.

Leech—The trailing edge of a sail.

Leech tension—The amount of downward tension exerted along the length of the leech; controlled by the mainsheet and vang on the main; controlled by the fore and aft position of the jib lead on the jib.

Leeward—Away from the wind, or downwind.

Leeward helm—When the keel, rudder and sails are working together in such a way that the boat's natural tendency is to want to change course to leeward.

Leeward mark—The mark at the end of the running leg of a windward-leeward racecourse, or following the second of two reaching legs on a triangle racecourse.

Leg—The portion of a racecourse between one turning mark and the next.

Lift—A windshift after which the wind comes from a direction closer to the stern.

Lifted tack/heading—In shifting conditions, the tack that is experiencing a lift at any given moment; the heading that is steered on the lifted tack.

Luff—Leading edge of a sail.

Luffing match—On a reach or run, a situation in which a boat to leeward sails a dramatically higher course to prevent another boat from passing it to windward.

Making land—In a crossing situation, the impression that another boat is moving astern relative to its background; indicates that it will pass astern when the two of you cross tacks.

Mark—A permanent or movable buoy or navigational aid designating the end of a leg or a turning point on the racecourse.

Marks to port—Describes the requirement whereby boats must sail to starboard of all the turning marks on a racecourse (leaving the mark on the port side); much more common than "marks to starboard."

Masthead rig—Rig in which the forestay runs to the very top of the mast.

Neutral helm—When the keel, rudder, and sails are working together in such a way that the boat's natural tendency is to want to sail a straight course.

Olympic course—A racecourse in which the first three legs form a triangle, followed by three legs going directly to windward and leeward.

One-design race—A race in which competing boats are of identical design; the first boat across the finish line wins!

Oscillating windshifts—Describes windshifts in which the direction swings back and forth.

Outhaul—A line used to control tension/draft along the foot of the sail.

Overlap—A condition in which any portion of one boat is abeam of any portion of another boat. An overlap is of particular importance when boats are establishing right-of-way at a leeward mark or jibe mark. An overlap exists whether the two boats are on the same tack or not.

Overstanding the mark—Sailing beyond the layline so it is necessary to sail a course lower than close-hauled to make a close rounding of the windward mark.

Persistent windshifts—Describes windshifts in a single direction.

PHRF (Performance Handicap Racing Fleet)—An administered handicapping system whereby a committee assigns a handicap rating based on a subjective evaluation of a boat's design and speed potential in local conditions.

Pin—The buoy designating the port end of the starting line, at the opposite end from the committee boat.

Pinch—To sail closer to the wind than one's usual close-hauled course, sacrificing speed in an effort to gain distance to windward.

Pinned—On a beat, a situation in which a boat sailing close to windward and astern of another boat prevents the lead boat from tacking.

Pitchpole—To heel so far to windward with the spinnaker hoisted that the pole is driven into the water.

Point of maximum draft—The deepest point in the draft of the sail. Often expressed as a percentage of total chord length: e.g., if a boat has its point of maximum draft 50 percent aft, the point of maximum draft is in the middle of the sail; if the point of maximum draft is 40 percent aft, it is slightly forward of the sail's midpoint.

Polar diagram—A diagram showing a boat's theoretical optimal speed at different angles of sail in different wind strengths.

Port-starboard crossing situation—A situation in which a pair of competitors on port and starboard tacks are on a collision or near-collision course. Occurs most often on a beat.

Prebend—Fore and aft curvature induced in the mast through shroud tension.

Prefeed the guy—To pull the spinnaker clew toward the pole before the actual hoist so it will fill more quickly as it is set.

Preparatory flag—The flag raised after a class flag to designate four minutes until the start; the flag is lowered one minute before the start. Generally consists of the "P" flag. The "I" flag also can be used to signal that no boats are allowed to cross the line in either direction when there is less than one minute to the start; a black flag can be used to signal that any boat crossing the line early at the start is automatically disqualified.

Pressure gradient—In meteorology, the rate of pressure change across an area of high or low pressure. The gradient can be seen by looking at isobars: closely packed isobars indicate a high pressure gradient, which generally results in stronger winds; widely spaced isobars indicate a low pressure gradient, which generally results in lighter winds.

Proper course—The course a boat would sail to finish as fast as possible in the absence of other boats; the most direct course to the next mark.

Rake—The degree to which a mast is set to lean aft of vertical; not to be confused with bend.

Rating—A number assigned to a boat that is used to adjust the boat's finish time when racing in a handicap fleet.

Reef—The act of reducing the amount of sail area exposed to the wind by cinching down a portion of the mainsail to the boom or rolling up a portion of a roller-furling headsail; the

area of sail cloth that has been cinched to reduce the overall sail area.

Rhumbline—The straight-line course from one point to another; e.g., the shortest distance between two marks.

Roll—To pass a competitor by sailing to windward.

Rounding—The act of sailing around a mark.

Run—To sail before the wind, with the wind coming directly from astern; on the racecourse, the leg that goes dead down wind.

Sailing high—Sailing to windward of an obstruction or competitor; sailing a course higher than proper course.

Sailing low—Sailing to leeward of an obstruction or competitor; sailing a course lower than proper course.

Sailing under the spinnaker—In rolling conditions, the principle of steering the boat in the direction toward which it is heeling to keep the boat as upright as possible and avoid a broach.

Sailplan—The overall sail configuration of a sailboat; on a sloop the sailplan consists of the main and headsail; on a yawl or ketch the sailplan consists of the main, headsail, and mizzen.

Scallop course—An irregular course that the helmsman steers to maximize overall speed; on a beat the helmsman steers low to build speed in waves, then steers higher in smoother water; on a reach the helmsman steers a slightly higher course to build up apparent wind, and then falls off to take advantage of this apparent wind while sailing a more direct course to the mark; when speed/apparent wind eventually fall off he once again steers a higher course.

Sea breeze—A local breeze resulting from

temperature and air pressure differences between the air over the water and the air over the land.

Seamanlike rounding—At the leeward mark or jibe mark, a rounding in which the helmsman steers the boat as close around the mark as possible, as opposed to a tactical rounding.

Section—*see* Class.

Sheet tension—The amount of force applied to a sail via the sheet.

Slot—The area between the main and jib when sailing on a beat or reach.

Steerage—The condition whereby a boat is moving with enough speed to generate the amount of water flow over the rudder that is necessary to control the direction of the boat; a boat that is moving so slowly its rudder is no longer effective is said to have "lost steerage."

Steps—Combinations of wind speed and angle of sail at which some sailboat designs will experience a small burst in boat speed.

Tack—To alter course (when sailing to windward) so the bow passes through the eye of the wind; the course on which a boat is sailing as defined by the side of the boat over which the wind is passing; the lower, leading corner of a sail.

Tactical rounding—A situation in which a boat comes in to a leeward- or jibe-mark rounding a couple of boatlengths wide so it can cut close to the mark as it finishes the turn, steering onto the next leg without having to make a sharp turn (thus killing boat speed). *Also see* Wide-in and tight-out.

Telltales—Light pieces of yarn or fabric (often nylon) attached to a sail that indicate how wind is flowing along the sail's surface.

Time allowance—The amount of time by which a boat's finish time is adjusted according to its handicap rating.

Time-on-distance correction—In a handicap system, time allowances that are calculated according to the distance raced.

Time-on-time correction—In a handicap system, time allowances that are calculated according to the elapsed time of a race.

Triangle course—A racecourse in which the marks are placed in a triangle pattern.

Trim—To use control lines such as a sheet or cunningham to adjust a sail; to tighten a control line.

True wind—The wind speed and direction you experience when standing still, as opposed to the apparent wind you experience aboard a boat underway.

Twing—A trimming device that moves a spinnaker lead forward; either a hook attached to the deck or a small piece of line with a block attached to the end, through which the spinnaker sheets are run.

Twist—The degree to which the trailing edge of the sail angles off to leeward.

Under load—Describes a condition in which a sheet, halyard, or the tiller is subjected to the force of the wind or water.

Upwash—The phenomenon whereby air ahead and to windward of a sail is "pulled" by the sail from the windward side to leeward.

Vang sheeting—A technique executed on a beat whereby the vang is used to control leech tension in the mainsail and the mainsheet is used to control the angle of attack; used in heavy air conditions on smaller boats, since it can be an efficient way to dump excess air.

Vector—A theoretical line showing the strength and direction of a given force.

Veer—When the wind direction shifts in a clockwise direction.

Velocity made good (VMG)—The progress you actually make toward the mark on a beat or when jibing downwind, as opposed to the speed at which the boat is traveling through the water.

Waterline length—The length of a vessel as defined by the most forward and aft points of the hull where they intersect the water's surface when the boat is afloat.

Weather—To sail to windward of a mark or obstacle when on a close-hauled course.

Weather helm—*see* Windward helm.

Weather side/end—The side or part of anything that is toward the direction from which the wind blows, or to windward.

Wide-in and tight-out—The principle behind a tactical rounding; designed to maintain boat speed when going around the leeward mark or jibe mark from a run or broad reach to a beat, or from a reach to a reach.

Wind shadow—The area of disturbed air to leeward of a boat's sails; its length is usually about ten times the height of the mast.

Windward—Toward or in the direction from which the wind blows.

Windward helm—When the keel, rudder and sails are working together in such a way that the boat's natural tendency is to want to change course to windward.

Windward-leeward course—A racecourse in which boats sail directly up- and downwind.

Windward mark—The mark at the end of the windward leg of the racecourse.

Index